TRIGGERED

TRIGGERED

HOW THE LEFT THRIVES ON HATE AND WANTS TO SILENCE US

DONALD TRUMP JR.

CENTER
STREET®

NEW YORK   NASHVILLE

Copyright © 2019 by Donald Trump Jr.
Cover copyright © 2019 by Hachette Book Group.

All rights reserved. In accordance with the U.S. Copyright Act of 1976, the scanning, uploading, and electronic sharing of any part of this book without the permission of the publisher constitute unlawful piracy and theft of the author's intellectual property. If you would like to use material from the book (other than for review purposes), prior written permission must be obtained by contacting the publisher at permissions@hbgusa.com. Thank you for your support of the author's rights.

Center Street
Hachette Book Group
1290 Avenue of the Americas
New York, NY 10104

www.CenterStreet.com

Printed in the United States of America

First Edition: November 2019

Center Street is a division of Hachette Book Group, Inc.
The Center Street name and logo are trademarks of Hachette Book Group, Inc.

The publisher is not responsible for websites (or their content)
that are not owned by the publisher.

Interior book design by Timothy Shaner, NightandDayDesign.biz

Library of Congress Cataloging-in-Publication Data has been applied for.

ISBNs: 978-1-5460-8603-1 (hardcover), 978-1-5460-8602-4 (ebook)

Printed in the United States of America

LSC-H

10 9 8 7 6 5 4 3 2 1

I dedicate this book to the DEPLORABLES. While the elite of the other party look down on you and would rather you stay silent, I salute your work ethic, patriotism, and values. America wouldn't be great without your blood, sweat, and tears. I will always stand with you! I am proudly one of you.

CONTENTS

1. TRIGGER WARNING 1

2. COUNTERPUNCH 7

3. CRACKS IN THE FOUNDATION 23

4. CLASS WARFARE 47

5. GAP YEAR 67

6. NOT EXACTLY THE STATUE OF LIBERTY 87

7. NOT YOUR GRANDFATHER'S DEMOCRAT PARTY 109

8. BACK TO SCHOOL 123

9. ELECTION NIGHT 145

10. A DEADLY FORM OF HATE 159

11. MISS GENDERED 173

12. THE ENEMY OF THE PEOPLE? 185

13. SHADOW BANNED: HOW THE LIBERALS' GRIP
    ON SOCIAL MEDIA CAN RUIN YOUR LIFE 205

14. THE LATE-NIGHT KING OF COMEDY WITH JUSSIE
    SMOLLETT AND THE FAUXTRAGE ORCHESTRA 225

15. JOE CHINA 243

16. THE OPPOSITION 253

17. TRUMP2020 267

   Acknowledgments 285

   Endnotes 288

TRIGGERED

1.

TRIGGER WARNING

I'M NOT MAD.

Look, everybody is called a traitor once or twice in their lives, right? Everybody gets falsely accused and wrongly investigated by the FBI and has to testify in front of Congress for over thirty hours, answering the same stupid politically motivated questions over and over again, don't they? And, everybody has an army of social justice warriors combing through every word they've ever said online to find something to be offended by, correct?

Why should I be mad? I'm not mad. In fact, my plan was to write a feel-good book about forgiveness and healing, sort of a *Chicken Soup for the Political Soul* type of story. I was even going to call it *Kumbaya* instead of *Triggered*, but it seemed that title was already taken, probably by one of the 2,467 Democrat candidates currently running for president.

So instead of chicken soup, over the next 300 pages or so, I'll take you on a tour of all the craziest, most destructive ideas that the left has come up with in the last decade or more. Think of it as a trip through Jurassic Park, only instead of dangerous dinosaurs, you get to see sleepy liberal losers, socialist crybabies, and hypocritical politicians and media. If you decide to come along, I promise that nothing will jump into the car with us.

You'll also get to find out a little about me during the ride, if only as a way to dispel the conspiracy theory on the left that I was born with horns.

Before we get going, however, I need to make a few disclaimers. If you've been around lawyers as much as I have lately, you begin to think like them.

First: I am not operating in my official capacity as a spokesman for my father's campaign in these pages. So if I were to say something like, oh, I don't know, "Adam Schiff is a lying ass clown" or "Robert Mueller is a feeble old fool who got used by the Democrats"—you know, if I were to *hypothetically* say those things—that's all just my opinion. No one on the campaign has been consulted, and I doubt any of them would care very much anyhow. I'm just saying what they all know to be true but don't want to take the heat for saying in public. I guess that's just one of those things that got passed down in the genes!

Second: As much as I might joke around, I am not actively trying to offend anyone with what I'm about to say. I'm just making arguments, backing them up with facts, and putting them out into the world, the same way millions of people have done with millions of books before mine. I would actually like to think of this book as offering a reasoned antidote to all the hysterical bullshit that's flying around right now. That used to be called discourse. But today, "discourse" exists only for leftists. When conservatives do it, they call it "hate speech." I also know that as the son of a rich white guy living in 2019, I'm essentially not allowed to have an opinion anymore, let alone express that opinion in public.

Finally, I guess I should probably include a note about the title of my book, because it's probably not a term you hear every day. In fact, if you're over the age of about thirty-five or you haven't spent the last few years on a college campus, on Twitter, or in an asylum (and really, who can tell the difference anymore?), you probably have no idea why this book is called *Triggered.*

Allow me to explain.

Today, as it appears on the internet at least, the term "trigger warning" is used to describe something, say a tweet from my dad, that blows up the fragile sensibilities of the liberal Twitterverse. At the very least, it sets their hair on fire and creates a minor news story for a few days. But at the worst, it moves them to real-life outrage and organized violence. And before you ask, the freaking out is wildly disproportionate. While conservatives usually get worked up over important things—such as the killing of babies or the stripping away of our natural rights as human beings—with liberals the "triggers" tend to be much sillier. If you say capitalism is better than socialism, they freak out. If my father says America is the greatest country in the world, they lose it. If you tell them the cat video they posted isn't that cute, they have a complete breakdown.

With every passing day, the bar for what's considered "triggering" gets lower and lower. For example, have you ever asked someone where they're from? Well, according to liberals, you can't do that anymore. It's called a microagression. (Don't worry, I'll explain these terms as we go.)

And when Robert Mueller says the president of the United States is *not* an agent of Russia—which, call me crazy, seems as though it should be good news for everyone—they melt down and console each other like they did when they found out Al Franken was a creepy pervert.

So, because my book will contain sections with a number of these so-called dangerous ideas, I thought it best to include a little warning of my own. Though it isn't illegal—yet—to discuss triggering ideas like this in a book, who knows where we'll be by the time this goes to print. I could be brought up on charges just for having a an opinion or a picture of myself on the cover.

———

YOUR TRIGGER WARNING

Do not continue reading this book if you don't like conservative ideas or if the thought of reading bad words scares you. Do not continue reading if you don't have a sense of humor or are American but somehow, magically, Donald Trump is not your president. Also, if you find any of the following even remotely offensive: patriotism, masculinity, hunting, MAGA hats, the American flag, guns, sex, religion, Roseanne Barr, criticism of stupid ideas, capitalism, skyscrapers, or the use of the word "Christmas" during the Christmas season, then you should *definitely* stop reading.

In fact, if you're a dyed-in-the-wool liberal or a social justice warrior, why don't you go ahead and put this book down altogether. Just close the cover, march right back to your local bookstore, and hand it back over the counter. Better yet, buy it and throw it away. Put it in the recycling bin if that makes you feel better. Maybe your favorite vegan restaurant can make menus out of it. Either way, you'll be engaging in capitalism, which is a good thing, whether you like it or not.

———

Are they gone?

Good. I thought I'd have to break out my MAGA hat.

Now that it's just you and me, my fellow patriots, Trump-supporting Americans, and those from the whisper campaign who actually like our president but are afraid to tell people, I think we can finally get down to the heart of this book.

Things have gotten way out of control in this country. We've elected socialists to our Congress, allowed anti-Semitism to run rampant throughout our government, and allowed our most important media institutions to be run by angry mobs and leftist activist "journalists" on Twitter. Worst of all, we have completely ceded control of what we can and cannot say in public to the left, who are just a bunch of oversensitive babies who find everything offensive. If a liberal declares that something is racist, it is. If a liberal says he or she is offended by something, that thing, no matter what it is, is suddenly unspeakable. My father says a place is infested with rats, the mob cries racism. My father says he likes taco bowls from Trump Tower, the left cries racism. Since my father announced his run for the presidency, screaming racism has become the Easy button of left-wing politics, just like in those old Staples commercials. It's the liberal "trump card," if you will.

Facts aren't working for you?

RACIST!

Math is hard?

IT'S RACIST! Obviously.

The problem with using racism as a label for everything you don't like, of course, is that racism is still a real problem that persists in this country—not nearly to the extent that the left would have you believe, of course, but it's still one of our major issues. Real people face real racism every day. And when you use it as a buzzword to try to win a losing argument, it does a disservice to those who live under it. People have become numb. When they hear "racist," they roll their eyes because that term has been so over-played on such a vast scale, always hurting the real victims along the way.

The left has also gone crazy with its newfound powers of censorship. Things have gotten so bad that the list of what we are no longer allowed to discuss in this country has gotten longer than the Mueller Report. There are stacks of books we're no longer allowed to read, public figures who are no longer allowed to speak in public, and crucial debates we are no longer allowed to have—all because they might hurt someone's feelings. Even what passed for rather amazing comedy just a few years ago is now considered offensive and regressive by the left. Just ask Dave Chapelle, who's fighting off an online outrage mob as I type these words over a comedy special he just released. So many people have been "canceled" by the left for minor offenses against "wokeness" (I'll explain these terms as we go) that I can hardly keep track anymore. What's next? Book burning?

So before they light the bonfire, I decided to write a book that includes just about every subject that the left believes we shouldn't talk about. I've also decided to call it *Triggered*, because, well, why not? Anything that makes the veins in a few liberal foreheads bulge out is fine by me.

Okay, now that you've had the appetizer, let's get to the red meat.

2.

COUNTERPUNCH

I DON'T KNOW if you've heard, but the Mueller Report is out. Turns out I'm not a Russian agent after all! After spending almost $40 million in taxpayer money, employing nineteen of the most prejudiced Democrat lawyers they could find in Washington, DC (some of whom had worked for the Clinton family and others who had been at her "victory party"), magically without a single Republican, and taking nearly two years to do an investigation that anyone with half a brain could have done in five minutes, the Mueller team found absolutely *zero* evidence of collusion or obstruction.

Now, most people would have been willing to leave it at that. Most people would have been relieved to have their name cleared in public after so many years of having it dragged through the mud. And if I were "most people," this chapter might be a little different. Maybe it would open on the afternoon the Mueller Report came out. There'd be some vivid writing about how relieved I felt, how I could breathe easily for the first time in years. Or maybe there'd be scenes from right in the middle of the whole ordeal, and

I'd tell you about how I'd curled up in a corner every night with a teddy bear praying that I wasn't going to go to prison over this made-up nonsense. I might include some tear-filled speeches from my friends and family about how they were going to stick with me till the end, how they brought me strength in troubled times.

If that's what you're expecting, you'd better go buy a different book.

I'm not "relieved" to have the Mueller investigation over with. I don't feel as though a weight has been lifted off my shoulders, and I'm not breathing any easier than I was on the day that old, over-the-hill puppet was first appointed. I'm not relieved because I know that it was never about Russia or collusion or obstruction. It certainly wasn't about "the integrity of our elections" or "national security." If the Mueller investigation *had* been about any of those things, the Democrats would have been celebrating along with everyone else when we learned that the President of the United States had not colluded with a foreign power. But they didn't celebrate. They waved the report in the air like a bunch of lunatics and claimed that *You have to read between the lines, man! It's all in there!* They had officially joined the ranks of the tinfoil hat brigade who think the moon landing was staged in a television studio or who think we're keeping aliens in Area 51 (if you really want to see aliens, the first place I'd look would be in Nancy Pelosi's office).

From the day the Mueller investigation began, it was about one thing and one thing only: taking down my father, the only president in the history of this country who was elected without the approval of the ruling class. He was a populist candidate who spoke for real Americans, and that meant he had to go. The investigation was, and always had been, a complete farce. It was started by people who hate Donald Trump more than they love America.

But for some reason, we were all expected to stay quiet and let the Mueller team carry out their crooked investigation in peace. While the Democrats were telling outright lies about us on the floor of Congress during the day, then moving their clown show over to cable news and doing the same thing every night, we were just supposed to just nod along and not say a word. Sorry, not the way I operate. Throughout the entire investigation, I kept up the heat on television and on Twitter, calling out all of the lies Adam #FullofSchiff was telling about me—which, by the end of the whole thing, got to be like a full-time job—and taking shots right back at the Democrats who were trying to remove my father from office.

You might be shocked to hear, but not everyone was pleased with my combative stance. One afternoon, right in the heat of the Russia hoax, even my lawyers approached me and said, "Don, you might want to slow down on social media, maybe not be so aggressive." I politely declined. Shortly after that, my father—yes, my *father*, Donald J. Trump, our tweeter-in-chief, the so-called Shakespeare of 140 characters—told me that I might be getting "a little too hot" on my social media accounts.

I respect the heck out of my dad, and when he gives me advice I take it ninety-nine point nine percent of the time. This, however, was probably the one time I decided not to listen! He knew as well as I did that there's no such thing as being "too hot" on social, at least as far as I'm concerned. I consider myself a shit-talker par excellence.

Plus, I knew that when it came down to it, all the morons in the House and the Senate—these clowns like Eric Swalwell and Ted Lieu who were attacking me every day—would throw me in jail themselves if they had the power to do it. They didn't give a damn about investigations or getting to the truth. They just wanted to get my father out of office and punish anyone who supported him— starting with me and my family.

So, no, I didn't think it was the time to "slow down" or "take it easy." I still don't. . . . and I won't.

Throughout the entire Russia investigation, it seemed, the Democrats in Congress had only one reason to exist, and that was to try and make my father and me cower in a corner, curl up in a ball, and die. Well, that had about as much chance of happening as them finding proof of collusion. My lawyers could've talked to me until they were blue in the face, which they pretty much did, but my attitude wasn't going to change. Not one bit. Because I fight back. That's what we do.

I wasn't surprised when those same lawyers came back to me at the end of the investigation, when the report was out and everyone was beginning to learn the truth, and told me I had probably been right all along to hit the Democrats so hard. I don't blame them for being skeptical, though. None of them were actually there when this supposed collusion took place.

I was.

Like the rest of my family, I worked on the Trump campaign. I know what it was like in the early days before the primaries, when the whole world was against us and we were struggling just to compete in a crowded Republican field. As I've often said, we couldn't have colluded to order a cheeseburger, much less coordinated an espionage campaign with a foreign power.

Especially in the beginning, the Trump campaign was filled with political neophytes, and I mean that in the best sense of the word. Almost all of us came from walks of life other than politics, meaning we were used to actually working for a living. All of us were accomplished, just not in the political arena. While the other campaigns were wasting time with polling data and staff shake-ups, we were figuring out ways to streamline the process and reach as many voters as possible. No one had time to reach out to foreign governments and ask for help. I mean, look, candidly? I got one unsolicited email. The Clinton campaign sought out and *paid for* foreign operatives to do research on its opponents. That's a big distinction.

If you were a liberal in early 2017, the Russia collusion story was really all you had left to cling to. It absolved you and your candidate of all blame for her defeat, and it gave you a perfectly sensible reason to reject the results of the election. All of a sudden, once Big Bad Russia got involved, Donald Trump became an "illegitimate president," and the whole getting-elected thing was just a colossal misunderstanding. It was the do-over they all wanted so desperately. Not only did Democrats get to carry on as if their candidate hadn't lost, they also had free rein to take down just about everyone who had ever associated with Donald J. Trump, from his close associates and friends to the people who share his last name. Ask me how I know!

I mean, I'm old enough to remember when Barack Obama made fun of Mitt Romney by telling him "the 1980s called and want their foreign policy back." But now, miraculously, Russia could be brought back from obscurity to be the villain in the Democrats' assault on democracy. They always get to have it both ways.

Thank God we're on the other side of the Russia hoax now. The reports have been written, the testimony—days and days and days of it—has been given, and we know the truth. There was no collusion. No obstruction. Not so much as an unpaid parking ticket as far as my father and his closest aides from the campaign are concerned. And finally, the liberal media have given up on the story.

Yeah, right.

They've kept up the delusion, assuring their disillusioned followers that more evidence is coming, more interviews are being unsealed, and there are more investigations to be done. No matter

how many times Robert Mueller tells them to shut up and read
the report—which, as my father has correctly said, exonerates him
completely—they keep bringing up the man's name as though
he's some kind of conquering hero, even dragging him in front of
Congress so he could stutter and babble his way through five hours
of testimony. Hell, I'm still waiting for all the evidence that Adam
#FullofSchiff claims he's been privy to over these past two years.
It seemed as though he was on television every night, claiming he
had "seen evidence" of collusion.

I have to admit that I almost felt bad for Robert Mueller during
that testimony. And if it weren't for the fact that I was probably
number two on the guy's kill list for years, I might have. I'm not
against old people; I've always respected my elders. But watching
those Democrats in Congress go at him, question after question, all
of them trying desperately to make him tell them about the smoking gun they all wanted so badly, was like watching a bunch of kids
find out Santa Claus isn't real. For years, they had been living in
their filter bubbles and echo chambers, able to spread lies about the
Mueller Report without anyone throwing any facts into the mix.
They had staked their entire reputations on the allegations being
true and gone all in. They'd chosen—or rather, they'd *used*—Mueller because they'd thought he was beyond reproach, someone whom
no one—not even my father—would dare attack. After all, he was a
former prosecutor, the former head of the FBI, a decorated Marine.
But it all came tumbling down when we realized he was nothing
more than a pawn for the leftists running the show—an empty suit
to fit their narrative and nothing more. Worst of all for Democrats,
in their hysteria to destroy Trump, they forced the man they had
elevated for two years to appear before Congress and he proved
what he and the MAGA-sphere had known all along: that he was
the author of his report in name only. Asked about key figures in

the report and dates that anyone who'd even been following the story on Twitter would have known, Mueller came up short again and again. *Oh*, he said, *I don't know, I need to check that, I don't know who that is . . . That's beyond my purview.* Seriously Mr. M? Well, it was right there on page 45, so it really isn't. You wrote the report and you can't tell me what's in it? You didn't know anything about Fusion GPS, the opposition research firm hired by the DNC to dig up dirt on my father? You didn't know that they were the genesis of the entire investigation and all of the FISA warrants? Sorry, I don't buy it. You spent two years and nearly $40 million and you didn't bother to learn how it all started? The genesis of the greatest hoax ever perpetrated on the American people is "beyond your purview"? G.T.F.O.

Tell you what: if you see me on the street, feel free to ask me questions about this book you're reading right now. I might not be a fancy former head of the FBI or anything, but at least I can remember things I've written myself.

In their desperate attempt to get him to testify beyond the report, the Dems actually did more to discredit the whole farce than anything before. And for that, I say: *thanks!*

But if you think a little thing like the debacle of Mueller's appearance before Congress is going to stop the Democrats, think again. They are obsessed. They'll believe anything that confirms what they already believe, and they'll call anything that contradicts what they already believe a lie.

———

If you're trying to find the starting point of this lunacy, look no further than the night of the 2016 election, right around the hours of midnight to six o'clock in the morning, when the craziest wing of the American left finally lost its mind for good. DJT has been living rent-free in their heads ever since—a strong real estate play from the best in the game.

It was in those few hours, right after the networks finally called the presidential election, that the liberal press and the Clinton camp first started groping around for anything that would explain their loss. For them, my father's victory was the worst possible thing that could have happened. The postmortem that immediately followed the election read as if the world had come to an end. "The world's shining light of democracy has gone dark," one journalist said. Paul Krugman, a columnist for the *New York Times*, wrote that markets were plunging, and that they would probably never recover (How'd that work out?). A few weeks later, Jeff Zucker, the president of CNN—who, by the way, has my father to thank for his job—blamed himself, saying that the network probably shouldn't have aired so many of DJT's campaign rallies. Yeah, right, Jeff. You could have filled the airspace with *New Year's Eve with Anderson Cooper* reruns, and my dad still would have won. I guess these days CNN is paying reparations by choosing to be the anti-Trump network at all costs—especially in the ratings. All the experts proved what we've all known all along. That they are full of shit. They all got it so wrong they needed cover and when they saw something, no matter how asinine, it became gospel to cover their abject failure.

Still, the left wouldn't feel sorry for itself for long.

First it picked up the Russian spy story and started pushing it to every devastated reporter who would listen.

Then it did everything it had told us the Trump supporters would do if Hillary won. Think about it. For weeks leading up to the election, we had been hearing about all the horrible things Donald Trump would force his supporters to do if he lost. DJT wouldn't accept the defeat they were all so sure was coming. The editorial boards at the *New York Times* and the *Washington Post* both ran many articles warning us about the chaos that was about to ensue. According to popular opinion, Trump supporters were going to riot in the streets, refuse to accept the results of the election, and begin some kind of underground coup against the duly elected president, Hillary Clinton. They would start a second civil war. The streets would become absolute anarchy.

And when things didn't go the way the Democrats had wanted them to go, what happened?

Let's see. They held riots in the streets. (Check.) They refused to accept the results of the election, cooking up one of the strangest spy-movie stories I've ever heard in order to maintain their collective delusion. (Check.) Then they formed an underground group of online keyboard warriors called "the Resistance," dedicated to taking down my father one stupid hashtag at a time. Prominent journalists, liberal activists, and actors have all identified themselves as proud members of "the Resistance" on Twitter. When I'm attacked by an outraged mob online, their voices are usually among the loudest. (And Check.)

The hatred that fomented online and in protests became hand-to-hand combat—and I mean real violence, the kind you usually see only in Third World countries. I'm not kidding. The same party that used to preach peace, tolerance, and inclusivity (mostly platitudes when you look at its history, which I will) has now become the party of hate, violence, and suppression of free speech.

So-called activists on the extreme left have moved from their safe spaces and the basements of their parents' houses out into the streets, usually clad in black hockey pads and carrying weapons. Sometimes they call themselves antifascists, or Antifa, but most of the time, they don't know why they're there or what they even believe. All they know is hate and anger. Time and again, these people try to shut down speakers with whom they don't agree. They attack journalists in the streets and threaten anyone who doesn't go along with their twisted sense of social justice and equality.

They're not exactly the most physically imposing people in the world (that's what happens when you live on nothing but soy lattes and veggie burgers), but the sheer force of their numbers is shocking. They have allowed hate to spread at a rate we haven't seen since the era of civil rights, when Democrats—the party that founded the KKK, in case you've forgotten—would organize lynch mobs and counterprotests all across the South, most of which ended in horrific violence.

These people are irrational, hysterical, upset, and out looking for enemies.

I should know. As of November 16, 2016, I became one of their top targets. Before the election, I was just a guy who appeared on television every once in a while, went to work, and went home at the end of the day and played with my kids. There were probably a few people who thought I was an asshole because I was blessed to have been born into a wealthy family. But no one was mailing suspicious powder to my home or screaming at me in a restaurant where I was celebrating my brother's birthday. No one was threatening my life. After the election, I became the guy who receives the second highest number of death threats in the country (according to the Secret Service, second only to my father). And that's a list that includes senators, former presidents, and ambassadors to several war-torn countries. Here's what the exploding letter filled with powder that sent my then wife and a member of my Secret Service detail to the hospital said: "You are an awful person. This is why people hate you. You are getting what you deserve. So shut the f—k up."

Keep in mind that I hadn't done anything to that person, who, by the way, turned out to be a liberal activist and an Elizabeth Warren donor. I've never had an actual physical confrontation with any of those lunatics in my life. All I do is give speeches, have opinions, run a business, and support the president of the United States, who also happens to be my father. For that, I get the second highest number of death threats in the country.

It gets worse. Much worse.

In June 2017, a left-wing activist, armed with a rifle and a 9 mm handgun, walked up to a practice for the annual Congressional Baseball Game and started shooting at Republicans. Sometime before, he'd tweeted: "It's Time to Destroy Trump & Co." My friend Republican Whip Steve Scalise was so badly injured he almost died. Matt Mikaf, a lobbyist and former legislative assistant, was critically wounded and underwent surgery. Another legislative aide, Zack Barth, was shot in the calf. Two Capitol Police officers, David Bailey and Crystal Griner, were injured just before they took down the shooter.

These days, anyone who supports my father is a target. Just as the anti-Trump revolution was beginning, Senator Rand Paul, one of my father's closest allies on Capitol Hill, was brutally attacked by his neighbor, an avowed lefty. The man ran down a steep hill to gain momentum and then blindsided Senator Paul, who had headphones on and his back turned. He never knew the man was coming. The senator had six broken ribs and blood in his lungs. Doctors who examined him said that the injuries sustained were more consistent with a car accident than a sucker punch. As he was recovering, the left celebrated. The celebration continues among some of the most callous and idiotic people on the left. Just a few months ago, the comedian Tom Arnold tweeted: "Imagine being Rand Paul's neighbor and having to deal with @RandPaul lying cowardly circular whiny bullcrap about lawn clippings. No wonder he ripped his toupee off." Within seconds, Representative Ilhan Omar had retweeted it, obviously gleeful that the attack had taken place. Nice, right? And they say Donald Trump is the one who's vulgar, but they won't say anything about Omar allegedly marrying her brother to enter the country illegally. Or, having an affair with a married paid staffer, or as someone hilariously commented on my Instagram feed, "She puts the infidel in infidelity." Whether it's true or not, she's not exactly the moral authority the media makes her out to be.

The left has become nothing more than a hypocritical caricature of itself—a *Saturday Night Live* clip gone horribly wrong.

And it's not just politicians who are targets. It's anyone the left doesn't agree with. As I was working on this book, my brother Eric walked into a bar in Chicago and a waitress there spat in his face. The Secret Service had to lead her outside before the confrontation could get worse. People get triggered simply by seeing a Trump. Last year Sarah Huckabee Sanders, my father's longtime press secretary, and her family were kicked out of a restaurant in Washington, DC, simply because she worked for the president. Her family was forced to leave another restaurant by an Antifa mob just minutes afterward. Democratic Socialists of America threatened former Secretary of Homeland Security Kirstjen Nielsen, White House adviser Stephen Miller, and Senate majority leader Mitch McConnell in restaurants. Senator McConnell has been targeted multiple times, including by left-wing extremists who stormed his home screaming "Just stab the m—f— in the heart." Then, when the senator posted a video of the incident, Twitter locked him out. They locked him out for showing an attack on his house directed by the left!

Even the vice president has been harassed. Instead of taking a curtain call, the entire cast of the musical *Hamilton* stood on stage and lectured Mike Pence, then the vice president–elect. Vice President Pence was at the show with his daughter and her cousins, who were upset at the public display of hostility.

As gracious as anyone you'll ever meet, the vice president excused the rudeness of the cast by telling his daughter, "That's what democracy sounds like." Everyone is entitled to his or her opinion, even if the left doesn't think we are. There are, however, appropriate times and places to express them. I don't know, but the cast of a show shouting at a man and his family who are sitting in a theater where tickets for the show cost hundreds of dollars doesn't seem like one of those times to me. If anything it shows most of America how uncivilized and deranged most of these lefties are. (By the way, though I use the terms "lefty, leftist, and left" interchangeably with "Democrat" in these pages, not all Democrats are leftists. Many are good people, some even voted for my father. Unfortunately, the party has lost its way and is now run by the leftists and the socialists.)

Last year, with a few friends, we were celebrating my girlfriend, Kimberly Guilfoyle's, birthday at a restaurant when a man came up to our table and started screaming "Shame on you!" Our friend Sergio Gor, who was with us at the table, asked the man to name one policy of President Trump's that he wasn't happy with. Instead of giving an answer, the man continued his irrational rant but now targeted Sergio.

"Is it the environment?" Sergio asked.

More incoherent screaming.

"Civil rights?"

Loud nonsense.

"Taxes?" Sergio pressed.

"I don't have to name one!" the man finally screamed and walked away.

It was a classic display of Trump Derangement Syndrome. He didn't know why he was mad; he just knew he was mad.

———

The attacks against us aren't random incidents. They're part of a coordinated plot to intimidate anyone into silence who doesn't agree with the radical left. Antifa is nothing less than a terrorist organization, and it's about time we started treating it that way.

Its members are certainly radical enough. In their own minds, they are part of a long line of brave, tightly organized "antifascists." They see themselves as being descended from those who took on the supporters of Benito Mussolini in Italy and opposed Adolf Hitler in Germany during World War II. In reality, they're just idiots who've played too many video games. They are people who have never gotten the chance to confront anything real in their lives, so they turn the real world into a fantasy land where they are good people fighting evil fascists. Oh, and in this little fantasy world, anyone who says things they don't agree with—or anyone who is white and male and happens to be within fifty feet of them when they hold their demonstrations—is a fascist.

I'm not sure if Antifa understands fascism all that well, because it sure as hell seems to be willing to employ fascist tactics on a daily basis. Maybe they should just call themselves "Fa," because from what I've seen they're far more fascist than anti-.

In April 2017, an Antifa mob wearing ninja black, ski masks, and sun goggles and carrying knives, clubs, and cans of Mace descended on the peaceful Patriots' Day "free speech" rally in Berkeley, California. Of all places—the home of the '60s hippies' crusade for free speech. One of the Antifa thugs began hitting people in the head with a large bicycle U-lock. He sneaked up on them and hit them from behind—the worst kind of coward. As many as eleven people fell from the blows. One man was so badly injured that he needed multiple staples in his skull to close the wound.

The police would later arrest Eric Clanton for the crimes. By day, Clanton was an "ethics" professor at Diablo Valley College.

By night, he was a leftist thug in the war against Trump. (Irony is lost on the left.) The ethics professor would receive just three years' probation. If the sentence seems a little soft to you, you're not crazy. Three years' probation for what amounted to attempted murder? Perhaps the scales of justice were tipped in his favor? Well, the court was in California's Alameda County, a place that had gone nearly 80 percent for Clinton. So you tell me.

At the end of June 2019, an Antifa mob attacked Andy Ngo, an editor for Quillette, on the streets of Portland, Oregon. Over the past few years, Andy had been doing some excellent reporting about a vast series of fake hate crimes that had been staged by various "oppressed people" in Oregon and elsewhere. His reporting, some of which had run in the *New York Post*, had exposed several people who had "Smolletted themselves," as I like to say, painting racial slurs and obscene images on their own houses and then blaming Trump supporters for it. In one case, a woman who had fallen while drunk blamed her injuries on a white supremacist. Andy's reporting had made him an enemy of Portland's liberal gestapo, whose entire narrative hinged on those horrible attacks being true.

When they found out about Andy's reporting, the leftist communities of Portland reacted violently, as they often do when you point out their blatant hypocrisy. On June 29, Andy tried to film a protest going on in downtown Portland, and the Antifa crowd turned on him. They allegedly dumped milkshakes on his head, punched him in the face, and beat him all over his body with whatever weapons they'd left the house with that day. Later, in the hospital's emergency room, doctors told Andy that he had suffered brain injuries from the attack. The attack is being challenged, of course, but only by left-wing rags that likely only want to hurt Ngo because he doesn't fit their desired mold.

If those had been isolated incidents, it'd be one thing. But they're not. All over the country, leftists are organizing marches, shutting down speakers, and committing horrible acts of violence when they don't get their way. And instead of calling out these atrocious acts for what they are, the media either ignore them or cheer them on. The *New York Times* referred to the widespread protests after my father's election—many of which had turned violent—as "peaceful." When Trump supporters gather anywhere, organizing in the same numbers for similar reasons, we're called "white supremacists" and "hateful fearmongers." This isn't because we're evil or even because we've upset the established political order. It's because we say things that the left doesn't like to hear—and in the era of Trump, there is no greater crime than to trigger someone.

In recent years, the left has come together and decided that words are violence, which, in the minds of its members, makes it perfectly acceptable to use violence against people with whom they disagree.

They have decided that there are some things you just shouldn't say anymore, and when you say one of those things, you become the enemy.

But words aren't violence. They're just words.

3.

CRACKS IN THE FOUNDATION

I WAS ONLY FOUR or five years out of college when I undertook my first major project as a VP at The Trump Organization. I had already learned a great deal about the business on a few smaller projects in New York City, but this was much different. Ninety-eight stories high, the Trump International Hotel & Tower now stands on the banks of the Chicago River. Luckily, I was alongside some of the most talented men and women in the business. We worked day and night on the project for close to five years. Because of the team's commitment to the company, we brought the whole thing in on time and under budget.

By the time we had our soft opening in 2008, I was almost thirty years old and fifty times more experienced than I'd been at the start. The lessons I learned on that job stay with me to this day. Maybe the most fundamental lesson was this:

You need a strong foundation.

Hidden from view, foundations transfer the weight of the entire building to the earth. As any good architect knows, a few centimeters of misalignment in the concrete subfloor can cause the structure to tilt or sink. If you don't believe me, look at the Millennium Tower in San Francisco. Finished in 2009, the fifty-eight-story tower has sunk seventeen inches and tilted a foot. Today, they call it the "leaning tower of San Francisco," and estimates are that it'll take more than $100 million to fix—not the best news for people who bought condos in the building, which have depreciated in value $400,000 on average. Like most things in life, tall buildings need a solid foundation. Without one, as they say in the trade, you're screwed.

I'm reminded of faulty foundations when I look at the modern Democrat Party. It built a political party on a foundation of Jim Crow–style racism, support of the KKK and slavery, and stark opposition to Abraham Lincoln. Every few decades it added a floor to that foundation. Those floors included a widespread welfare state, hindrance of businesses both big and small, and finally political correctness, Soviet-style socialism, and Antifa. They are the party of dependence. Without that, they have nothing.

It's a miracle that the party is still standing.

It's not as if it hasn't had several opportunities over the years to tear down and rebuild. After my father crushed Hillary in 2016, exposing an obvious flaw in the Democrats' way of looking at the world, they could have regrouped and figured out a way to become less radical.

But they didn't.

Instead of becoming more sensible after the 2016 presidential election, they shifted even further to the left, bringing the craziest fringe figures to the forefront of the party. In recent years, the Democrats have almost completely abandoned the principles of capitalism and democracy. Instead, they've begun embracing some of the worst ideas in the history of mankind: socialism, collectivism, class warfare, and the politics of fear and resentment. Some of their most recent proposals sound as though they came right out of *The Communist Manifesto.* They saw the 2016 election results, and they did exactly the opposite of what most reasonable people would have done.

Did you ever think you would live in a country where the president of the United States would have to stand up during his State of the Union address and declare that we "would never become a socialist country"? But here we are.

For my maternal grandmother, who lives with us for a few months every year, that line came as an incredible relief. For her, it was personal. She and my grandfather grew up in Czechoslovakia during the very worst of communism. Unlike most of these new-age Starbucks-chugging socialists in Brooklyn, they knew the horrors that can come from a state-run economy, and the scars of socialism are seared in her memory. I vividly remember speaking with her during the lead-up to the 2016 election, when she was watching neo-socialists such as Bernie Sanders on CNN almost every day. (We're working on getting her off the CNN train, by the way. But back in the Czech Republic, you pick up CNN early, like a drug addiction. Soon she'll be watching Fox with the rest of the sane people in the world.)

"Don, don't these people understand?" she asked, her voice quavering, tears coming to her eyes. This is a woman who hid from Nazis in the basement of her farmhouse as a child and lived under Communist occupation for decades. At ninety-three, she's still stronger and tougher than most. But she feared that her grandchildren and great-grandchildren might go through some of the same things she went through, and the thought of that had scared the hell out of her.

"They don't know how bad it can be. Please do something. Don't they know this is all lies?"

The truth is that most people probably don't know. They don't know that socialism—especially this new, hip version of it that's being pushed by the Democrats—is all just a bunch of nice-sounding lies. They're happy to buy the rosy picture that the current Democrat Party is pushing. When Democrats tell them that what they're proposing isn't "real socialism," they're happy to go along with that, too. But socialism has been lurking on the left of the US political system for decades, spreading like a crack in the foundation a few inches every election cycle.

In the aftermath of John F. Kennedy's presidency and assassination, something called the New Left emerged in American politics. Much like Bernie's following, the new left found its strength on college campuses across the United States. Organizations such as Students for a Democratic Society (SDS) populated the movement.

Meanwhile, in Washington, Lyndon Baines Johnson, perhaps to provide cover for his failing war in Vietnam, tried to appease the New Left by ushering through a socialist agenda. Among the programs he supported were food stamps in 1964, Medicaid in 1965, and the Gun Control Act of 1968. By the early 1970s, the hippies of the New Left had traded their peace signs for raised fists and terrorist organizations. Among them was the Weather Underground, which was responsible for more than two thousand domestic bombings. The Weather Underground's manifesto, called *Prairie Fire: The Politics of Revolutionary Anti-imperialism*, is dedicated to Sirhan Sirhan, Robert Kennedy's assassin. Then there was the Black Liberation Army, which murdered seventeen American police officers in the 1970s, including six in New York City alone. There was the Symbionese Liberation Army, of Patty Hearst kidnapping fame. On the other side of the spectrum was the United States Christian Posse Association, a precursor of Aryan Nations, which preached violent white supremacy. It was domestic terror groups such as these that led the assault on the United States. In one poll taken at the time, more than 3 million Americans favored a revolution.

The election of Ronald Reagan as president in 1980 and the strength of capitalism brought an end to the socialist insanity that marked the prior decades. Even Bill Clinton tried to ride the prevailing winds. The Personal Responsibility and Work Opportunity Reconciliation Act he signed in 1996 sought to combat the cycle of poverty by putting limits on welfare. Still, under the surface, the cracks in the Democrats' foundation spread and deepened.

Out of those cracks, hidden socialists crawled.

I'm not sure anyone was paying attention in 1988, for example, when Bernie Sanders took a little jaunt over to the Soviet Union to meet with some of the party leaders he admired so much. Anyway, why would they have noticed? In those days, Comrade Bernie was still just the hippie mayor of Burlington, Vermont. No one took him seriously.

Less than four days into his trip, he found himself in a sweaty Russian sauna singing "This Land Is Your Land" with a bunch of bare-chested Communists. I know that sounds like a nightmare, but I can assure you that it is all too real.

It used to be the case that most people—even other crazy liberal Democrats—would just look the other way when Bernie started talking. I don't know if there was two-camera programming on C-SPAN back in the early 2000s. But if there had been, today you would be able to find clips of Crazy Bernie ranting to an empty Senate chamber, going on about socialized medicine while the janitors came through and scraped gum off the bottoms of the desks.

Next to not having him in the Senate at all, leaving him alone was probably the best way to deal with the guy. Maybe we should have taken him more seriously.

Many people saw Sanders's run for the presidency in 2016 as a joke. But his crazy socialist ideas of free college, free health care for all, higher minimum wage, income redistribution, and tearing the heart out of capitalism almost gave him the Democrat Party's nomination. It's hard to run against "free everything." Even if that is a pipe dream, it's appealing to those who don't get or choose not to realize that nothing is free. He won twenty-three primaries, 13.2 million votes, and 1,865 delegates. Though he ultimately lost to Hillary, in what was really a stolen and rigged primary, his success gave birth to a new generation of socialists who now threaten to take over the Democrat Party—and the country, if they ever find their way to power.

———

A few years before Bernie took his little Soviet vacation, I was on my first-ever plane ride to Prague. I was five years old, going to with my grandfather to visit his home in Communist Czechoslovakia. I had already been once when I was two years old, but this was my first trip without my parents.

Looking back, I guess the trip to where my mother had grown up served two purposes. First, it gave my parents a little peace and quiet for a couple of months, and second, it allowed me to see what life looked like outside a Fifth Avenue penthouse. My parents didn't believe that a childhood of privilege would do anything good for my development as a human being. My father actually had the conversation with my grandfather, and they both agreed that I needed to see the other side.

My maternal grandfather put in as much work raising me as anyone else in my family. Dedo, Czech for "grandfather," was tall and handsome with a long, lean body that he'd built by swimming laps in the public pool as a competitor. According to my grandmother, he had been a Czech national team swimming contender as a teenager, but I never got the full story about that. He had dark hair and rough workingman's hands that were about as big as my whole face. In Czechoslovakia, he was a blue-collar electrician. He was very much his own man in everything he did.

Throughout my entire childhood, Dedo would tell me how lucky I was to live in the United States, a place where a man could get whatever he wanted through hard work and perseverance. I had the kind of freedom he had yearned for his most of his life. But he also warned me about growing up rich and how easy it would be for me to become complacent.

Given that the left will tell you that I was potty trained on a solid-gold toilet, I guess I got his point.

Zlín was a three-hour drive from Prague. The building my grandparents lived in was gray and drab, twelve stories of cheap concrete-and-metal construction. It was designed in the old Soviet fashion, not to make money or push architecture forward but to keep the status quo. The apartment was a one-bedroom, as were all the apartments in the building. They were barely big enough for a couple, let alone a family. I don't remember the structure having an elevator. I made a friend on the tenth floor, and we would run up and down the stairs to see each other.

Visiting my grandparents was like going back in time sixty years. Most of the people who lived there kept chickens in the backyard. I would help my friends pluck and butcher them—I butchered hundreds of chickens in my childhood. Milk was sold in glass bottles with foil seals. Although the apartment was in the city, it was on the outskirts. Three hundred yards or so from where they lived was a tree line to a small forest we called "the woods." After breakfast and the wood chopping, Dedo would point to the woods and say, "There's the woods. Go. I'll see you at dark." I'd spend all day in the woods trying to master the things my grandfather had shown me how to do: shoot a bow and an air gun, make a fire, swing an ax, and throw a knife—all that guy stuff. There were aqueduct tunnels that my friends and I would explore, holding up homemade torches made with pine sap. It was during those early experiences that I first began to love the outdoors, a love that's a fixture of my life to this day.

Though I treasured the great outdoors, I wasn't crazy about speaking Czech at first. My mother and grandparents had started speaking it to me so early that by the time I was three, I was completely fluent. Sometimes I couldn't tell the difference between Czech and English. I only knew that my friends back in New York would laugh at me when I slipped into speaking Czech by accident. To this day, I have a clear memory of sitting in my grandmother's kitchen one night and screaming "Nechci mluvit česky!" at the top of my lungs. It means "I don't want to speak Czech!" in Czech. I totally didn't realize I was doing it.

(Just as an aside, I'm sure if anyone heard me speaking Czech, they'd take it as some kind of proof that I had colluded with Russia. I've actually heard pundits on television using my second language as proof that I must love "Mother Russia." Not only is the Czech language different from Russian, the Czechs have no love of Russia. If those crazies had bothered to learn the history between the two countries, they would have known that the Soviet Union occupied Czechoslovakia from just after World War II to the fall of the Berlin Wall. The Russians destroyed many things in the country. So, there's certainly no love lost there, to say the least. But these days, the narrative rules the facts.)

Still, there was something about life in Zlín that I found comforting. Around a campfire, I developed amazing friendships that I've kept to this day. In Czechoslovakia, I learned the value of friends over tangible objects. Despite the difficulties they endured, the people there had great relationships, great families whom they cared about. They just had to do it somewhat hidden from the Communist Party, I guess. Eastern Europeans are some of the hardest-working people in America—once they get here. The thing that they were missing in Czechoslovakia was motivation.

My grandparents lived practically their whole lives around people who relied on the government for everything. When Czech citizens wanted a new house, they talked to the government. When they wanted a new job or a promotion, they spoke to the government. Health care and elder care and retirement funds, all low quality compared to their counterparts in the United States, came from the state. In Czechoslovakia, the government gave the people everything they needed to exist (barely) and then asked for a small amount of labor in return. People worked in careers that would maintain the status quo and provide for the state, and everyone made roughly the same amount of money. No one could make a higher wage just because he or she worked harder. There were no incentives, so there was no economic growth. The only people with any money were the people who had connections to the top ranks of the Communist Party, and most of that money was either dirty or stolen.

If you weren't in the Communist Party, things were harder. My grandfather refused to join the Party and got away with it only because of his expertise as an electrician. Because of their non-Party status, my grandparents were always last in line for everything. The government issued tickets for food, but by the time my grandmother got her turn, there would be nothing left. My grandfather once waited eight hours for an orange. My grandmother made all of my mother's dresses by hand because the store shelves were empty when she was allowed to shop.

On my visits to the country, I experienced the bread lines and the poverty myself. When I talk about why socialism is bad, it's not because I've read articles about it or seen people talking about it on Twitter. I've been there, and I know why no one who's actually lived under these systems ever advocates for them.

Because my grandfather wasn't in the Party, he and my grandmother felt the stifling grip of communism even more than most. The whole time Czechoslovakia was a Soviet state, they were under constant surveillance. I'm sure if you look back in the Party archives, you'd find a file about each of them. If my grandparents came to see us in the United States, they would always be questioned extensively upon returning home to Czechoslovakia.

So, I guess it's not just me and my father. People in my family have been getting spied on by governments for generations!

———

Stepping off the plane that first time, I came face-to-face—well, face-to-hand, really—with life behind the Iron Curtain. The line for customs was long and moved slowly; the Communist Party of Czechoslovakia was about as easily offended in those days as your average American liberal is today. Customs agents, dressed more like soldiers, searched everything. If they found anything offensive on your person, you were either arrested or, in my case, reprimanded.

At the time, I had a favorite jacket that had blue and white stars on the back like the American flag. Though I can't remember, I would imagine my mother had bought it for me. When it was my turn, the customs agent glared down at me as though I were a tiny spy (I guess there's something about the way I look).

"You can't wear that here," he said, pointing at my jacket.

Though I understood the guard's Czech, I didn't realize what I had done wrong. I didn't know that the jacket was too American for a Communist country.

I remember looking around the room and seeing how afraid all the Czech citizens were on my behalf. I'm sure they had seen similar scenarios play out much differently, especially when the offender wasn't a five-year-old kid. My grandfather told me to take the jacket off, and then he talked to the guard. Whatever he said, it was enough to appease the agent, and we made our way through. In the car, on the way to my grandparents' apartment, I asked my grandfather why the man didn't like my jacket.

"Things are different here," he said.

As much as I look back fondly on all the time I spent with my grandparents in Czechoslovakia, that incident with the jacket remains one of my earliest childhood memories. I think it's because of how serious things got all of a sudden. Even after all the fun memories fade away, I'm sure I'll still have the feeling of what it was like under the stare of that customs officer.

It didn't take me long to notice how dull and similar everything in Czechoslovakia was. Compared to the view from the roof of Trump Tower, where I went many times as a kid, New York City was an IMAX movie while Czechoslovakia was a black-and-white photograph.

Every new building was made of the same gray concrete. All the clothes were the same colors and the same styles. Even the appliances in my grandmother's kitchen looked as though they had rolled off the same drab assembly line. There were only two channels on television—one cartoon for kids called "Vechernczrk," which aired every night around dinner time, for a total of ten minutes and another news station for adults.

Soon I began to see the dichotomy between the two countries. I could sense that there was something underneath all those tall buildings and twinkling lights in Manhattan that was absent in the Soviet Union. The engine that made it all run. Later, I would learn that the engine was called the market and the missing piece was called capitalism.

———

I was eleven years old in 1989 when the Berlin Wall fell and the Communist government of the Soviet Union started to crumble. The change came rapidly to my grandparents' hometown. By 1992, Czechoslovakia was being called the Czech Republic. The government embraced the principles of democracy and capitalism. Suddenly it was time for the Czech people to work hard and build an economy that could compete on the world stage. It was a tall order, and not everyone was happy.

My friends in the Czech Republic would tell me how hard it was to make the transition from a command economy, where the state makes the rules and requires the bare minimum of its citizens, to a market economy, where citizens get only what they work for and government handouts are slimmer. Much like people who depend on welfare in the United States, many had gotten used to not working and getting everything for free. Teaching them to start businesses and earn money for themselves was more difficult than anyone had expected—although for those with the ability and the willingness to work, the possibilities were endless.

Though it wasn't an easy transition to make, it was a good one. As long as a country is continually moving away from socialism, away from free rides and handouts from the state, and toward the free market, that country will always be better off.

———

The story of the Democrat Party is the exact opposite of Czechoslovakia's. Instead of embracing capitalism, they've descended into socialism. This would be bad enough if the people who were pushing socialist policies had any idea what socialism is or how horrible it is for people who have to live under it, but it's much worse that they don't. Maybe Bernie Sanders and his acolytes in Congress do but don't care. That makes their actions even worse.

Socialists have taken advantage of every crisis to promote their policies and spend millions of dollars on marketing (oh, the irony) to convince young people that socialism can take care of everything for them. Bernie Sanders alone has three houses. He's made millions of dollars under capitalism while preaching like a crazy person for its opposite. Let's call him the "Commie Capitalist." People like him say that socialism can pay off student loans, provide a universal basic income, even provide free college and health care. In 2016, a YouGov poll found that 44 percent of young people between the ages of sixteen and twenty-nine would rather live in a socialist country than a capitalist one like the United States. As if that weren't scary enough, only 33 percent of the people could even describe with any accuracy what the word *socialism* means. This is precisely the way Bernie Sanders has wanted it all along: push lies for years until you make a majority of the population ignorant enough to believe those lies.

I have to admit that for a socialist, he's come up with a pretty good business model.

If Democrats had taken some action to rein in their craziest member a few years ago, they might have been able to fix their problem and regain some degree of sanity. Today, the chances of that happening are about as good as the chances of Bernie ringing the opening bell at the New York Stock Exchange. The midterm elections of 2018—which, by the way, were unfairly influenced by the baseless Russia collusion investigation—was a turning point. As soon as the new class of freshman socialists rolled into the Capitol building (once they found it), any hope of reconciliation went out the window.

Now the Democrat Party has tilted so far left that it threatens to collapse any day. Just look at what remains of the party's presidential hopefuls. Elizabeth Warren wants to arm the IRS (not literally but with more pencils) to punish the wealthiest people in the country. It doesn't matter to her if they made their money by working hard, then creating jobs. She believes that the money belongs to the government. Of course, that didn't stop her from making almost $500,000 a year from teaching one class at Harvard. It's no wonder why college tuition is through the roof!

Kamala Harris wants to get rid of all private health care and replace it with a single-payer government-issued model. The fact that the US government owes $122 trillion in unfunded liabilities such as Social Security and Medicare doesn't even faze her. Just dump more debt on the pile, and let our children figure out how to pay for it.

Then there are the future leaders of the Socialist, I mean, Democrat, Party. Alexandria Ocasio-Cortez, Ilhan Omar, Rashida Tlaib, and Ayanna Pressley, or "the Squad," as they're commonly known, stand somewhere left of Chairman Mao. Their radical beliefs have real-world consequences.

As you might remember, a few years back, Amazon, the world's largest internet retailer, announced it was beginning a search for a new headquarters. The announcement was big news and caused quite a stir. Nearly every major city in the country wanted to be picked, with most offering Amazon billions of dollars in tax breaks and subsidies. One smaller city even promised to change its name to Amazon and proclaim Amazon CEO Jeff Bezos its king—a little excessive, if you ask me, but you really couldn't blame it. After all, the proposed headquarters promised to be one of the largest corporate investments in US history, creating fifty thousand high-paying tech jobs.

After a fourteen-month search, Amazon decided on two sites instead of one. The lucky winners were northern Virginia and a neighborhood in Queens, New York, called Long Island City. There was a lot of disappointment across the country, but for Queens and New York City, it was like hitting the lottery. Not only did it mean twenty-five thousand high-paying jobs—six-figure jobs in a city that badly needed the revenue—but also union construction jobs, service industry jobs, and a massive infusion of cash into the local economy. Any way you looked at it, it was a good deal—at least to people who know what a good deal looks like.

Obviously, Alexandria Ocasio-Cortez is not one of those people. Here's what the princess of the socialist Democrat Party had to say: "Frankly, if we were willing to give away $3 billion for this deal, we could invest those $3 billion in our district, ourselves if we wanted to. We could hire out more teachers. We can fix our subways."

Apparently, AOC was under the impression that New York City was going to write Amazon a check for $3 billion. She had no idea what a tax incentive is or what it does. The $3 billion Amazon would save in taxes would go toward construction and salaries that would, in turn, be taxed, creating nearly $30 billion in revenue for the city and community by some estimates. When Amazon saw the socialist stink that AOC and others put up, the company backed out of the deal quicker than Bernie Sanders can comb his hair. Uh-uh, the folks there thought, no way are we going to build in Queens, not when two hundred other cities are lining up to give us tax breaks. On February 14, 2019, Amazon officially pulled out of the deal. Although it didn't mention AOC by name in the announcement, it was pretty clear who it was talking about. It read in part: "a number of state and local politicians [who] have made it clear that they oppose our presence and will not work with us to build the type of relationships that are required to go forward with the project we and many others envisioned in Long Island City."

Now, I'm not saying that Amazon was an innocent bystander in the collapse of the deal. It is a ruthless corporation that has practices that you don't have to be socialist to dislike. It turned their back on the people of Queens without giving it so much as a second thought. Jeff Bezos, the supposed champion of the free press, had about as much compassion for the people of Queens as a Mafia hit man.

The main villain, however, was the freshman member of Congress who couldn't name the three branches of government when she was elected and didn't know the basic economics of a tax break.

People who think socialists who shut down deals like the Amazon one in Queens are working for the greater good have it backward; AOC is working against the interests of the people she represents. Nearly single-handedly, she ruined a deal that would have brought tens of thousands of jobs to her neighboring district, tens of billions of dollars to the city she represents, and the headquarters of one of the biggest tech companies in the world to Queens.

She was only getting started.

———

The idea for the Green New Deal began with a group called the Sunrise Movement, started by recent college graduate environmental activists who drew inspiration from Occupy Wall Street and Black Lives Matter. Some even say their roots can be traced back to Saul Alinsky, the gift to the right who keeps on giving. Alinsky, as you might remember, wrote a book back in 1971 called

Rules for Radicals in which he cited Lucifer as the father of the radical movement. Barack Obama and Hillary Clinton both idolized Alinsky.

The Sunrise Movement started to get notoriety when some of its members staged a sit-in in Nancy Pelosi's office. It is also the group responsible for the famous YouTube video in which Senator Dianne Feinstein scolds a bunch of children as young as seven. The children were recruited by the movement as a publicity stunt and to put pressure on the senator to back the Green New Deal.

"You know better than I do, so I think one day you should run for the Senate and then you do it your way," Ms. Feinstein told one of the girls.

"Great," she replied. "I will."

But it was when AOC joined forces with Sunrise that the group's Green New Deal really gained momentum. Along with her cosponsor in the Senate, Edward J. Markey, a Democrat from Massachusetts, AOC introduced the ridiculous resolution to Congress.

If you're not familiar with the details of the proposal, allow me to give you some of the high points. First off, it would cost US taxpayers almost $100 trillion dollars—$93 trillion to be precise, since I've stumped a lot on it. That's trillion with a *t*. To put that number into perspective, the US government has annual revenues of about $6 trillion. So AOC and her socialist pals want to spend what would be the equivalent of about fifteen years of the US government's revenue to stop cows from farting, eliminate air travel, build an underground tunnel from California to Hawaii, and fund people who don't want to work.

If we spent nothing on the military, nothing on entitlements, and nothing on education and focused only on farting cows, in fifteen years we might be able to pay for AOC's Green New Deal.

In the meantime, we would wreck the US economy and actually do little to clean up the environment. The proposal calls for covering hundreds of thousands of acres of land with windmills and solar panels, which would do irreparable damage to land on which wildlife is protected by federal statutes. It also addresses only the United States' carbon emissions and gives countries like China and India a pass for a decade. I'm no scientist, but I'm pretty sure we can't keep China's dirty air from sneaking into the atmosphere over the United States. I am pretty good at economics, though, and economists have a term for that type of thinking: freaking stupid. AOC once said that people her age should reconsider having children because of global warming. Can you imagine? I think the best answer to that ridiculous statement was by my friend, Jerry Falwell, Jr., "People her age should reconsider having children if people like AOC ever get to be in charge of this country."

Still, just about every Democrat presidential candidate jumped on board the AOC crazy train because they were unwilling to take on a freshman congresswoman who was elected in a district that Nancy Pelosi said a glass of water with a "D" on it could win—and who, after being sworn in, could not name the three branches of government. This is who they wouldn't stand up to? There needs to be an adult in the room, but there isn't.

Of course, they had ulterior motives, as most career politicians do. The Green New Deal is less about the reduction of fossil fuel and more a progressives' letter to Santa with a list of all the gifts the liberals want for Christmas. If they couldn't stand up to AOC, good luck with standing up to China and North Korea.

In an article she wrote for The Intercept, Naomi Klein, an author, anti-Trump feminist, and AOC supporter (and Canadian, by the way), explained the reach a select committee steering the deal would have: "By giving the committee a mandate that connects the dots between energy, transportation, housing and construction, as well as health care, living wages, a jobs guarantee, and the urgent imperative to battle racial and gender injustice, the Green New Deal plan would be mapping precisely that kind of far-reaching change."

Did she mention everything? Let's see: Medicare for all? Check. Minimum wage? Check. Police reform, voting rights, pay equality regardless of merit? Check, check, and check. Economic security for all those who are unable or *unwilling* to work? A big, fat check!

———

When you strip away the naiveté of a freshman congresswoman from the proposal, what's left of the Green New Deal is a Hollywood-fueled publicity stunt. As Saul Alinsky wrote: "The threat is usually more terrifying than the thing itself." Mitch McConnell exposed the sham when he said, okay, sure, let's bring the Green New Deal proposal to the floor of the Senate for a vote. When he did, the only ones who would go on the record with a vote were Democrats Joe Manchin of West Virginia, Kyrsten Sinema of Arizona, and Doug Jones of Alabama, together with Angus King of Maine, an independent, and all of them voted against the resolution. McConnell was accused of participating in "political theater" for doing his job and bringing the bill to a vote. Imagine! Allowing them to vote on their own bill was political theater!

It seems that for Democrats, knowing what they're talking about is not as important as looking as though they know what they're talking about. Sometimes they don't even care about looking good.

With all her talk about saving the planet, AOC has put a new spin on the phrase "limousine liberal." According to a story in the *New York Post*, she runs up Uber tabs like crazy. It wouldn't be so bad if she had no other way to get around. But her congressional district, which includes parts of Queens and the Bronx, has about five or six subway lines.

She responded to the article in typical sanctimonious fashion: "Living in the world as it is isn't an argument against working towards a better future."

Hey, listen, girlfriend, you want to get driven around by Uber, go for it. But if you're going to keep telling people the apocalypse is upon us, you might want to think about carrying a MetroCard.

And then there's Maxine Waters. At a House Financial Services Committee hearing in April 2019, Waters, the Democrat chair of the committee, grilled banking CEOs about their role in student loan defaults. "What are you going to do about it?" she demanded of one banker. The banker sat there for a moment, perplexed. "We stopped making student loans back in 2007," he finally answered. "So you don't do it anymore?" Waters wondered aloud. Embarrassed for her, the banker shook his head. During the Obama administration, all student loans had been taken over by the federal government. So just to be clear, the congressional chairperson of the committee that oversees federal student loans didn't know that the government she worked for was in charge of all student loans. Now you know why my father says she's a low-IQ person.

With ignorance at the wheel of a see-through proposal the size and audacity of the Green New Deal, only bad things can happen. When pressed, Democrats can't even defend it. All they can do is point fingers at the right and say ridiculous things like "You don't love the planet." Right. That's it.

———

Though some people dismiss AOC as a flash in the pan, or the flavor of the day, they shouldn't. With more than 5 million Twitter followers and more than 3 million Instagram followers, she's a socialist star. She's been on the cover of a half-dozen major magazines. If people think she and her socialist plans are going to disappear, they have another thing coming.

Today, she's the leader of many socialist and socialist-leaning Democrats. Her squad of socialists is pushing an agenda that includes abolishing Immigration and Customs Enforcement (ICE), the Department of Homeland Security, and the Electoral College, expanding the Supreme Court from nine to fifteen justices to ensure a liberal majority, mandating a $15 minimum wage (which would eliminate 4 million low-paying jobs), and paying for the health care of illegal immigrants. And that's only some of the destruction it's planning.

For instance, the Squad does little to hide its disdain for Israel. We should probably rename them "the Hamas caucus." Omar opened a recent panel discussion by saying, "I want to talk about the political influence in this country that says it is okay for people to push for allegiance to a foreign country." Her inference was that Jewish members of Congress were more loyal to Israel than to the United States. Earlier, she had tweeted that politicians support Israeli causes because Jews have money to donate. The House of Representatives voted to condemn anti-Semitism in response to her remarks. Both Omar and Rashida Tlaib are supporters of the Palestinian-led Boycott, Divestment, Sanctions (BDS) movement. Endorsed by the Democratic Socialists of America, BDS pressures economic leaders to withdraw support from Israel and to support reparations for the descendants of slaves.

Pressley, the least scrutinized of the Squad, is no better. Though the Squad is quick to play the racism card under any circumstance, Pressley engages in a sort of in-kind racism, demanding that people of color follow the Socialist Party line. "We don't need any more brown faces that don't want to be a brown voice. We don't need any more black faces that don't want to be a black voice," she said at a Democrat activist convention. Can there be only one black or brown voice? Can they not have different opinions? Well, it seems not, at least not according to the radicals.

That rhetoric and those views might seem radical to a normal person, but they've already entered the mainstream of the Democrat Party. Twenty-one of the thirty-two candidates the Democratic Socialists of America endorsed in the past midterm election won. According to a recent Pew Research Center survey, 84 percent of Republicans have a negative view of socialism, while nearly two-thirds of Democrats (65 percent) have a positive one.

Socialists have made America's youths their prime target. The magazine *Teen Vogue* spreads the propaganda and has become a socialism influencer for teenage girls. Along with flattering profiles of Karl Marx and Bernie Sanders, it has run articles that criticized capitalism, promoted prostitution as a career choice, and described anal sex. The Socialism 2019 conference in Chicago, which had the tag line "No Borders, No Bosses, No Binary," invited the magazine to hold a panel discussion.

Like the weaponizing of the new left in the late 1960s, today's radical left has resorted to terrorism. We'll talk a lot about Antifa in the pages ahead, but for now, please know that AOC and her Squad are perfectly fine with the deadly violence the organization engages in. Last July, an Antifa activist showed up at an ICE facility in Tacoma, Washington, armed with a rifle and incendiary devices. Washington State Patrol police shot him dead as he was trying to blow up a propane tank next to the facility with a Molotov cocktail. When asked on Sunday-morning news shows if they condemned the terrorist attack, none of the Squad would answer the question. Then, in reference to the terrorist attacks of September 11, 2001, Ilhan Omar brushed them off by saying, "Some people did something."

You tell me which side those people are on. People like Omar were literally saved by the United States, and she repays the soldiers who will help keep her safe by insulting them. As I said on Twitter, I'll bet that when Omar watched Black Hawk Down, she roots for the Somali warlords.

President Trump knows foundations as well as anyone and certainly better than anybody else in the political world. Over the course of his first term, he's built a solid foundation on which America can soar, bringing us back to the glory we once had. Solid construction is the enemy of socialism. Democrats will do everything they can to sabotage what my dad is building. We can't let them worm their way in.

4.

CLASS WARFARE

AS YOU CAN PROBABLY GUESS, my father and I didn't spend a whole lot of time tossing a baseball back and forth in the backyard. When your backyard is a busy patch of a Fifth Avenue sidewalk, playing catch isn't an easy thing to do. It seems that Manhattan pedestrians don't take kindly to getting whacked in the head by flying objects.

Instead, during our weekends and summer vacations, my father would take me, my brother, and my sister out to his job sites, letting us trail alongside him the way his own father had done with him. We would arrive early in the morning as the crews were setting up, and I would walk with my dad while he inspected the concrete foundations and metal stairways. Whether it was a golf course or a building, he would walk every inch of it. He has an incredible attention to detail—from the quality of the cement to how many dishes cabinets will hold to the depth of a sand trap. If there were any imperfections, no matter the size or the significance, he would notice. He could figure out how to do the best job at the lowest cost, something the government doesn't seem to think about very much. He would spend a whole day on the site, then come back the next day to make sure he hadn't missed anything. He looked—well, you've seen the photos: dark suit and long overcoat, out of context on a job site. But there was nowhere my father was more at home. He loved talking with the men and women who made it all happen for him. Many of those men and women, by the way, occupy senior positions at Trump Tower today. The same people who taught me to swing a hammer now help me make major decisions about new projects.

During lunch breaks, I would sit with the union contractors and plumbers while they ate. We would talk about sports and the events of the day, and my brother and I would ask every question about power tools and construction equipment we could think of. I was always amazed by heavy machinery and, in fact, would go on to learn how to drive bulldozers and maneuver cranes. I always said that Eric and I were the only sons of billionaires who could drive D-10 Caterpillars and run chainsaws. We had done just that before we could even drive a car, at least legally.

In the afternoons, I would hear my father talking with the men and women who were in charge of design and development. Those conversations could get tense, especially when they were about deadlines or budgets. But there could be laughter, too. When my father talked to me about the construction business, he would emphasize the need to be both precise and flexible, and to be physically on the site and not in some boardroom listening to people read from spreadsheets. He didn't lock himself in an office and look at monitors all day. He was on the ground. It was good advice, both for the construction business and for life. It's also pretty good advice for running a country. Not only should you do a better job, you should do a better job for less money. To paraphrase Ronald Reagan, this is even more important when you're spending other people's money.

To give me my own solid foundation, my father made my brother and me get jobs as soon as we could lift our own tools. He put us in the care of a couple of his loyal employees, Brian Baudreau and Vinny Stellio. Brian would drive me to school when I was a kid, and had little or no experience in construction when he began working for my dad. But Dad saw something in him that wasn't on his written résumé. My father promoted people based on their character, street smarts, and work ethic, people—as I said in my 2016 Republican National Convention speech—with doctorates in common sense. Brian went on to head the construction of our hotel on the Las Vegas Strip, bringing it in on time and under budget in the middle of the financial crisis. Now he runs the hotel, and he does it better than those who had been doing the job for decades. Vinny Stellio started as a bodyguard for my father and rose to become one of his most trusted advisors in Trump Org. Sometimes he would drive us to school, too. They were smart guys—brilliant, even—but they didn't have the right degrees or the right acronyms behind their names to get a good start in most businesses. Most executives wouldn't even have given them the time of day. But DJT was different. He saw their talent, work ethic, street smarts, and he allowed them to run with those qualities.

Learning the business also came naturally to me. For generations, the men in our family had worked construction jobs. As I mentioned, my grandfather on my mother's side was an electrician in Communist Czechoslovakia. He kept the lights on—or at least flickering—in the shabby gray buildings of the area, a job that paid enough to put food on the table and to rent his small apartment in the city. He had a huge impact on my life. As I have come to learn, my Czechoslovakian grandparents were very important to my development as a person and to my politics.

On my father's side, of course, we had the famous Fred Trump, a man I know means as much to my father as my father does to me. Throughout my life, I would hear my father hold his father up as the shining example of work ethic and business acumen.

So when it came time to get a job, I figured I would do something with my hands. It seemed only natural after all the time I had spent hanging around job sites as a kid. By that time, I could tell the sound of a Sawzall from a circular saw. I could hang Sheetrock, pour concrete, and get a stripped Phillips-head screw out of a wall without much trouble. Though I might forget which fork you were supposed to use with salad at a dinner party, I did know what grit sandpaper you'd use on the table. My mom eventually got some of the etiquette to stick, but it took a while.

Though I mowed lawns in Connecticut in my early teens, my first real job came when I was fifteen. I worked the summer at my father's casino on the marina in Atlantic City. There were docks outside, and the beautiful people docking boats in the harbor kept me busy all summer. Some days I would be a dock attendant, throwing ropes over the boats for pretty good tips. For a while, it was a good time. I hung out with pretty girls, made a bunch of friends, and had plenty of spending money. Then, a couple of years later, I got what I thought was a promotion and ended up out in the woods with a chain saw in my hands.

Clearing land for a development, I discovered a very different world from the one I had known on the docks. All of a sudden, the pretty girls were gone, I was making no money in tips, and every human being in sight was a sweaty man in work boots.

Not exactly what you'd call a promotion. But I learned everything I could about doing manual labor and soaked up all the norms of behavior that came with being around working men. It was good for me to be working and making my own money, especially because a lot of the kids who grew up like I did went the route of the spoiled brats you see in movies: taking limousines to school, partying in the New York clubs, and going away to expensive resorts for spring break. (Although I may have done some of that myself. I never said I was perfect, did I?) Getting away from all that every summer was good for me. To this day, Eric and I are probably the only sons of a billionaire who could parallel park a Caterpillar D-10 in Manhattan if we had to, because that's what we did all summer as kids.

It was during that "promotion," however, that I got my first hard lesson in negotiation—and the lesson came from none other than Donald J. Trump. Looking back, it was a little like playing your first pickup basketball game against Michael Jordan.

My father did not operate at half speed when it came to deal-making, even with his kids—and he still doesn't. He wasn't going to pull punches. That's how we were going to learn—the hard way. Going in, I'm sure I thought, *Hey, I'm this guy's kid, he'll go easy on me, cut me a break, treat me different from everyone else.*

I was very wrong.

Here's what happened. Hanging around the job site one day, I started doing a little math (which was never my best subject as a youngster, but when it came to money, I was able to figure it out). I thought, *I used to make hundreds of dollars in tips, smelling nothing but sunscreen and salt water, and now I'm in mud and sawdust up to my knees, wiping dirt out of my eyes, and working around sweaty dudes for less money.* I decided I would tell my father that weekend after dinner what I had realized about my paychecks. I assumed that he would immediately raise my pay and commend me for realizing how unfair the system was to working guys like me.

Easy.

What actually happened was much different. But to this day, I'm grateful that it did. It was a light-bulb-over-the-head moment for me. Here's how it all went down, written as a one-act play, just so you get the full experience that I did (notice that "Don Jr." does not have a major speaking role).

> *[Interior, dinner table. Donald J. Trump seated at the head.]*
> *[Enter Don Jr. with very long hair, probably wearing cargo shorts and a camouflage T-shirt.]*
>
> **Don Jr.:** Dad, I've realized that even though I'm doing more work on the job site, you're paying me way less money for it. Why didn't I get a raise?
>
> **Dad:** Well, you didn't ask me for more money, so I didn't give you more money. That's how the world works. Why would I give you more money than you're willing to work for? That would make me an idiot.
>
> **Don Jr.:** I, uh—
>
> **Dad:** Why would I do that? You think people are going to give you more money just because you're a nice guy? They're not, Donnie. Anything you want, you have to go out and get it. Nothing is going to be handed to you. Nothing. You have to earn it before you ask for it! Always remember: you don't get anything you don't ask for.
>
> *[End of scene.]*

Over the next few minutes, I think I tried negotiating for a retroactive raise. I may have even pulled some pie charts out of my shorts. My father found it amusing, but he didn't budge. That day I learned a few lessons that have stuck with me. Number one: You shouldn't expect to get anything in life that you didn't work for. Number two: If you don't ask for it, don't expect it. And number three: When someone goes around offering things for free, don't believe them. In most cases, that person is either a liar or an idiot.

Or a leftist, which means they're both.

This is as true in the boardroom of Trump Tower as it is out on the campaign trail. As I learned time and time again in 2016, if you want someone to vote for you, you have to go to work and earn that vote. If you want a donation, you need to explain where the money is going to go and why you need it. You shouldn't take anyone's support for granted. And once you get that support, it's time to enact policies that will make the people who gave you their vote proud that they did.

By the way, throughout this book, I'm going to tell you about all the "regular Joe" things I did, such as hunting, driving heavy construction equipment, and sleeping on my buddies' couches. I know the trigger-happy people on the left will pop a cork and accuse me of trying to be somebody I'm not. To be honest, I don't give a crap what they think. But I don't want to give you, my faithful readers, the wrong impression. Though I did spend a lot of my childhood in the woods in Czechoslovakia and I did learn how to drive one of my dad's Caterpillars, I did my fair share of rich-kid stuff, too.

I grew up in an enormous triplex at the top of Trump Tower and spent a lot of the year in Greenwich, Connecticut. I really *could* play football in the living room, and I could see almost the entire island of Manhattan from the windows of our apartment. One day, my sister Ivanka was kicking a beachball around the living room of our house in Greenwich, and she shattered a big chandelier. There were pieces of glass everywhere. When my mother came into the room and saw the mess, Ivanka told her it was me who did it. I wasn't even there! My mother proceeded to beat the crap out of me (she broke a wooden spoon on my ass, if I remember correctly), even though I had no idea what was going on. By the time she was done and Ivanka fessed up, my mother was too tired and over it to do anything to her. As usual, Ivanka got off scot-free, and I've been plotting my revenge ever since . . . Ivanka if you're reading, when you least expect it, expect it!

Most mornings, I was driven to private school, and we had nannies. And, oh, by the way, in the winter we would go to a place called Mar-a-Lago.

My father bought the massive mansion in the late 1980s. It might have been the greatest deal ever recorded in Palm Beach: twenty acres on the Atlantic that stretched to the Intracoastal Waterway in one of the richest zip codes in the country. The main house had fifty-eight bedrooms, thirty-three bathrooms, and an 1,800-square-foot living room with a forty-two-foot-high ceiling. Dad bought it from the federal government for about $7 million, or about the price the original owner, cereal heiress Marjorie Merriweather Post, had paid to have it built in 1923. The asking price was sweet enough, but the deal became even better when the untapped value of the house was calculated. Ms. Post had collected antique furniture from all over the world, including from European castles. Though beautiful and very expensive, the furniture wasn't practical. Dad sold most of it and almost paid for Mar-a-Lago with the proceeds.

Though my father's entrepreneurial spirit would eventually kick in and he would turn the mansion into a club, when we first moved to Mar-a-Lago, it was our winter home. I was seven at the time, Ivanka was four, and Eric was two. For us, it was like the movie *Night at the Museum*. We explored every inch of the mansion. Hide-and-seek games were epic. You could put a full-grown palm tree in the living room, so for us it was like having our own private indoor stadium. When my parents had parties, I would climb up onto the rafters over the entranceway of the living room with a handful of raisins. As the guests passed by underneath, I would fire the raisins at them, trying to land them in their drinks. More than once, guests looked at their cocktail and thought there were spiders falling from the ceiling.

———

To be honest, I was much more comfortable in the rafters than down with the people in the living room. I didn't take to the opulent lifestyle the way some children of billionaires do. It's not that I despised my father's money, because I really didn't. Even as a kid, I sensed that wealth and opulence were DJT's brand. I saw it as part of his job. Later, I would realize that it was the reason he had become so successful in the first place. Without his solid-gold image, I doubt there would be Trump properties all over the globe today, all of them rated among the highest quality in the world. That's not a plug, that's the truth.

Still, there was something that made me feel uncomfortable around the people who populated the rich circles my father lived and worked in. Even when Dad would bring home a celebrity, which he did often, I would usually run in the other direction. Although I did become friends with a few of them, including Herschel Walker, the Heisman Trophy winner who played for my dad's team in the USFL, the New Jersey Generals. When I was six, I took a trip to Disney World with Herschel and his family. He used to come to our house in Greenwich. His wife at the time once took a ride on my motocross bike and crashed it, seriously injuring herself. We remain friends to this day. There was also Michael Jackson, who lived in Trump Tower and with whom I played video games. One day in Eric's room, my father saw how much Michael enjoyed playing Teenage Mutant Ninja Turtles with us on Nintendo and told him he could take the game home. My game! To this day, Eric says it was his game because it was in his room, but I know whose game it was. I'd worked a summer job to pay for it! And here was Michael Jackson, probably a billionaire at this point, and he took it! The recent revelations about Jackson came as a shock to me. My experience with Michael does not include any of what he's been accused of. Oh, and by the way, given all the things my father has been called, particularly a "racist," it sure sounds odd that he'd let his son vacation with a black man or hang out with Michael Jackson, doesn't it? If he's a racist, he's sure not very good at it.

I'd like to say I wasn't impressed by social standing or celebrity, and certainly I would feel that way later on. But maybe the real reason was instinctual. I was much more at ease with the folks who worked for my dad. I became close with a number of the security guys at Trump Tower and other properties, most of whom were former New York City cops. I'm still friendly and go shooting with a few of them. For me, their stories from behind the scenes were always more interesting. Maybe the most productive relationships I had were with the chefs my parents hired. We always had world-class people who cooked for us. Having them cook for *me* was always way less comfortable. Within a few years, I was caramelizing onions and making soufflés right along with them, even taking over the kitchen and giving some of their dishes a shot on my own. All through my childhood, I cooked for myself alongside some of the best chefs in the world, and I learned a lifelong skill in the process. As a result, I can now cook some pretty impressive meals, and I've been teaching my kids to do the same thing. Even the fried eggs and bacon we cook over our campfires upstate have a few secret, chef-approved spices thrown in for flavor. I also try to help out with the more serious events when I'm not busy. When

Prince Charles came to Mar-a-Lago, for instance, I made him a nice meringue cookie. (If you're enjoying this book so far, keep an eye out for my self-help/cookbook, *Cooking Through Collusion with Junior!*, coming in 2024.)

I also spent as much time with my grandfather as I could. Half the year, my Czechoslovakian grandparents would stay with us in the United States. In Mar-a-Lago, I would find Dedo at the seawall, where he fished and smoked cigarettes. We would sit together for hours until our bucket was filled with pompano and jack. It was during those times that my grandfather impressed upon me that a man shouldn't get used to being dependent on anything or anyone— not the government, not his company, and certainly not his father. When things got too rich for me, I could always count on Dedo to remind me of what really mattered in life and to keep me grounded.

In the early 1980s, my father bought a twelve-acre estate on the water in Greenwich, Connecticut. We would go there in the summer, when Florida was too hot. It was an amazing house with eight bedrooms, indoor and outdoor pools, and a bowling alley in the basement. With Dedo, I would ride Suzuki motorbikes and dirt bikes around the grounds. We'd shoot bows and air guns. My grandfather had a little dory, and we would fish for bluefish and striped bass in Long Island Sound. It had a motor, but if I went out with him I would usually row (good practice for when I rowed at the University of Pennsylvania). It was Dedo who taught me to use everything we caught or hunted. Together, we built a smokehouse where we would smoke our catch. When I was with my grandfather, there were also plenty of laughs. Some of them came at my expense.

When I was six or seven, I decided one night to camp outside on the grounds of the Connecticut home. In my own mind, I was already a pretty experienced outdoorsman, so I figured there wouldn't be any problems. Dedo helped me put up a tent about three hundred yards from the main house. In Czechoslovakia, when I camped out, I had my friends with me. In Connecticut, however, I was all alone. I was in the tent only a few minutes when I heard howling. At seven, I didn't know that the only wolves in Greenwich worked on Wall Street. It turned out that my grandfather was the hidden howler, and he laughed as he watched me break the land speed record back to the house. You never saw someone run three hundred yards that fast in your life!

That's why it came as such a blow to me when in 1990 I got the call that Dedo had died of a sudden heart attack in the Czech Republic. I guess that medically, it wasn't that big of a surprise. He'd been smoking a couple of packs of cigarettes a day for most of his life. Emotionally, however, it was as though Mike Tyson had punched me in the gut. The funeral was in the Czech Republic, and the whole family went over.

From the day Dedo died forward, I felt slightly adrift in the world. It was as though I had been living my life on a pair of stilts—one anchored to the woods of Czechoslovakia, the other to the gridded streets and swanky apartments of Manhattan—and his death had knocked one of them right out from under me. As if Dedo's death weren't bad enough, my parents were going through a divorce that was playing out on the front pages of the New York tabloids. Every day it seemed that there was a new story about them or a new rumor just beginning to spread. I can only imagine what it would have been like if Twitter had existed when I as a kid.

If any good at all came out of my parents' divorce, it was the deeper bond that I developed with my sister and brother. Though we are very different people, we had always gotten along very well. We've always made a great team.

After the divorce, we sort of locked arms and got through it together. To this day, Ivanka, Eric, and I rib one another good-naturedly. When the news about this book leaked just after I signed the deal, liberal Twitter was pretty brutal to me. No surprise there. But even my sister had some fun at my expense.

> **@IvankaTrump:** When **#DonJrBookTitles** is trending on Twitter... **@EricTrump @LaraLeaTrump @TiffanyATrump @kimguilfoyle** and I are having some fun with this one!

I tweeted back that I was going to include some scandalous secrets about her. There's a lot of material from Ivanka's teen years. To be honest, however, there really isn't much bad to say. My sister was always able to handle life as a child of Donald Trump, along with all the press, paparazzi, and gossip that came with it, with the kind of grace and calm I could never muster. Anyone in my father's social circle during those years would have told you in a second that they wanted their daughters to grow up and be just like Ivanka. Later on in this book, when I tell you about fake news and its agenda against my father and his family, I'll show you what Ivanka has to endure. The constant onslaught by the media is incredibly unfair and cruel. Yet she's able to rise above the vindictiveness. So if you're reading this, Ivanka, don't worry. Your secrets are safe with me. I won't even write about how I stuffed one of your boyfriends into a suitcase and flung—or, um . . . gently rolled—him down the stairs. I'll keep my powder dry for the next Twitter attack.

———

The other good thing that came out of that horrible time was boarding school.

In 1990 or '91, my parents gave me the opportunity to go away to school in rural Pennsylvania, and I jumped at the chance. I've learned that sometimes the best decisions come out of the worst circumstances. The Hill School would change my life in a couple of very important ways, although not at first.

A feeder school for the Naval Academy and West Point, "Hill," as we called it, was an old-school type of place. There, it didn't matter one bit that I was Donald Trump's son. In fact, if anything, being a rich kid from New York got me my ass kicked more than usual. But guess what? I learned a lot from those beatings. I gave away eighty pounds to the seniors, so they weren't fair, but they were deserved. (I'm sure you're shocked to hear that.) My mouth developed faster than the rest of me. Stories about my parents' divorce ran in supermarket checkout publications such as *People* and Page Six of the *New York Post* all the time. The day they dropped me off at school, we stopped at Kmart to pick up some things for my dorm room. Someone took a picture of the three of us in front of the store, which ran in the local paper. We also stopped at Taco Bell, where my mother ordered a glass of chardonnay which was really, really awesome for a guy just trying to fit in. Really awesome, Mom. Thanks. When people in school read about those moments, it didn't make things any easier.

Luckily, the dean of students at Hill, a man named Gordon McAlpin, took me under his wing. The school had a small rifle range for small-bore shooting and another one just off campus for skeet and trap shooting. I had shot an air gun with my grandfather but had never done any shooting with a real firearm. Mr. McAlpin took me to the range my first time. Most of the students went there once or twice as a novelty. From the first time I went, however, I was hooked and went back as much as I could. You couldn't find a better outdoors mentor than Mr. McAlpin. He was the consummate outdoorsman, the kind of guy who could shoot a perfect skeet score with a .410 pump-action Winchester Model 42. Soon I started showing my own talent for shooting.

One Saturday in school, Mr. McAlpin told me to meet him in the parking lot the next morning at 6:00 a.m. and to dress warmly. That might not fly in today's world of helicopter parenting, but I thought it was awesome. Along with another student a couple of grades higher, I climbed into his car and we drove about an hour outside the campus to shoot birds. In the woods, I remember thinking that this was the coolest thing in the world. Afterward, I read every book I could about hunting and took every opportunity to shoot and hunt. Mr. McAlpin arranged for me to take my hunter's safety course so I could get licensed. We went hunting on opening day of Pennsylvania deer season. It was the quintessential American hunting experience: I carried an old-school 30-30 lever-action rifle and it was on public land, which forms the basis of so much American outdoor life. It's the reason I fight so hard to this day to preserve public land, and the lifestyle that comes with it.

There was also a teacher at Hill who taught me the basic fly-casting motion. I got an L.L. Bean starter kit and went from there. I knew so little about it that for the first couple of years, I was reeling in the fly line instead of stripping it in because I didn't know what I was doing. In time, however, I taught myself and became pretty good at it.

I guess I was seventeen when I got my first car, a Jeep (I had the Jeep and then two Dodge Durangos in a row, and that was pretty much the extent of my car history for the first twenty years I drove). The last two years at Hill School, I took solo hunting and fishing trips. I'd work for my father for the first two months of the summer and then jump into the Jeep and drive to parts of Pennsylvania, upstate New York, and New England.

The summer after I graduated, I headed west to the Rockies. That time of the year isn't hunting season, so I hiked and fished.

I didn't want to be around tourists, so I would find what looked like a good high-mountain lake maybe fourteen miles away from my location on a map or atlas. (For you younger folks, those were things we used to find our way around when dinosaurs still roamed the earth.) I had learned orienteering from my grandfather, so a map and a compass were usually enough for me.

I would throw my pack on and go spend a few days up there. Sometimes I'd lose my bearings, come out somewhere completely different, and have to hitchhike my way back to the Jeep. Then, I'd drive somewhere else and fish a different river or lake. I'd live out of the back of my truck for a couple of weeks at a time and go for days without seeing anyone. Sometimes I would come upon someone and share a camp for a day or two.

I continued my trips out west throughout college. I've driven across country four or five times by myself. I have fully covered Wyoming, Montana, Colorado, Arizona, and New Mexico. I hiked much of the western Rockies, wherever there was good fishing.

———

While attending the Hill School, I also learned a lesson courtesy of Donald J. Trump.

I was a very average student until the end of my freshman year. When my father read my report card, he sat me down.

As disciplinarians, my parents were completely different. My mother had old-school Eastern European ideas about raising a child. If she thought you'd done something wrong, she'd whack you before she said a word. My father used a more psychological technique: he'd have one of "those" talks with you, and you'd walk away thinking that whatever you'd done wrong was the stupidest thing in the world. He was good at guilt trips.

"These grades are fine," he said, "if you want to be average."

He knew exactly how to motivate me. When I went back to school, it was as though he'd put a rocket in my butt. Whereas I had crammed for maybe an hour for a test, I'd now spend eight hours studying. I'd put in thirty hours for an exam. I went from being an average student to getting nearly straight As. I became the editor of the school's literary journal and yearbook. By my senior year, I was mentoring other students. I rose to the top of the GPA rankings in my class. In fake news hit pieces about me, you'll read that the only reason I got into the Wharton School at the University of Pennsylvania was that my father went there and has donated to the school. Maybe that had something to do with it, although all of them say the donation came after I had already gotten in. But in my heart, I know that even if I wasn't my father's son, I had the grades to get into Wharton.

The last big lesson I learned at Hill had nothing to do with the school at all.

The campus of the school sat on the very eastern edge of the Rust Belt. There was a closed Firestone Tire plant in nearby Pottstown, Pennsylvania, and Bethlehem Steel, which would close just after I graduated, was about an hour's drive away. The juxtaposition was not lost on me. Here you had a wealthy boarding school up on a hill surrounded by the modest homes of blue-collar workers, many of whom were out of work. I didn't know it then, but the men and women who had once worked in the now-shuttered factories, who staked their family's future on those same factories, were the same people I would later meet at Trump rallies all around the country. They're the ones who would tell me stories about their lives and families as they waited for my father to arrive and deliver the message that they had been waiting to hear. I lived with those people. I had local friends, dated local girls. After a while, I started feeling as though I was more from Pennsylvania than from New York City, and I was proud of it.

Even in 1990, when I began boarding school, we had already begun the process of exporting the American dream all over the world, sending the jobs that used to belong to hardworking Americans of all colors, creeds, and genders to countries that couldn't have cared less about our values. They were our biggest export. In some cases, we sent those jobs to countries that hated our guts, and then we paid the price for it later. At Hill, I could already see some of that anxiety and desperation building around me.

In my junior year, Bill Clinton signed one of the most disastrous trade agreements in the history of our country. Democrats promised that the North American Free Trade Agreement would usher in a golden age for US business and send our economy skyrocketing. Instead, NAFTA did the exact opposite: it caused a huge trade deficit, hollowed out Detroit, and sent US companies scrambling over the border to exploit cheap labor.

It wasn't only the Rust Belt that suffered. American farmers did, too. Before NAFTA, farmers had been $200 million up in the balance of trade with Mexico and Canada. A few years after the deal was signed, they were minus $1.5 billion. Maybe even worse was the fact that the crops we were importing were displacing the crops we grow here. Avocados, berries, and tomatoes flooded our market and came without any tariffs, quotas, or quality food safety restrictions.

Whatever way you looked at it, NAFTA was a disaster. Everyone knew it. During the campaign, my father said over and over that he was sick and tired of watching us export the American dream to our competitors while Americans—good, hardworking Americans—suffered. He was sick of watching countries live our

American dream while our jobs went down the drain because of stupid, gutless Democrat decisions. The United States–Mexico–Canada Agreement (USMCA) will bring much of those dreams back. It will increase US auto parts production. It will force Mexican companies to pay their autoworkers at least $16 an hour, which will help keep factories here in the United States. It will open up the Canadian market to US dairy farmers. Yet, at this writing, the Democrats continue to slow-walk ratifying the deal. Why? Because they hate my father more than they love the American worker—and don't care if the American worker is collateral damage for their gains. For years, Democrats did a great job to build up the manufacturing base in other countries. In America? Not so much. They sat on their hands and watched the factories of iconic manufacturers such as Firestone and U.S. Steel empty and rust. As of right now, Nancy Pelosi won't bring the trade deal up for a vote simply because she doesn't want my father to have any credit. Can you imagine that? Because of her jealousy of DJT and his success, she will continue to strangle the American dream. The Democrats would much rather see America fail than for it to succeed with Trump at the helm. My father has done everything he can to keep Democrats from hurting the American worker. Later in this book, I talk about his being a blue-collar billionaire for just that reason: he understands workers, and would never think of them as pawns in trade deals that literally take away their jobs. The Democrats can give you all the talking points in the world, and their partners in crime, the liberal media, will run stories to support them. (Please don't be swayed by the liberal media. Read @realDonaldTrump and @DonaldJTrumpJr's tweets. They're the unfiltered truth.)

But sound bites are not policy. Sound bites do not help the American worker. Sound bites don't bring back jobs.

What will bring the American dream back to America will be someone with the balls to say, "Enough!" Someone who will say, "The days of us being a doormat are over." Someone who knows the art of the deal.

On the campaign trail, my father promised American workers that one of the first things he would do as president would be to renegotiate trade deals that ignored their needs. That promise was the reason he won Pennsylvania, Wisconsin, and Michigan, a feat not accomplished since Ronald Reagan in 1980. I've been Donald J. Trump's son for forty-one years and counting, and I can tell you this with complete confidence: He will never stop fighting for the American worker. He will never give in to Democrats at the expense of the American worker. He will bring the American dream back to our shores.

5.

GAP YEAR

FROM THE MOMENT the nurses at New York Hospital inked the name "Donald John Trump Jr." onto my birth certificate, you might say I've been following in the footsteps of my father. Even when I didn't know it (and most of the time, I didn't), I was picking up his mannerisms, learning his lessons, and trying to live up to his example.

Take the moment of my birth, for example: December 31, 1977, just a few hours before the stroke of midnight. By the time I was swaddled and sleeping in my crib, there were fireworks exploding outside the delivery room window, champagne corks popping in the streets, and music blaring from the rooftops—all while millions of people in Times Square screamed their heads off.

If that's not an entrance fit for a Trump, I don't know what is.

In the years since, I've started joking that the precise hour of my birth was no accident—that my father wanted to claim me as a dependent on his tax returns for 1977, so he told my mother she

had to get me out by midnight or she could go back to the apartment in a cab. (I'm completely kidding about the second part, of
course. On the tax return thing, who knows, it's been a family joke
for years.) I can also confirm that he wasn't always so hot on letting
someone else have his full name, even his own firstborn son. When
my mother first approached him with the idea of naming me Don
Jr., my father is rumored to have said, "We can't do that! What if
he's a loser?" Again, no idea whether my father ever really said this,
but it sure sounds like him.

When you're Donald Trump's son, you get used to that sense
of humor. As you can probably tell, it's one more of the things I
picked up from him. But believe it or not, there was a time when
most people didn't believe that my father and I were very much
alike. Even after I had gone to college at his alma mater, studied
the same subjects, and prepared myself for a career in real estate,
I wasn't so sure I wanted to go into the family business—at least
not right away.

So after college graduation, I loaded up my Jeep and pointed
it toward the Rocky Mountains.

———

I guess there is a conception of a certain privilege attached to taking
a gap year. Not everyone can afford to take a year off to backpack
through Europe before entering the work force or going on for an
advanced degree.

My gap year, however, didn't come attached with a whole lot
of privilege. When I decided I was going to spend my first year out
of college bartending and enjoying the great outdoors, I called my
father to let him know. I would tell you exactly what he said during
that call but . . . well, let's just say it was less than awesome—after
all, I was about to become perhaps the only Wharton grad to ever

go off to work in a bar. By the end of the call, we had decided that I was free to do what I wanted, but as far as paying for it? Well, that was up to me. He was cutting me off. I rented a room in a small house in Aspen, Colorado with a few roommates. My budget might have gotten even tighter if my parents had remembered the Mobil card I had. I kept the gas tank in the Jeep full, and was able to buy a meal with it every now and then.

As a family, we'd gone to Aspen many times, usually spending Christmas and New Year's there. I thought I might get a job as a ski instructor. My mom had been on the Czech national ski team, and all of the Trump children were on skis soon after we learned to walk. I didn't end up teaching snowplows to eight-year-olds or parallel skiing to rich divorcées. Instead, I landed the perfect job for me at the time.

The Tippler had been a celebrity hangout in the 1980s and '90s, attracting stars such as Jack Nicholson and Sylvester Stallone. By the spring of 2000, when I began working there as a bartender, however, it had officially achieved dive status, just the way I liked my bars.

In fact, I started to like them a little too much.

Although I'd had fairly good grades in college, I had partied my ass off. Once I got going, it wasn't easy to stop me—which, when you're in college, isn't a huge problem, as long as you're getting your work done. But once I started thinking about a career and a life beyond school, it was. To be honest, I didn't know how to drink in moderation. I have an all-or-nothing personality; just ask anyone who knows me. Being compulsive works for some things—give me a job to do, and I'm going to get it done—but it's not so good for vices.

I guess I should have known that drinking wasn't going to be good for me. There were warning signs in my family.

As you probably have heard, my dad has never had a glass of alcohol in his life. He watched his brother, Fred Trump Jr., die from alcoholism at the age of forty-three. My father had loved his older brother, and Uncle Freddy's death affected him greatly.

So, in a couple of ways, my gap year was a kind of turning point for me. Though I continued to party throughout my time in Aspen, it was in the mountains surrounding the ski resort that I began to realize that with my personality, drinking alcohol was a recipe for disaster. One thing about us Trumps is that we have plenty of willpower. I would come to find that it was easier for me to ignore alcohol than it was to try to control it. Eventually, I would give up drinking for good.

The other awareness I experienced in Aspen was actually something I had known all along.

The mountains and rivers surrounding the Colorado ski resort provide some of the best fly fishing and elk hunting in the country. The Tippler was often slow during the week, and I'd spend three or four days in a row out on the mountain with a fly rod, or a rifle, or a bow. And it wasn't just the western states. If I had a few days off, there was absolutely nowhere I wouldn't drive. Once during that year, I went twenty-eight days straight hunting elk. Out in the woods, no one knew I was Donald Trump's son, and I don't think anyone would have cared if they did know. As it turned out, that was just what I needed.

For a moment or so during that year, the thought of staying in Aspen for an extended period of time might have crossed my mind: a bartender at night, ski bum and outdoorsman by day kind of life. I have friends from back then who are still out west and still doing exactly that. To this day, whenever I travel out to Iowa and Montana for campaign events or stump speeches, I sleep on one of their couches or in one of their guest rooms. It didn't take me long to realize that as passionate as I am about the outdoors, I wasn't going to make it my life's work.

There was another path for me, and that path—the one that led toward business, capitalism, and self-reliance—was practically written into my DNA. I needed more—more of a fight, more of a challenge. Looking back, I think that's why I took so readily to campaign politics.

My grandfather Fred Trump grew up in a working-class section of Queens called Woodhaven. When he was a little boy, he sold a local newspaper, making a half-cent a copy. Once he became strong enough to carry a golf bag, he caddied at the nearby Forest Park Golf Course. His building career began in his early teens. It was then that he took a job as a carpenter's assistant. In the 1920s, Woodhaven was booming. New manufacturing offered plenty of jobs, and improved transportation made it attractive for commuters into the city. Houses went up by the hundreds. My grandfather learned the building trade on the job site and from the ground up. It was a good thing that work was steady. When he was just thirteen, his father passed away, making him the man of the house. He was responsible for putting food on the table for his mother, sister, and brother.

When I was young, my parents would take us—my sister, brother, and me—to visit my grandparents in Jamaica Estates once a month. In the house my father had grown up in, my grandmother would make a big Sunday dinner. Sometimes during those visits, my grandfather would take me to visit job sites or collect rents at some of his properties. The job site stuff was fun; the rent stuff, not so much. My grandfather had strict Germanic ways, and because he had become the man of the house at thirteen, he had a different perspective on life. It was a perspective that not a lot of people have today. His motto was "To retire is to expire." He really didn't know how to have fun. Even late into life, in his 90s with Alzheimer's disease, he went into the office because that's what he knew and loved. My uncle kept him busy with older expired contracts because work was his life.

I don't know if I ever fully enjoyed most of the time I spent with him as a kid. As a child, it was tough to relate to him. But I would come to respect and truly appreciate the drive and work ethic I saw in him—the pure survival mode he had to take on when he was a small child changed him permanently. It was unlike anything I ever could have imagined.

By high school, Fred Trump had started his own construction business. He built a garage for a guy and did it better, cheaper, faster than any of his competitors. Then he built another one. And another one, putting them up so fast it was as if he were trying to keep up with the production of Henry Ford's Model T, which was then coming off the assembly line. He called his company E. Trump & Son. His mother's name was Elizabeth, and she took care of the books until Fred was legally old enough to do it himself. By then he was already well on his way to putting up twenty buildings. His properties weren't fancy, but they were "spic and span," functional, and solidly built. "Mint condition" was the phrase he would use to describe them. He paid the same attention to small details that my father would, only Fred Trump's focus was on non-luxury products. Because of that, he would go on to become one of the biggest developers in Brooklyn. His was the quintessential Horatio Alger story, one of hard work, determination, and opportunity.

As a young boy, my dad would go to job sites with his father, just as I did with both of them. I guess you could say my future was cemented during that time.

Now, it's not as though I was destined to become Donald J. Trump 2.0. There's only one of that man. The idea, however, that I wouldn't work for The Trump Organization now seems preposterous, although it took me a year out in the woods to realize that.

It was never a question of whether I would go back to New York City, just when.

The "when" came on a Tuesday in the second week of September 2001. I was coming out of the woods in Colorado, fresh off a morning elk hunt during archery season, when I heard the news on the radio driving over Independence Pass back into town. Like many people, when I first heard that a plane had flown into the World Trade Center, I thought it was a small single-engine. I figured it was small and hard to control, like one of the planes I used to fly. When I found out it was a terrorist attack, and the towers had collapsed, killing nearly three thousand people, there was only one place I wanted to be.

A day or two later, I packed up the Jeep and headed back home.

———

My first job in the real estate business after college was on a project called Trump Place that now sits on a seventy-six-acre plot of land on the banks of the Hudson River. I was working on the building with some of my father's partners, Hudson Waterfront Associates. Once the New York Central Railroad yards, it was the last undeveloped tract in Manhattan. I learned about "ground-up" construction. The project included a combination of very-high-end condominiums and rental apartments.

Along with construction, I learned marketing and leasing. My next assignment came two years later and was a completely different kind of construction from the first job. We bought an existing seventy-five-year-old building on Park Avenue and turned it into high-end condominiums. The old adage "They don't build them like they used to" doesn't necessarily mean what you might think. The building had been the Hotel Delmonico, and there was a surprise behind every wall. There were rent-controlled apartments that we had to retrofit around, floors and walls that didn't match the building drawings that we had. We also had a couple of partners, including General Electric Pension Trust. There were lots of balls in the air. Because I was young enough and dumb enough, I did all the jobs no one else wanted to do. I knew that everyone on the project had about 10 percent of his or job they hated doing. During those first years, I made it my business to take that 10 percent off their hands. An executive was too busy to handle some aspect of the construction or marketing? I'd gladly take it off his or her plate. Because of my willingness to work and learn, I went from a project manager to basically having owner-ship of all aspects of the job.

Another old adage is "Responsibility is taken, not given." I took that one to heart.

The next job I worked on was the Trump International Hotel & Tower in Chicago. Here again, the project was a totally different animal than the other jobs. The plans called for a ninety-eight-story tower with a hotel, condominiums, and retail space includ-ing restaurants and a spa, built on the banks of the Chicago River. With the world-renowned architect Adrian Smith we came up with a fabulous design built on the site of the former *Chicago Sun-Times* building. Long considered an eyesore on a beautiful riverside plot of land, it was the only project I ever worked on where no one was upset that we were demolishing a building.

With a growing family and commuting two or three times a week to Chicago, I wasn't watching intently what was going on in Washington, DC. My interest in politics, such as it was, was mostly local, fiscally conservative, and seen through a business lens. I'd show up at certain events and support certain politicians who could give us support when we needed it during every project. I didn't necessarily have to believe in the person's politics (I'm in

New York City, after all, so most times I didn't) or particularly love the politicians with whom I dealt. But as Michael Corleone said to his brother Sonny in *The Godfather*, "It's not personal, it's strictly business." At least most of the time, that is. Every now and then you ran into a politician who took things very personally.

In the mid-eighties, when my father first began planning the development of the West Side Yard, a local state assemblyman from the district fought the project as though he had a personal vendetta. Even more curious was that his opposition to the plan made no sense. The land was desolate, crime-ridden, and an eyesore. DJT was going to turn it into a beautiful, thriving business and residential community. My father even scaled his plans down to appease the assemblyman and others, to no avail. Then, in 1993, the assemblyman ran for Congress and was elected to represent the Tenth District on the west side of Manhattan. He took his hostility toward my father with him to Washington. One of the aspects of the planned construction involved moving the West Side Highway. In order to do so, DJT needed federal approval and funds. The congressman from the west side went out of his way to make sure the federal government would not give my dad a dime.

Why a politician, whose job is to serve the people he represents, would spend so much of his time and energy fighting a developer who wanted to improve that politician's district is a mystery. Except, that is, when you learn that the politician's name is Jerrold Nadler.

Since his first day as an assemblyman, for whatever reason—jealousy, probably—Nadler has hated my father. While my father was trying to rebuild the broken parts of New York in the same way he's rebuilding the broken parts of the country right now, Nadler stood in his way. To this day, the man will go to any lengths to stop anything that Donald J. Trump does.

In 1998, Nadler was a member of the House Judiciary Committee, the committee he now chairs. Kenneth Starr was the special
counsel for the investigation into President Clinton, which led to
impeachment proceedings. Nadler was perhaps the most vocal
opponent of the release of the Starr Report. He called his opposition "a matter of decency."

"It's grand jury material. It represents statements which may or
may not be true by various witnesses," he said. "Salacious material.
All kinds of material that it would be unfair to release."

That quote comes from the same man who, at this writing, is
still fighting for the release of grand jury testimony in the Mueller
Report: Jerry Nadler, the Babe Ruth of hypocrisy.

Luckily for Trump Org, the mayors of New York City for most of
the 1990s and through the 2000s were business friendly. In 1993,
Rudy Giuliani held the top city post. He inherited a New York
from Democrat David Dinkins that was like a war zone. In 1990,
New York City had over twenty-two hundred murders. To give
you some idea of just how bad it was, the city with the highest
murder rate in the country today, Chicago, only sees around 700
homicides per year. Times Square was one big X-rated pit. The
brave few who would come into the city to see legitimate theater
would fear for their lives. Business and construction barely had
a pulse. The Crown Heights race riots in 1991 threatened to tear
New York apart. A *New York Post* headline at the time read "DAVE,
DO SOMETHING!" Then Rudy rode to the rescue. He cleaned up
Times Square, oversaw a remarkable decrease in crime, and became
a friend to builders. His leadership during and after the 9/11 attack
on the World Trade Center was nothing short of heroic. During his
mayoralty, people started moving into the city instead of out of it

for the first time in years. Companies such as The Trump Organization put up buildings that soared to the sky.

In 2002, Michael Bloomberg carried on what Rudy had started. Bloomberg is a businessman, and his relationship with builders was good. He once called us "the great Trump Org." It was only when my dad ran for president that Bloomberg's attitude toward him changed. Again, jealousy is probably the reason. My father got the job that Bloomberg desperately wants but will never have. It takes guts to do it as a conservative, and most people—even accomplished people—can't or won't take the heat required, so they just sit and throw stones from the sidelines.

———

It was around 2008, after the Chicago tower and hotel were completed, that we started our branding business, offering our name, expertise, and value engineering and marketing ability to developers around the world. One of the first deals we made was in Sunny Isles, Florida, which turned out to be very successful. It was around then that we saw the promise in a much wider market. Though our brand was very New York–centric, after a couple of successful ventures in Florida with our friends, Michael and Gil Dezer, we began to believe we had something that would sell all over the world. It was also an opportunity, first for me, but for Ivanka and Eric, too, to start doing deals internationally on our own. Over the course of the next ten years, I made deals all over the world and built a major book of business.

Throughout that time, national politics existed somewhere in the background for me. Had I been watching Washington more closely, I would have seen what government looked like with the Republican establishment running things. You might have noticed that I've been beating up on the Democrats pretty good, and they deserve every punch. But they weren't the only political party screwing up Washington. The establishment Republicans had a big hand in populating the swamp, and when DJT became the party's nominee, they wanted him to lose to Hillary just as badly as the Democrats did.

One of the ways they tried to sabotage my father's candidacy was by using the conservative press. Though later in this book I dedicate a chapter to the biased liberal media and fake news, the Republican establishment had its own propaganda machine. One of it most notable propagandists is Bill Kristol, the editor of the failed *Weekly Standard*. Once thought of as a lion of conservative politics, Kristol was one of the first rats to attack my father. It's hard to believe he was ever relevant, but then again, maybe that's why we always lost.

Along with Kristol, establishment columnists such as the *Washington Post*'s Jennifer Rubin, the *New York Times*' Bret Stephens, and Jonah Goldberg from *National Review*, just to name a few, furiously wrote columns trying to derail the Trump train.

It was Sarah Palin, perhaps, talking about the Tea Party, who first talked about the relationship between the establishment and the press it controlled. "The Republican establishment which fought Ronald Reagan in the 1970s and which continues to fight the grassroots Tea Party movement today has adopted the tactics of the left in using the media and the politics of personal destruction to attack an opponent," she wrote on Facebook.

She was right.

Just like the mainstream media, however, the establishment press seriously underestimated DJT's ability to punch back. My father called them out for what they are: irrelevant. Existing in a bubble floating high above what was happening on the ground, they championed policies that kept the status quo or tried to talk us into another unpopular war. Meanwhile, down here on the ground, real people watched the middle class dwindle, the borders get thrown wide open, and the United States get clobbered in trade while our factories turned to rust.

When it comes to handling the press, my father is the undisputed heavyweight champ. It really wasn't a fair fight.

There's no better example than Bill Kristol to show you how badly the establishment press lost to DJT. His high-profile career has hit the canvas with a thud. Today, you might catch him doing a Sunday-afternoon hit on MSNBC. The only thing lower than that is maybe an infomercial for wrinkle cream on Sunday morning. Keep an eye out for Bill holding up a jar to the camera.

Still, getting rid of the entire establishment Republicans political-media-industrial complex is like trying to pull an oak tree out of the ground by its roots. Back in the early 2010s, the Tea Party gave the Republican establishment a pretty good shake. Rand Paul, Ted Cruz, Mark Meadows, Jim Jordan, Mike Huckabee, and Sarah Palin led the revolution. But it was DJT who took a buzzsaw to it.

If you remember back to the beginning of the campaign, the Republican establishment called themselves "Never Trumpers." Made up of RINOs (Republicans in name only), huge money donors, and a variety of interest groups, the list of them is as long as John Kerry's face. In March 2016, 122 "Members of the Republican national security community" signed a letter denouncing my father's candidacy. The following August, 50 "Republican national security officials" signed a second letter announcing that they would not vote for Trump under any circumstances. According to a *Washington Post* article from last July, many of those same people are now looking for jobs in the Trump administration. Magically, DJT's foreign policy has started to look pretty good to them.

After my father was elected, some members of the establishment weaseled their way into the White House. They were supposed
to act as "the grown-ups in the room" or "guardrails" to keep the
Trump presidency from driving off a cliff. Yeah, right. When DJT
got into that car, it was just about to do a Thelma and Louise. He
was the one who slammed on the brakes just before it went over.
He was the one who got us back up onto the highway. One by one,
DJT got rid of the guardrails—or speed bumps, as we like to call
them—and got the West Wing humming just like Trump Org, or
the 2016 Donald J. Trump for President campaign: lean and mean.

In less than three years, my father has almost completely recon-
figured the Republican Party, a political entity that, frankly, was
headed toward extinction. In less than one term, he's torn down
an establishment structure that took fifty years to build. Today,
most establishment Republicans have little or no significance in the
political world, certainly not the ones who oppose Donald Trump.
Some saw the error of their ways and joined the Trump team (I'm
sure there's a phony or two in that group, but they always eventually show their true stripes). Others, it seems, have fallen off the
face of the earth. Today, Bob Corker and Jeff Flake couldn't get
elected dog catcher. Paul Ryan got so embarrassed by how out-of-
touch he'd become that he had to retire. Out of all the establishment Republicans who didn't understand my father, Paul Ryan
was by far the most confused. Good riddance. Whether relevant
or not, most members of the Republican establishment now realize that the Trump administration is a once-in-a-lifetime chance
to right the wrongs of a couple of generations of Democrat and
old-guard Republican rule. The ones who don't will be unem-
ployed soon enough.

It's been amazing to watch.

———

Until my father announced that he was running for president, the idea of my entering politics was about as remote as my becoming a vegan. Sometimes, however, circumstances direct the roads you take. If you remember back, the press and the political world at large didn't take my father's campaign seriously at first. They called it a publicity stunt that would last a couple of weeks at best. That belief was pervasive and didn't help our recruiting efforts, so we did it ourselves, our way, without the so-called experts. We weren't exactly the Jeb Bush juggernaut. Without political professionals, we did what we always do as a family: we filled the voids. I had experience on TV, so I became a surrogate before we even had surrogates. I still had responsibilities with Trump Org, but I helped as much as I could. So did the rest of the family. That's the way we are. We just did more and slept less . . . a lot less.

Along with being pretty handy in front of a camera, I also brought something else to the campaign. Like everyone in the beginning of the race, we focused on the Iowa caucuses, the first of the presidential primaries. It was in Iowa that I began to realize that my life up until then had prepared me for my father's campaign.

In January 2014, Terry Branstad, then the governor of Iowa, invited me to his annual deer hunt in Centerville, Iowa. The hunt is sponsored by Knight Rifles, which is located in Centerville. It hooked me up with a volunteer guide named Doug Hurley. For the last twenty-five years, Doug's been a special agent with the narcotics division of the Iowa Department of Public Safety. He and I hit it off right away.

As it happened, the day of the hunt, a polar vortex from Canada descended over Iowa. Saying it was cold that week is a distinct understatement. I'm sure Doug thought that some Fifth Avenue billionaire's son wasn't about to go out and hunt with a −50° F wind-chill factor. I might have surprised him when I showed up, ready to go.

For five hours, we stood on a hillside with the wind in our faces, waiting for the deer to come through. Doug was behind an evergreen tree, while I used a fence post for protection. When we called it a day, Doug came over and fist-bumped me. "New York City!" he said. "I never thought you could handle this!"

I stayed in touch with Doug and called him before the Iowa caucuses. I flew into Des Moines about one in the morning and drove down to Appanoose County, where he lives.

Doug was nice enough to let me stay on his basement couch for four or five days. I'd do radio hits in the morning; then we'd go hunting the rest of the day or just hang out with his pals. The governor's deer hunt was held that week also, and we hunted again in that.

A few weeks later, I was with Doug again. This time it was a pheasant hunt, and Maggie Haberman from the *Times* and a couple of other reporters tagged along. By then my father was locked in a tight race with Ted Cruz and Marco Rubio (and about one hundred other people) and, though biased, the press was all over our campaign.

I don't know what Maggie and her reporter friends were expecting. Maybe they were hoping for me to shoot myself in the foot or pull a Dick Cheney and shoot a pal in the face. At one point, one of the reporters asked how they would know I was for real—meaning, not just one of these politicans who shows up with a smile on their face and brand new hunting gear looking for a photo-op.

"How many birds did you see go up?" I asked.

"Nine," they said.

"How many shots did I take?"

"Nine," they answered.

"How many birds am I holding now? I asked.

"Nine."

"Do you have any other questions?" I said, smiling.

"Damn, you're a pretty good shot," Doug said afterward. "Especially under pressure with camera crews and Jake Tapper in tow." It was high praise coming from a hunter like him.

The ease I had around people like Doug and his friends started to multiply on the campaign in ways I couldn't have imagined. Look, I know my appearances on *The Apprentice* gave me a touch of celebrity, and I also know that my father's message was like water in the desert for his people. They wanted it that much. But I was able to talk to people who came to events in a way the other surrogates, even candidates, couldn't. I had spent most of my youth out in the Rust Belt. In a very real sense, these were my people. Unlike many New York City socialites, I didn't have to try to connect with them. I was one of them. They saw that I'm not an out-of-touch elitist, that I relate to people and people relate to me. They liked that I was a hunter and that I had a good sense of humor. They liked that I felt at ease in front of a crowd. When I added it all up, I realized that I brought something to the campaign that no one else on our team could. Although I didn't know it then, because of that something, I would become the tip of the spear of the greatest political campaign ever. I distinctly remember the moment I began to sense something special was happening. It was in the Western Slope of Colorado, doing a solo event in a gym auditorium where Hillary had spoken a few days before. The state campaign people called me and said, "Don, we have a problem. We have to move the venue." I thought they were going to tell me that not enough people were showing up.

"We were hoping for three hundred," they said, "and we've already got twenty-four hundred."

"Do they know it's Donald Trump *Jr.*?" I asked.

"Yeah," they said. "Your photo is on the advertisement."

"Okay," I said, "But I don't want to get sued for false marketing. Don't want people to think it's the old Donald Trump bait-and-switch."

When I found out that Hillary had drawn only 150 or so when she had done her event, it just about knocked me over. I felt the same way when I started having people come and help me out on the stump. All throughout the campaign, I had some terrific opening acts. Mark "Oz" Geist is one. A retired Marine, Mark was a member of the annex security team in Benghazi and survived to tell the story. Mark would show up and campaign with me all across the United States. He introduced the campaign to countless veterans and current active duty members. A true patriot, Mark is who you want next to you in battle.

Soon I learned that when it came to campaigning, the only place it made absolutely no sense for me to be was wherever my father was. We were only wasting our resources by going to the same cities. Plus, in case you haven't noticed, wherever my father goes, all eyes are on him; when he's talking, no one really cares who else is there. He's a big personality, and only a certain kind of person can complement that. In some sense, this is the dilemma we faced when trying to decide on a running mate during the campaign. We'd had a lovely breakfast with Mike Pence and his family, during which we noticed that the Pences' approach to life was a lot like ours—no cooks and maids doing everything for them, just dinner every night like a normal family. Bear in mind that this breakfast occurred in the Indiana governor's mansion. The Pences could have had dozens of aides and staff members catering to their every need, but they chose not to.

But we had also been considering Newt Gingrich, who seemed like a viable choice. After all, Newt was a tremendous Speaker of the House and a great advocate for my father during the early days of the campaign. While we were in Indiana visiting the Pences, Newt Gingrich met us in a hotel room. A few minutes into the conversation, though, I noticed that Newt seemed hesitant about the whole thing. I finally decided to mention the elephant in the room.

"Mr. Speaker," I said, feeling slightly awkward. "Forgive me for asking, but . . . do you really *want* this job?"

Newt was very gracious in his response, but the bottom line seemed to be that no, he really did not. Over the next few minutes, he explained that if he was asked, he would give the vice presidency 110 percent of his energy, and would be happy to do it. But he also said he could probably be of more help to us on the outside, where he could be as brash and abrasive as he wanted to be without worrying about the political ramifications. When it comes down to it, I'm happy he decided that. We already had one pirate on the ticket; we didn't need two.

Still, I knew drawing crowds meant nothing if you didn't have a message. I had one that was set in stone.

During my speech to the Republican National Convention, I brought that message to millions of people across the country. Even *Politico,* no fans of me or my father, said that a "political star may have been born" that night. I don't know about that, but I do know something got started. That convention speech was the spark that lit the fire of my political life. But all I did was speak from the heart, saying what I knew to be true about my father that I didn't think anyone else knew. I barely had to write it down.

Left-wing pundits and fake news told you that my father was making promises on the campaign trail just to be provocative, just for the attention. Those who said and wrote that, however, were about to experience a rude awakening.

6.

NOT EXACTLY THE
STATUE OF LIBERTY

GIVE US YOUR HUDDLED MASSES—OH, AND
YOUR GANGS AND DRUGS, TOO.

IT WAS ON JUNE 16, 2015, a two days after Flag Day and his birthday, when my father announced that he was running for president of the United States. Fifty years from now, they'll be talking about the escalator ride he took with Melania. Among his many talents, DJT certainly knows how to make an entrance. What people don't know, however, is what happened right before that entrance. It was then when my father said what might be the most prophetic statement he's ever made.

Melania and Barron, Ivanka and her husband, Jared, Eric and his wife, Lara, my kids Kai and Donnie, my then wife, Vanessa, and I had gathered in his office. Together we rode the elevator down to the first-floor atrium with my father. People have asked me if we had a family sit-down like you hear about, where the candidate discusses the decision to run or not with his family. Doesn't happen like that in the Trump family. DJT is his own man, and when he makes a decision, we all do whatever we can to help him. Just before the doors of the atrium opened, my father turned to me and said, "Now we find out who our real friends are."

———

His announcement speech, one still played all the time as proof my father is racist, didn't, at first, cause a blowback in the press. Almost all of his remarks that day, even the most controversial, came off the top of his head. He had a sheet of paper with a few notes scratched on it in his suit jacket pocket, but I don't think he looked at it once. What caused the left to explode in outrage came a few days later. It was then that Hillary Clinton all but blamed my father for the actions of a maniac named Dylann Roof who had walked into an all-black church and shot nine people to death. This is a common theme for Democrats. Anytime anything horrible happens, such as a mass shooting, my father is to blame. It's insane and insulting.

Two things happened at that moment. First, the presidential election essentially became a race between Hillary Clinton and Donald J. Trump and, second, the press began to invent a racist narrative about my father, one that would become an avalanche of lies.

A little more than a year after my father made his famous proclamation about the scourge of illegal immigration, I stopped in a hotel outside Denver, Colorado, to catch a few hours of sleep between campaign events. By then, the race truly was between Hillary and my father. It had been a brutal couple of weeks out on the trail, and both campaigns were feeling the heat. (By that point, DJT was doing multiple events each day, including major rallies, and shaking a few thousand hands at every stop; Hillary Clinton was collapsing into her SUV from sheer exhaustion after trying to keep up for a few hours.)

I'd realized how crazy our schedule was on a stop in Detroit (where, by the way, no one thought we should be). It was 9:30 p.m. I remember the time because I was doing a hit on Sean Hannity's TV show later that night. We'd already done a couple of rallies and stopped at a Muslim-owned eatery and then a college campus. I looked over at Tommy Hicks, my friend since my early days in New York after college. Tommy had left a very lucrative job with his family's business to join me on the campaign and had then stayed with us every step of the way. Tommy was a lifesaver. He helped us with everything from crowd control to fund-raising at a time when the Republican National Committee wasn't exactly breaking its neck to support us.

"Man, I'm hungry," I said.

He looked back at me as though I were nuts. "That's because we haven't eaten since breakfast yesterday," he said.

It had been almost forty hours since my last meal, and I hadn't thought about eating once. It wasn't just me. All of us—family members and a handful of surrogates—were stretched thin across the country and running on fumes. We spoke at rallies, sat in on meetings, took pictures, did radio and TV hits, county fairs, fund-raisers—you name it, anything that might enable us to scrape up a couple more votes, and having a meal stole valuable time. If we were going to lose—which, if you believed the mainstream media, was exactly what we were going to do—we wanted to go down fighting.

The hotel lobby in Colorado was starting to come to life. It must have been around six in the morning. There were newspapers stacked on the front desk, but they were all folded up and unread, meaning that the hit pieces and liberal tirades about my father hadn't yet been disseminated. I was grateful for the quiet. Part of being on the 2016 Donald J. Trump for President campaign was keeping your guard up. For the tens and tens of thousands of supporters we saw every week, there were plenty of haters, people who bought what the fake news peddled hook, line, and sinker.

But here in the semi-solitude of the lobby, I had a chance to take a rare deep breath. Maybe have some coffee. Just as I was feeling comforted by the calm, however, I saw a cashier in the coffee shop staring at me. Her eyebrows were arched as though she were ready to give a big speech. I immediately assumed that it would have something to do with my father and his immigration stance. There goes the coffee, I thought. But then the woman smiled and leaned over the counter toward me.

"You know," she said, lowering her voice to a whisper and looking around, "my husband and I voted for your father yesterday in early voting."

She was a recent immigrant from Ethiopia who, along with her husband, had gone through the proper channels and filled out all the paperwork required of them. She said it was something they were proud to have done.

"Your father's right," she said. "People who think they can just come into America and get whatever they want makes it so much harder for people like me."

Her smile was so genuine, her handshake so warm, it nearly made up for all the smears and slams we had taken for months.

"Thank you," I said. "You don't know how much this means to me."

Over and over during the campaign and after the election, people came up to me, people of all nationalities and from all walks of life, to tell me how proud they were to have come to the United States legally.

These are the people that the liberals would rather not talk about. They like to pretend that there's no difference between a good immigrant and a bad one. In other words, someone who enters the country illegally, carrying ten pounds of heroin, should be afforded the same rights as someone who has come in to be a doctor. Their rationale is ridiculous. We should be supporting those who followed the rules to come here, not criminals whose first act on US soil is a violation of our laws.

———

Like many Americans, I come from a family of immigrants. As I've mentioned, my mother grew up in a small village in Communist Czechoslovakia. She came to the United States legally through Canada to escape the Communist ideal that so many of the liberal elites are now espousing. My father's mother, Mary Anne MacLeod Trump, the youngest of ten (apparently I'm an underachiever; I have only five kids!), came to the United States from a small island off the coast of Scotland during the Great Depression.

Maybe my favorite family immigration story was that of Frederick Trump. In 1885, my great-grandfather came to America from Germany at sixteen years of age with nothing but the clothing he could fit into one small suitcase. He lived in New York City with his sister, who had come over a year earlier, and her husband. In those days, there was no social safety net like there is today. Even if he'd wanted to exploit the system, he couldn't have. There was no system to exploit. It was only work and survive. So he went to work instead. Seven days a week, for twelve hours a day, he worked as a barber in the city. He learned English by listening to the customers, and he saved his money. When he had enough, he decided to strike out on his own, chasing the American dream as so many immigrants had before him.

In the early 1890s, with $600 in small bills he'd saved from the barbershop, he moved to Seattle and opened a restaurant in that city's red-light district because he had been told that that was where the business was. In 1892, he became a US citizen and voted in his first presidential election. Around the same time, there was a gold rush in the Northwest. Braving the harshest elements, he made his way to the Yukon—but not to pan for gold. He did what he knew how to do: he opened restaurants, first in tents and later in buildings made from timber. He would go on to serve thousands and thousands of meals to prospectors in Whitehorse, Yukon Territory.

My family risked everything to come here and kept taking risks to rise up in American society. Our stories are not unique. They've been replicated millions of times. They are the stories that made America great. Make no mistake, I come from a family of immigrants. My girlfriend, Kimberly Guilfoyle, comes from an Irish-born father and a Puerto Rican mother (you don't want to make her mad). I have many good friends who are immigrants, and I have met thousands of immigrants who contribute financially, socially, and educationally to this great nation. That's just not the case with far too many illegal immigrants.

———

The left will argue that today's immigrants pull their own weight, but the facts tell a different story. The immigrants of the late 1800s and early 1900s legally entered an America that was experiencing a spectacular rise in industrialization. There was a great need then to fill entry-level jobs, and our ancestors gladly filled them. Today, no such job pool exists. So instead of a hardworking, grateful pool of workers, there are people who evade the law to enter the country, pay minimal or no taxes, and then rely on government handouts to survive. This invasion—and that's what it is using any metric—

doesn't hurt people like me. I have private medical insurance, and my kids all go to good schools. The people who really get hurt are the ones on the lower ends of the economic ladder. They are the ones who will experience the decline in the quality of health care that will come about when the system is overstressed by illegal immigrants who have no insurance. They're also the ones whose children will see the quality of their education declines with over-crowded classrooms. They will face competition with entry-level workers and workers who work for cash off the books.

Now, I don't blame illegal immigrants for trying to come to the United States. Who wouldn't want to with all we give away? But comparing today's illegal immigrants to the ones who built this country is ludicrous. In fact, the immigrants of today never had the chance to replicate the experience of our grandfathers and great-grandfathers mostly because of legislation championed and passed by Democrats more than fifty years ago.

After President John F. Kennedy was shot in Dallas in 1963, the sympathy of the nation was with the Kennedy family, particularly his brother Teddy, who was then the newly minted senator from Massachusetts. At the time, Ted Kennedy could have proposed a bill that required all men to wear pink pants with little whales on them, and Congress would have passed it.

The younger Kennedy, undoubtedly a smart fellow (except when he was drunk behind the wheel in Chappaquiddick), knew that the population of the United States was growing and pros-pering, which was not necessarily the best thing for the Demo-crat Party. Soldiers who had returned from World War II bought houses, built businesses, and began voting Republican because Democrats had nothing to offer them other than higher taxes and more spending on government programs that didn't work (sounds all too familiar, huh?).

So Senator Kennedy hatched a plan to get some new voters. In short, he would need poor people who spoke very little English and who would want to take advantage of some of the massive welfare programs the Democrats were selling to the American people. That year, he proposed a bill that would do away with the old quota system used to govern immigration, which gave equal weight to immigrants from stable, friendly countries and blew the doors wide open for people from Third World countries. Not only would poorer immigrants flood our shores and social services, but Teddy's plan also enabled the families of those people to be brought in for generations, beginning what we now call "chain migration."

By the way, the idea of not wanting immigrants who would drain our social safety net is nothing new. A good friend recently took a tour of Ellis Island, where this quote about the Immigration Act of 1882 was displayed:

> Any immigrant deemed "liable to become a public charge" was denied entry to the United States. To Ellis Island inspectors, this clause, which has been a cornerstone of federal immigration policy since 1882, meant those who appeared unable to support themselves and were therefore likely to become a burden on society. Influenced by American welfare agencies that claimed they were being overwhelmed by requests for aid from impoverished immigrants, the Ellis Island inspectors carefully weighed the prospects of new arrivals, especially those of women and children intending to rejoin husbands and fathers in this country.

Those words were in force during a time when immigration truly made our country great. (And I'm sure the sign will be removed about five minutes after this book is published. Facts hurt!)

You have to give him credit: Teddy was playing the long game. He knew that the Democrats needed poor immigrants if they were going to stay in power. He knew that the trap of the welfare state was waiting for them. Once they started to feed off the system, they would start families who would be Democrats forever. That is what Democrats won't tell you, and it might trigger many of them: they *want* immigrants to rely on welfare. They *want* individuals to depend on the government from cradle until grave. Forget upward mobility; Ted Kennedy had his yacht and his parties, but he envisioned a dependent class that would forever vote Democrat. Without dependence on big government, the Democrats have nothing to offer. It's their power source, and self-sufficiency and independence are their Kryptonite. I believe the saying goes: *teach a man to fish, and he'll probably still vote for the guy who gives him a fish for free.*

Ted and his brother Robert Kennedy, who happened to be the attorney general of the United States at the time—something I like to remind people of when they start talking about "nepotism" in the Trump White House—helped draft the legislation. But I digress. No one pretends that we will be held to the same standards.

Although debate on the bill raged for months, it ended up passing by a good majority. When Lyndon Johnson signed it into law in 1965, Ted Kennedy assured the American people that "Our cities will not be flooded with a million immigrants annually" or "cause American workers to lose jobs." Nothing could have been further from the truth.

The result of the bill was the single most significant wave of immigrants entering the United States in modern history—more than 18 million legal immigrants and "uncountable numbers of illegal immigrants," according to the Center for Immigration Studies.

Many of those immigrants came from poor Third World countries. Few of them could read and write in English. Because of provisions added late in the game, early versions of "chain migration" were incentivized, meaning that for every immigrant who came into the country, a whole family was waiting to come in behind him or her. Subsequent studies have also shown that the bill increased the education gap between citizens and noncitizens by close to 50 percent and that it decreased the number of immigrants who eventually returned to their home countries. In other words, thank the Kennedys for enabling a permanent welfare state for which their Democrat descendants blame us.

———

Today the cost of illegal immigration to the American people is staggering. According to a recent report by Fairness and Accuracy in Reporting (FAIR), a supposed media watchdog that is actually fair only to the left, taxpayers "shell out approximately $134.9 billion to cover the costs incurred by the presence of more than 12.5 million illegal aliens, and about 4.2 million citizen children of illegal aliens." The real number might be $250 billion.

Forget about a wall; with that kind of money we could build a dome! The bottom line is that the cost of illegal immigration is unsustainable. And the strain on our social services is only part of the price we pay for illegal immigration. Those most hurt by it are not the rich and powerful. Candidly, they often benefit from cheap labor. It's hardworking, everyday Americans who foot the bill.

According to the Center for Immigration Studies (CIS), the percentage of Medicaid funds that were paid to illegal immigrants rose from 6 percent in 2007 to 17 percent in 2017, while the increase of US citizens on Medicaid was half that or less.

"The average immigrant household consumes 33 percent more cash welfare, 57 percent more food assistance, and 44 percent more Medicaid dollars than the average native household," according to Jason Richwine, an independent public policy analyst for the CIS.

———

More than just our money, however, illegal immigration and its by-products take the very lives of our children. According to the State Department, about 90 percent of all heroin consumed in the United States comes from the same three or four cities in Mexico. The death toll in the American opioid crisis has now reached just over 72,000 people a year. When you consider the violence of the people who produce and sell the drugs, the Mexican cartels and their loyal soldiers, the need to act now increases dramatically. As more drugs pour over the border, more people become addicted, the demand for heroin and other drugs increases, and those brutal groups grow more powerful. As they grow more powerful, the violence expands.

Just last year, there was record-breaking bloodshed and death in Mexico, much of it occurring less than a few hours' drive from the southern border of the United States, much of which, because of Democrat inaction, is little more than a negligible line in the desert. The Mexican Ministry of the Interior estimates that there were 29,168 murders in Mexico throughout 2017, most of which were committed by members of drug cartels. And that's not even counting the number of murders carried out in secret and never discovered by the government. When it comes to the cartel's unique brand of brutality, much of the horrible stuff isn't in the statistics—that's the stuff that corrupt officials and criminals bury with the bodies.

There are five or six cartels that are always at war over who gets the rights to ship drugs and other contraband into the United States. Battles with firearms and other military-grade weapons regularly occur in public places and spill out onto the streets. The streets of many Mexican cities are filled with blood, and because of a recent shake-up involving the Sinaloa Cartel, the battles are only getting worse—and they're spreading to the United States.

Members of these cartels come to the United States by both illegal and legal methods, including through our seriously flawed "amnesty" and "sanctuary city" policies set up by local Democrat administrations. Not too long ago, in Huntsville, Alabama, a thirteen-year-old girl was beheaded by Sinaloa Cartel soldiers after she watched them stab to death her grandmother, a woman with ties to the drug trade. The Sinaloa Cartel is known to hire members of the MS-13 street gang to do "wet work" for them in the United States. MS-13, you might remember, is another notorious organization of ruthless, bloodthirsty thugs who come into the United States from Central American countries such as El Salvador. Once existing mostly in Los Angeles, MS-13 has spread to other cities with high populations of illegal immigrants. Many MS-13 members came into the United States as "unaccompanied minors." They are children who, during the Obama administration, were sent alone to the border, where the US government was legally required to take them in. According to the Obama administration, not to take those minors in and give them free food and shelter for eternity would have been a severe human rights violation.

Since 2015, there has been a dramatic spike in the number of "unaccompanied minors" who show up at the southern border. Studies have shown that many of them are sent by relatives who have ties in the United States and want to take advantage of the system. Many are used as pawns by violent gang members who claim the child is theirs to get in. Many of the children have ended up in communities that already have very high populations of immigrants from Central America, particularly towns on Long Island such as Huntington Station and Brentwood. This means that the kids don't have to learn English or assimilate into their new communities because there are already subcommunities there for them to join—little clubs that are often ruled by violent members of MS-13. According to multiple studies by experts in gang activity, these new unaccompanied minors are the best pool of recruits MS-13 has ever had.

Gang members often approach new immigrants in the hallways of Long Island high schools, taking them in and promising a sense of belonging and protection. The new kids have no way of knowing the bloody history of groups such as MS-13 or the Mexican drug cartels whose dirty work they so often do inside the United States. They don't know, for instance, that MS-13 kills women and babies, usually using machetes to do it. In Nassau County on Long Island, there is an abandoned lot near a mental hospital that has become known as "the killing fields" because of the large number of dead bodies that has been dumped there by local members of MS-13. Last year, Long Island *Newsday* reported that police have identified roughly five hundred members of the gang, about three hundred of whom are still active in Nassau County. In Suffolk County, which sits right to the east of Nassau, there are three hundred more. This is a criminal gang that has been allowed to infiltrate some of the safest communities in the United States because of bad immigration policies.

If we allow this trend to continue, members of Mexican drug cartels will soon be fighting it out on the streets of this country rather than their own. What's MS-13's motto? "Kill, rape, control"? Its members specialize in bestial acts. They decapitate victims and tear their hearts out. They sound like wonderful people, right?

Yet when my father called them animals, the left lost its mind. In response to my father, Nancy Pelosi reminded us that we are all God's children and wondered if my father believed in "the spark of divinity."

Give me a f**king break.

Today, the Congress of the United States is the last real obstacle to full border security for our country. The Democrats need to stop the nonsense of investigating nonexisting and disproven conspiracies and instead do something that will keep Americans safe and allow people to sleep safely at night, knowing that the violence in faraway places such as Mexico and El Salvador has no chance of reaching our homes. Unfortunately, the Democrat lawmakers—most of whom live in houses surrounded by lovely big gates and go to work every day in a building staffed by dozens of armed guards—don't like talking about the American lives that illegal immigration endangers, the strain on our health care system illegal immigrants cause, or the jobs the illegals take. Instead, with their allies in the mainstream media, they reframe the discussion so that when my father talks about the emergency crisis at our southern border, he's labeled a racist or heartless or both.

The Democrats and their cohorts in the media are always engaged in a spin cycle that goes something like this: an illegal immigrant commits a crime, sneaks a few hundred kilos of heroin into the United States, or votes illegally. Prominent Democrats stay silent, preferring to focus on important issues such as how cow farting is harming the ozone layer. Next, a conservative points out that we might have a problem with illegal immigration, maybe after mourning the death of an innocent kid whose life was taken by MS-13. But then the liberal machine fires up, and dozens of members of Congress start yelling about how racist and evil the Republican Party is. There is no such thing as a

substantive immigration debate in this country, and the Democrats have done a brilliant job ensuring that there never will be.
Say what you want about them, but when it comes to vindictive
politics and obstructionism, they're good as it gets. Meanwhile,
two hundred American children are dying of overdoses each day.
Two hundred a day.

The crisis has especially crippled Pennsylvania, where the over-
dose rate has climbed to nearly twice the national average. Whereas
some places around the country have seen a slight decrease in
opioid-related deaths, the rate in Montgomery Country, where the
Hill School is located, has recently spiked. First the Democrats sent
the residents' jobs overseas; now they sit and do nothing as parents
bury children there at unprecedented rates.

———

The other thing the Democrats are good at is hypocrisy.

In 2013, Speaker Nancy Pelosi, Cryin' Chuck Schumer, and just
about every other Democrat senator voted for a bill that included
seven hundred miles of border wall. Obama agreed to sign it
and said that the bill was "consistent with the key principles for
commonsense reform that I—and many others—have repeatedly
laid out." Allow me to repeat what Obama called a border wall:
"commonsense reform."

In 2016, the former president—that's right, Obama—went on
to say, "Because we live in an age where terrorists are challenging our borders we simply cannot allow people to pour into the
U.S. undetected, undocumented, and unchecked. Americans are
right to demand better border security and better enforcement of
the immigration laws." And by the way, this whole hysteria about
kids in cages? Well, it began under Obama. Liberals seem to have
conveniently forgotten about that.

In 2014, our old Hillary had this to say: "We have to send a clear message: Just because your child gets across the border, that doesn't mean the child gets to stay. We don't want to send a message that is contrary to our laws or will encourage more children to make that dangerous journey." Weird, right? Sounds just like my dad, but when Hillary says it, no problemo!

———

So what happened to the Democrats, you ask. Well, my father was elected president, and they decided they hated him more than they wanted to protect the United States. So with the help of the mainstream media, they got to work at making the wall into a racial slur. Under Obama, nearly two-thirds of Americans supported building a wall or fence at the border, according to an ABC News/*Washington Post* poll. Now that number is below 50 percent. It dropped for one reason: a concerted effort to spread misinformation and lies by Democrat politicians and fake news.

Nancy Pelosi calls my father's actions on the border "barbaric," but I don't remember her saying anything like that about Barack Obama's immigration policy, which included separating children from their parents, keeping the kids in tent cities, and deporting 2.5 million of them! Remember who started this crisis! Funny how no one on the left mentions that, isn't it?

Then there's Democrat Dick Durbin, who called my father a racist because he used the term "chain migrations." But then Durbin had to apologize when a video was found showing him using the same words in a speech on the Senate floor. When Gavin Newsom was elected governor of California last January, he vowed to make his entire state a sanctuary for illegal immigrants, even promising them state Medicaid. In Nancy Pelosi's hometown of San Francisco, illegal immigrants are allowed to vote in local elections.

Yet when my father proposed sending illegal detainees to sanctuary cities, Democrats cried bloody murder. Julián Castro, the
ex–San Antonio mayor who's one of the six thousand Democrats
running for president, called the proposal "cruel." So did Nancy
Pelosi's spokesperson. House committee chairs Jerrold Nadler and
Elijah Cummings wanted to launch—wait for it—an investigation!
You'd think they'd have run out of paper for subpoenas by now.

One of the most prominent Democrat hypocrites is Cher. Back
in 2017, she urged all her fellow Hollywood types to open their
homes as minisanctuaries to protect Dreamers. Then, in April 2019,
she sent a tweet saying that her city, Los Angeles, "ISN'T TAKING
CARE OF ITS OWN," adding "If My State Can't Take Care of Its
Own (Many Are VETS) How Can It Take Care of More."

Here's my response:

Donald Trump Jr.
Amazing, simply amazing. I guess the leftists are only pro
illegals when they can lay the huge burden on someone
else.

Amazing, simply amazing. I guess the leftists are only pro
illegals when they can lay the huge burden on someone else.

————

Dems want it both ways. They want to be seen as the compassionate party, welcoming illegal immigrants with open arms, but they
don't want to be the ones who have to take care of them. Well, you
can't have it both ways. Money doesn't grow on trees.

When you clear away all the hysteria surrounding the wall,
it turns out to be part of a compassionate immigration strategy.
The United States can't solve the problems that today's immi-

grants experience. Those problems have to be addressed in the immigrants' home countries. My father is right to get tough on Mexico. It's in countries like our neighbor to the south that the answer to the illegal immigration problem lies, not in the United States. When DJT cut off aid to a lot of those countries, even some honest leaders on the left said it was a smart move. Much of the money we'd sent to those countries had never made it to those who needed it. Instead, it had been syphoned off by dictators and crooked politicians.

Ever since Ted Kennedy, Democrats have been wrong on immigration. Their strategies have only kept poor countries poor and overwhelmed the United States with desperate people in need of help. As a result, we have a shortage of skilled workers and far too many unskilled immigrants in need of government assistance.

Even if you ignore the moral side of the argument—that it's our job to be nice to the world and take care of everyone, which is ridiculous—there's a set of dire economic circumstances here. The United States cannot afford to pay to take care of the world when we can't even care for our own citizens. I can hardly count all the people who came up to me on the campaign trail lamenting the sad state of our VA hospital system, a system that is finally being addressed by my father. He believes that our veterans should be taken care of before even one dollar goes to helping an illegal immigrant on food stamps or paying for undocumented students to go to college.

How can that be controversial?

Does this mean we need to shut down all immigration? Of course not. We can continue to allow refugees into the United States to live and work if they show genuine respect and admiration for America, as my friend in the coffee shop from Ethiopia did, and strive to make our country better. There is a system in place whereby each new immigrant is given a visa that allows him or her to remain in the country for a specified period—usually one to two years, longer if he or she has a job or plans to attend college. The H-1B visa gives preference to people in foreign countries who excel in specialized fields such as medicine or engineering. This enables us to fill our cities with qualified professionals from other countries, some of whom may bring outside expertise or a different point of view. In the last few decades, this visa has allowed doctors and surgeons from all over the world to come in and provide much-needed relief to US cities whose health care systems are on the verge of breaking under the weight of our swelling illegal immigrant population.

This visa system has been especially helpful in towns such as Brownsville, Texas, just a few miles north of the Mexican border. In Brownsville, people are twice as likely to have diseases as the average American, and nearly all the doctors and nurses who treat them are here on visas. To the hysterical left, these "best and brightest" visas are racist and exclusionary; to the Trump administration, they are a model around which we should design the rest of our immigration system. My father recently introduced an idea to overhaul our immigration policy using a merit-based system instead of the chain migration system that is now in place. The reaction by the left, and even by some on the right, was as if he wanted to put machine-gun turrets on the border.

I have five children. As they grow up, the people a merit-based system would draw would be their direct competition. Theoretically, I should think of this as a negative. But it really isn't. Competition is good, and it forces parents and students to make wise choices, such as not going $300,000 into debt for a PhD in underwater basket weaving. I don't think there's any such thing as a wasted education, but if you can't pay off your debt with the job that education trains you for, I'm not sure what else to call it.

Even with careful vetting and a lengthy application process, it is far too easy for bad actors to squeak past our visa safeguards without setting off any alarms. Terrorists such as ISIS members can exploit these lax borders. This is why, in a perfect world, the US government would be able to keep track of each and every visa it issues—and, more important, the people who hold those visas—using the best technology available. Unfortunately, the technology in use by Immigration and Customs Enforcement (ICE) today is about as up to date as Nintendo. I know, having worked on a mostly privately funded national campaign, how easy it is to get your hands on technology that keeps incredibly detailed information on people. In presidential politics, this is the name of the game. If our federal government had even a small percentage of the technological capability of the average private sector corporation or political campaign, finding potential terrorists in a pool of 1 million visa applicants would be easier than locating Elizabeth Warren on an Indian reservation. Instances of Islamic terrorism on US soil—which have already declined sharply since Democrats lost control of the White House—would almost certainly fall further, and we would free up space for more bright, competent immigrants to obtain visas.

But our government doesn't have access to that kind of system—not even close.

When ICE wants to check on the status of a foreigner staying in the United States, it has about twenty-seven different databases to comb through, all of which are supported by ancient computer systems and run by people who have no idea how to use them. As a result, more than 700,000 people who are granted temporary visas for work, study, or asylum disappear into the system every year, moving away from their last known addresses and effectively dropping off the federal government's radar.

So when ICE wants to look for a visa holder who's gone dark, it's faced with the choice of either searching through dozens of old databases, interviewing sources, and combing neighborhoods looking for one person or just giving up in the hope that nothing terrible will happen. This is all made much worse by the fact that to the hysterical Democrats in Congress, ICE might as well be the Gestapo. When DJT was elected and promised to give more funding to ICE so it would be able to carry out its duties effectively, protests broke out in the streets, mostly in communities that aren't affected by the scourge of illegal immigration. Three of the Democrat presidential hopefuls want to either abolish or gut ICE. "We should probably think about starting from scratch," Democrat senator Kamala Harris said. Elizabeth Warren wants to shut the agency down altogether.

The good news is that the American people are awake to what's happening with immigration. Democrat rhetoric and fake news might be able to fool some people for a while, but it can't do so forever. Just as in the real estate business in Manhattan, the market always figures it out. The American people know there's a problem at the border. They know that everyone who's coming over isn't a good actor. They know it's not the American dream that many of today's immigrants seek but the easy American dollar. And that, as my Ethiopian friend said, makes it harder for those who come here legally. But the American people see through all the lies of the left.

The market always knows.

7.

NOT YOUR GRANDFATHER'S DEMOCRAT PARTY

I'VE LEARNED A THING OR TWO about politics over the past few years. For instance: never trust the polls; don't believe what you read in the newspaper; and never, ever underestimate the people in Michigan, Pennsylvania, or Ohio (hear that, Hillary?). Maybe the most important thing I've learned, however, is that there's no substitute for getting out on the road and shaking hands with real people, not just the paid seat-fillers and people who show up for the free coffee and donuts. You can learn more from one hour in a parking lot outside a campaign event or while filling up at a local gas station than you can in a hundred strategy meetings at campaign headquarters. From our first moment on the campaign, my brother Eric and I have always had a rule that we won't leave a room until we've shaken every hand extended to us. The same is true of taking pictures, signing hats, and hearing stories. Our motto is that if there is anyone left in the room, we're still in the room. My father got that from his very first seconds on the campaign stage. He used to poll people by listening to their applause, and he'd know what policies were working based on how loud they cheered. He didn't need a team of data scientists to know the people were behind him.

Follow this principle and you might lose some sleep and miss a lot of meals, but you also might just help your father win the White House. So it's kind of a good trade-off.

One morning in 2016, a few minutes before one of my many solo campaign events, I took a walk around the rope line outside a large venue in Wisconsin. I would like to tell you that I drew bigger crowds than Hillary Clinton in Wisconsin during that campaign, but I can't. That's because she didn't draw a single person. She didn't visit the state even *once*! (I'm sure the Dems will fix that this time around—not because they want to but because they have to. Thanks to my father, they learned that they can't take those votes for granted anymore.) My speech was only a few days before the election, so I'm sure I was running on pure adrenaline fueled by about 100 calories (mostly from Red Bull) and something like two hours of sleep. Looking back, those last weeks on the campaign run together like one very long day. Not that I'm complaining. As you might imagine, it was a pretty exciting time, and I loved the action and the fight. One thing about being on the Trump train is that it's never boring.

Beyond the rope, toward the front of the line waiting to get into the event, there was a rowdy group of guys in orange vests and soiled carpenter jeans. A few wore yellow hard hats, while the rest sported the classic red MAGA caps. It's the kind of gathering you don't come across too often at Manhattan dinner parties. It's also the kind of group, I came to find, that will tell you exactly how they feel and what's on their minds. So I went over to hang out for a few minutes. They couldn't have been nicer. For a while, it was the

2

usual stuff: "We can't wait for you to make America great again!" "Your dad's the best!" "We hate Hillary!" and so on, all smiles. They told me that they were all union carpenters and they all loved my father's message. I posed for a few pictures and was about to take off for the backstage area when I noticed a guy off to the side.

He was dressed in pretty much the same manner as the other carpenters, but he wore no Trump swag and he didn't seem all that happy to be there. Honestly, he looked as though his pals had stuffed him into the trunk against his will and forced him to attend. I went over to him and shook his hand. As I did, he shook his head and laughed. "Sorry, man," he said. "It's just that if my grandfather knew I was about to vote for a Republican, he would roll over in his grave."

I could appreciate his concern. Both my grandfathers are heroes of mine. I've lived my whole life with their examples in mind, and my views on politics are pretty similar to what theirs were. I'd also heard a similar line from other union workers.

"Just curious," I said. "Why is that?"

In response, my new friend—let's call him "Rusty"—went on to tell me that he and his buddies were all from the same union local. They'd traveled more than a hundred miles to come hear my dad's speech. Rusty in particular had come from a long line of union people, mostly carpenters and electricians from Wisconsin, who'd all followed the same path in life. They'd grown up in small towns around the smell of cut lumber, gotten jobs on the same crews as their fathers, then gotten their union cards on their eighteenth birthdays—right around the time they cast their first votes for Democrats.

For Rusty's grandfather, that Democrat was probably Franklin D. Roosevelt, the man who practically invented the labor union and brought the whole American working class out of the Great Depression. At least it can be argued that his vote made some sense at the time. Then for his father, it would have been John F. Kennedy (JFK would be considered alt-right today) or LBJ. In keeping with family tradition, Rusty joined the local and cast his first vote for Barack H. Obama, a man who took more money from the paychecks of blue-collar workers than any president since the Great Depression. Clearly, Rusty's presidential votes to that point were votes against his own self-interest. It wasn't really his fault, though. From the days when he was playing with his first Fisher-Price hammer-and-nails toy set, his father and grandfather had been telling him about how Democrats were the only true party for the working class. According to that line of reasoning, Democrats cared about wages and benefits, while Republicans cared only about lining the pockets of the corporate overlords and company bosses. And why wouldn't he believe them? To that point, the guy's life had been like one long Bob Dylan song (the early stuff). And it hadn't been only his grandfather and father feeding him the line. Fat-cat Republicans taking advantage of poor workers played on a loop on television news and in Hollywood scripts. It appeared in liberal newspapers on a daily basis. I've always said that if you actually work for a living and don't have time to scour the world for the few shreds of actual real news that remain, it can be very difficult to determine what's true and what isn't.

What is true is this: His grandfather and father hadn't been lying to him. For much of the twentieth century, the Democrat Party really was the party of the labor unions and blue-collar workers. No doubt about it. Sure, at first, the party opposed civil rights legislation and had some pretty big problems letting black people actually *join* those unions, but it did a lot to lift the American working class out of poverty. It's the reason we have a forty-hour workweek, a two-day weekend, and benefits programs for workers. If you were an electrician or a plumber in the 1930s—again, as long as you were white and male didn't have any black friends—you'd have been forgiven for voting Democrat all the way. But somewhere in the late twentieth century, the liberals changed their tune on working-class voters. During the administration of Lyndon Johnson, when the Democrats started to realize that pretending to be for civil rights reform would keep them in office, they started to replace their support for workers with a *support system* for workers. Instead of pooling resources so they could cut taxes and grow US businesses, the federal government under Democrat control started to promote public spending and enormous welfare programs. Instead of enacting pro-business policies that would enable American workers' wages to go up, they put those workers on welfare. Then they raised taxes to pay for bloated programs, such as food stamps and federally funded housing, that work only to keep poor people poor. Democrats wanted and still want to keep the masses dependent. Their party became the party of dependence, because without dependence, what else did they have to offer?

The logic in this may have been devious, but it certainly wasn't stupid. Like the Democrats of today, those liberals realized that when people are dependent on you, they're much more likely to go to the polls and cast a vote for you. It's just basic psychology. It is not in the best interest of the Democrat Party to give workers money and let them make their own decisions. If they do that, the Washington establishment that creates wasteful spending programs and doles out food stamps to out-of-work coal miners would become obsolete, and there would be no reason for those coal miners to get out to the polls and vote for a Democrat next November. The Democrats also managed to create a split between the leaders of labor unions and the actual members. A big part of the reason for that divide is the rampant corruption in union leadership. More than ever, union leaders have become part of the

Washington establishment—veritable swamp creatures in their own right—while the actual workers continue to suffer through flat wages, high taxes, and glacial economic growth. Along the way, union bosses realized that they could "represent" the membership by doing nothing: not working and being completely subsidized by the workers of their own unions! Meanwhile, they threw their support behind a party that did nothing for them but ship union jobs overseas. They were literally helping to export the American dream that they were initially created to protect.

For example, take John "Johnny Doc" Dougherty. As of this writing, the boss of the Philadelphia Building & Construction Trades Council and Local 98 of the International Brotherhood of Electrical Workers is awaiting trial on a 116-count federal indictment that includes the embezzlement of more than $600,000 in union funds. According to the *Wall Street Journal*, Dougherty had union workers power wash the sidewalk in front of his house, water his tomato garden, and make sports bets for him. For the past fifteen years, he practically ran the Democrat Party in Philly and its suburbs. So deep into the Democrats' pocket was he that he made sure his union local did the wiring for the 2016 Democrat National Convention at the Wells Fargo Center in Philadelphia. He met with Hillary Clinton during the campaign. Dougherty might be a throwback to the days of the movie *On the Waterfront*, but he isn't an anomaly. Union leadership across the country is rife with corruption. According to data released by the US Department of Labor, since 2001, the Office of Labor-Management Standards has investigated and prosecuted union leaders for embezzling more than $100 million in union dues. Union leadership also spent something like $100 million in collected dues on Hillary Clinton's campaign while supporting an agenda (immigration reform, climate change, and other Democrat favorites) that sounds like talking points for a Bernie Sanders speech.

To be honest, Rusty probably knew all that better than I did. He just needed someone to tell him what he already knew. By the time I went inside the venue for my speech, he was looking a little more secure about the vote he would cast in a few days.

When I asked Rusty what modern Democrat policies or leading ideas, from socialized medicine right up to giving amnesty to millions of illegals, he couldn't name a single one. "How about keeping more of the money you earn from working?" I asked "How much more of your paycheck do you want the government taking away?" Rusty shook his head and said, "None." I smiled. "Look, Rusty," I said, "I understand the tradition. I understand that being a Democrat is all your family has ever known. But, man, today's party is not your grandfather's Democrat Party." You could almost see the light go on behind his eyes. I put my hand out and he grabbed it. "Welcome to the GOP," I said. "We're glad to have you."

I've had this talk many times since then, and I'm sure I'll keep having it.

BLUE-COLLAR BILLIONAIRE

In the aftermath of the election, the so-called experts and geniuses on TV were shocked to find that my father had gotten unheard-of levels of support from voters who belonged to labor unions. In fact, the only Republican presidential candidate to get a larger percentage of the union vote had been Ronald Reagan in the 1984 election. For weeks, op-ed writers and data journalists seemed baffled that in all the years that Republicans had been running for president, the candidate who had finally broken through and gained the support of rural union workers was a billionaire who lived on the top floor of a Fifth Avenue high-rise. They pored over my father's life story, trying to find some way to explain it all away, even saying that the voters must not have had all the information, that they had gone with Trump only because they were "non-college-educated," or that they just hated Washington and wanted to burn it down.

What all those morons with Ivy League journalism degrees failed to see was right there in plain sight. As I've often said, if you want to wear yourself out, follow Donald J. Trump around a job site someday. My father doesn't just visit a construction project; he stays the whole day and then comes back the next day. By the time he's through, he knows most of the workers' names, every problem they've encountered, and just about exactly how much he's spent. At The Trump Organization, we've hired thousands and thousands of union workers over the years, including Teamsters, union carpenters, and union electricians. Thanks partly to my father, many of them kept working for years, bought homes, and sent their kids to college. Democrats can pretend to be the party of the American working class, but those men and women aren't easily fooled. To voters like Rusty, the billionaire from Fifth Avenue is just as blue collar as they are. To the idiots on television who ended up with egg on their faces: shame on you. The same goes for the executives who kept these idiots employed. Only in the world of fake news can someone get something so wrong, such as the 2016 election, come back the next day, and pretend nothing ever happened! Where the hell is the accountability, people? Heads should have rolled! Do you remember the meltdown on CNN? What a glorious early morning as those who had predicted for weeks that Hillary would win by double digits had to eat their words. Still, they got away with all their lies. Trump exposed the supposed experts for what they are: full of shit.

It all reminds me of another trip I took early on in the campaign, this one to Trump Turnberry, my father's golf course and country club a few miles from Glasgow, Scotland. We were about to reopen there after a year of extensive renovations. As it happened, the trip took place just as British citizens were getting ready to vote on whether or not their country would leave the European Union. As we were getting ready to cut the ribbon at one of the famed golf holes, I was hanging around with some of the guys who look after the course—people from the local towns who drank in the pubs and worked all day out in the sun (and the rain . . . it is Scotland, after all.) As usual, they were the people I spent most of my time with. In my years of going to Turnberry for Trump Org, I'd gotten to know most of them well.

A few yards away, a group of reporters was gathering around the stage. Most of them had come to ask my father questions about his presidential campaign and his views on Brexit, which was the big story of the day. None of them cared very much about the golf course. From where I was standing with the maintenance guys, we could hear the television news anchors giving some early poll results on the referendum that was going to happen later that week. According to those news anchors—a small subset of the British population, say 1 percent, who lived almost exclusively in London and other metro areas—there was no way their countrymen would vote to leave. That, they seemed to suggest, would be ridiculous and stupid—not unlike the election of a certain brash billionaire from Manhattan that was happening across the Atlantic Ocean.

When I turned to the guys I was talking with—the other 99 percent of the British population, the ones who'd actually vote and be affected by what they were voting for—they had a different answer.

"Absolutely no way we don't vote to leave," one of them said. "It's one hundred percent certain. We're out."

Across the golf course, there were dozens of reporters looking (or pretending to look) for the story on Brexit. When I asked one of these reporters before we left what he thought was going to happen with Brexit, he said the same thing as his buddies on TV: "We're staying. I don't know anyone who would vote to leave. Not a single one."

If he had wanted to meet one, all this guy had to do was walk a few feet and talk to some regular people. But he didn't. Neither did any of his counterparts in the British media or the United States. Then, when the unthinkable happened and the people spoke up for what they wanted, all the reporters were dumbfounded. *How could this happen? How did we get it so wrong?*

They got it wrong because they didn't get out and talk to voters. That's it. End of story. They knew the outcome they wanted and they wrote accordingly. But these words didn't give them more of a say than anyone else. They certainly didn't give them more of a vote.

And for all the things my father has supposedly "revolutionized" about US politics—all of which he deserves full credit for, of course—his most revolutionary tactic was a pretty simple one: he knew his voters, and he listened to them. I wish I could tell you there was some other big secret or a fifty-point strategy you haven't heard about for winning the presidency, but that's really it. When my father stepped out onto the stage for the first time, he was talking to people he had been working with his entire life.

No one else in the race could say that.

———

When my father emerged on the scene in early 2015, everyone assumed that the support of local unions and blue-collar workers belonged exclusively to establishment Democrats such as Hillary Clinton and Joe Biden. By all accounts, they had strong support in Pennsylvania, Michigan, and Ohio. They were going to take the entire black and Hispanic vote easily. No one even stopped to think about why that had always been the case or whether it made any sense anymore—at least not until my father started challenging the established norms of politics and speaking to voters who'd been ignored by Republicans and Democrats alike for decades. During that campaign, we all learned what could happen if you just sat down and *listened* to people, then came up with policies that addressed their concerns.

As is often the case with politics, this sounds simple. But the Republican Party had managed to screw it up in just about every election of my lifetime. No party had a more stellar reputation for losing big and ignoring the issues that mattered. The Republican Party under George W. Bush and Mitt Romney could snatch defeat from the jaws of victory better than any other organization in history. For years, the party had been refusing to speak to workers in small-town America who were getting laid off by the second. They were too focused on getting more donations or getting reelected to see that there was real pain in the center of the country that couldn't be fixed without major changes. Compared with past Republicans, we outperformed in almost every category and with every demographic despite the BS narrative the media was selling with such glee. All they had given was promises; we gave people real results.

Luckily for people like Rusty, my father came along. Now the working men and women of America actually have someone in the White House who knows what they need and how to get it for them. Ask yourself this: What politician today has a history of dealing with unions and labor in business? Who has done thousands of jobs employing union labor? Who has worked *with* labor and not *for* its leadership, as many Democrats have? Name one

substantive thing that Democrats have done for the union men
and women of America over the past decades. NAFTA was horrible. Democrats did a great job for other countries that wanted to
build up their manufacturing base. Meanwhile, union leadership
pretended that Democrats are good for union workers? Give me a
break! How dumb do you think we are? As I mentioned, my father
renegotiated NAFTA into a new deal, USMCA, which does so much
for American workers. Unions applauded that new deal, yet now
Nancy Pelosi refuses to even bring it up to a vote in the House! I
wonder why . . .

Before he was president, my father watched as Democrats
exported the American dream to our competitors while Americans—good, hardworking Americans—struggled, and it sickened
him. That dream was our only substantive export for decades. He
was sick of watching other countries who hate our guts prosper,
while our prospects went down the drain because of Democrats'
decisions. They were exporting the American dream to people
who despised our freedoms and our values, all while our citizens
suffered. Donald J. Trump brought that dream back to where it
belongs—right here in the U.S. of A.

——

After what my father and his administration have accomplished
for workers in their first three years—tax cuts, raises in workers'
salaries, historically low unemployment—there is absolutely no
defensible reason for a working-class voter to support any Democrat. By making ideas such as socialism and open borders mainstream tenets of the Democrat Party, Joe Biden, Bernie Sanders,
Cory Booker, Elizabeth Warren, et al, have made the United States
less livable than ever for members of the working class. Instead of
investing in workers, they have helped ship jobs overseas, cost-

ing the American workforce countless jobs and opportunities. They've also allowed thousands of people to enter the country as illegal immigrants—who take, far too often, from the system while contributing nothing. What better way to destroy American progress than by having overcrowded schools and health care systems that collapse under the strain of a growing population of dependents who won't ever pay into our systems? Only a Democrat could possibly think that's a good idea!

8.

BACK TO SCHOOL

YOU MIGHT BE SURPRISED AT WHAT THE MONEY YOU PAY FOR TUITION BUYS YOU.

So you disagree with someone.

Congratulations! You've officially taken your first step toward making the world a better place. In this country, disagreement and debate—especially in the political arena—are the two most important things we have. They are what made the United States of America great in the first place. Without them, we'd still be a British colony and learning how to curtsy to the monarch while sipping afternoon tea.

Still, this is 2019. Before you go disagreeing with someone, you should know that debate and disagreement aren't what they used to be. For instance, if the person you disagree with is a member of a minority group and you're not, you're going to have to shut up. Also, if that person is a woman and you're not, you'll have to shut up. Oh, and if you make more money than the person you disagree with, you'll have to shut up.

To make matters easier, I've compiled this handy checklist so you'll know the rules going forward.

Don's Handy Checklist for Not Getting Called Racist, Misogynist, Fill-in-the-Blank Phobic

Are you:

☐ White?

☐ Straight?

☐ Male?

☐ Christian?

☐ Cisgender? (This, as I understand it, is our new word for when you "identify" as being the same gender you were assigned at birth. In other words, if you have man parts and *feel* like a man, or woman parts and *feel* like a woman.)

If you answered "yes" to any of those questions, you may want to shut up. If you answered "yes" to all five, you *definitely* need to shut up (yes, even if your parts match the way you *feel*.)

If you answered "yes" to only one or two, hold on. We're not done yet. Here's the second part of the list:

Is the person you disagree with:

☐ African American/Asian/Hispanic/Native American?

☐ A woman?

☐ A Muslim?

☐ A Democrat?

☐ Poor?

☐ Transgender?

☐ Under a lot of stress right now?

☐ An illegal immigrant?

If you checked off any of these boxes, unfortunately, you're also going to have to shut up. In fact, why don't you just strap a dog muzzle on your face. These days, that's the only way you'll be able to make the radical left in this country happy. This kind of muzzling has been going on for so long that most people probably don't even realize the strangeness of it anymore. The left owns most of the space in the public square, having all the major news organizations on its side. It's the same with social (or not-so-social) media. They have a literal army of social justice warriors across every medium. They even have the vast majority of colleges and universities covered, to ensure that the next generation of voters are brainwashed young! Don't get me started on safe spaces, where you can express all your feelings in a three-foot-square designated box on campus.

But what happens if you reverse the roles?

Well, then, none of the above applies. If you're a black Muslim woman looking to criticize a white male, not only can you do so with complete impunity, you get to be a guest on *The Rachel Maddow Show*. And once you get there, whatever you say is gospel. Your feelings—and you—are infallible.

——

Today, those on the left are allowed to say whatever they want with zero consequences. They're allowed to question anyone, protest anyone, and start riots in opposition to anyone, and nothing will happen in return. The liberal press will make them look heroic. CNN, the *Washington Post*, and the *New York Times* have all used the phrase "antihate protestors" to describe Antifa thugs. You don't hear the press say a bad word about the extremely dangerous rhetoric that comes from Ilhan Omar, Rashida Tlaib, and the rest of the Squad. But if a conservative says or does something they don't like—such as, I don't know, getting booked to speak at the University

of California, Berkeley, or some other bastion of higher learning—
well, then, he or she is a racist or a sexist or a person without a soul.

Nowhere is this double standard more evident than on college
campuses, where everything is permitted and no one is in control.
During the time I spent on the campaign in 2016, I learned that
some of the most dangerous ideas that permeate our culture today
originate in the classrooms of our most liberal universities. That's
where liberals have their feelings coddled, their worst impulses
encouraged, and their brains warped by weird radical theories.
They want diversity in everything except thought. Conservatives,
on the other hand, are told to shut up and stay in the shadows.
Countless times on college campuses I've had scared conservative students come up to me to say thank you for making them
feel normal and welcome in their school. It is that bad and worse.
Below is the first paragraph of an op-ed piece written last year by
a student on the staff of the *Yale Daily News*.

> Republicans are single-handedly destroying the Yale
> community. They do not offer anything substantial to
> our campus. They are all racist, bigoted, homophobes,
> whose mere presence serves as an unwelcome reminder
> that Donald J. Trump is our president. The very idea that
> there are Republicans lurking among us is truly disturbing
> and offensive. I am tired of having to share a campus with
> people who hate minorities and support the patriarchy. If
> Yale is truly a progressive school that cares about the safety
> and mental health of its students, it will stop accepting
> Republicans.

The insanity probably reached a tipping point around September 2017, when a mainstream conservative named Ben Shapiro was

invited to speak at UC Berkeley. It had been a while since I had been on a college campus long enough to know just how crazy they were. But I was watching the news coverage in my office, and the whole thing seemed very familiar. As the event drew closer, protestors gathered where the event was going to take place. The crowd began chanting "No Trump. No KKK. No fascist USA!" in unison.

Around the building, there were police in full riot gear. Obviously, the Berkeley administration had learned from its mistakes. A few months earlier, it had allowed a speech by a conservative British political commentator, Milo Yiannopoulos, to be shut down by the social justice mob. Student activists and members of Antifa had shown up with weapons and wearing hockey pads, ready to rumble. The campus police hadn't been prepared to deal with that kind of assault. By the end of that night, the protestors had caused about $500,000 worth of damage and brutally assaulted dozens of people who had stood in their way—or, in some cases, people who had just happened to be walking by.

The next time someone tells you that free speech is not under assault or in danger in this country, remind them that we often have to deploy full SWAT teams to make sure it's protected, which is what was done at the Shapiro event. Combine that with the constant threat of doxing by the online outrage mob and you can see that the left has made great inroads to limit freedom of speech and thought. The threat is real. Watching the news coverage, I couldn't help but laugh. I met Ben Shapiro only once, but anyone who's read a few lines of his work can tell straightaway that he is not a "fascist" or a member of the KKK. In fact, he's among the few people in this country who have been willing to speak the truth about the Democrat Party's association with racism, slavery, and the KKK. He's also an Orthodox Jew, which would probably make it hard for him to be a Nazi, too. And, he's not a Donald J. Trump supporter.

But those distinctions don't matter to people who show up at speeches to protest, burn things, and cause violence. There's no nuance in their view of the world. To them, you're either with them or against them. And if you're against them, you're evil. (I've always found it funny that the same people who'll tell you there are something like fifteen genders are the same people who tell you that politics boils down to either "Nazi" or "not Nazi.")

Before Shapiro's appearance, the University of California, Berkeley, smugly released this message: "Our commitment to free speech, as well as to the law, mandates that the students who invited Shapiro be able to host their event for those who wish to hear him speak."

In other words, yeah, we're committed to free speech, and we're so gloriously tolerant of other opinions that we'll let this event go on as planned.

Also, we might get sued if we don't.

In the same statement, the university announced that it would offer counseling services to anyone who was traumatized or triggered by the speech, saying it was "deeply concerned about the impact some speakers may have on individuals' sense of safety and belonging. No one should be made to feel threatened or harassed simply because of who they are or for what they believe."

Bear in mind that we're not talking about people who were tied to a chair and had Shapiro's speech blared into their ears through headphones. We're talking about people who didn't even attend the speech, who just happened to be on campus (no doubt wearing scarves and tossing Frisbees) while the event was going on— people who probably wouldn't even have known Shapiro was even there if it hadn't been for the university-wide email blast about it. In some sense, it was almost as if the university wanted to make it clear how much it hated Ben Shapiro and wanted to suggest that anyone who *wasn't* upset like a little baby about it was some kind of moral Neanderthal.

This is how universities communicate passive aggression. This is how they become complicit in the stifling of free speech.

And the fact that it happened at Berkeley, the supposed bastion of free speech, is insanely ironic.

Back in the early 1960s, when students were marching for civil rights and trying to organize against the Vietnam War, the campus of UC Berkeley became the source of the Free Speech Movement. In those days, it was the university, not the students, that was trying to shut down certain speakers and stifle the free expression of ideas. In fact, the students had to hold peaceful protests to defend their right to express ideas that might be offensive or "triggering" or dangerous. They were willing to sit for hours, be arrested, and be ridiculed just to stand up for their right to free speech, no matter how disgusting or inflammatory that speech was.

Before the Berkeley Free Speech Movement, discussing politics on campus was all but forbidden. You couldn't have a rally or hold an event unless it was sanctioned by the university, and the university wouldn't sanction anything it thought was too inflammatory (read: interesting). After the Free Speech Movement, colleges became what they had always been supposed to be: places where your ideas are challenged, your mind is tested, and everyone is free to express his or her beliefs without fear of retribution from crazy people.

Sadly, that's usually not what happens anymore. Today, free speech is no longer free. Berkeley spent $600,000 for security for Shapiro.

At the start of the campaign, I didn't plan on visiting a whole lot of college campuses. I assumed that stump speeches happened mostly in parking lots and diners, all the places where middle-aged working-class voters hung out and talked. But after the first few events I did in support of my father, we started to notice that the people coming to see me were pretty young. Some were still in high school and college. I don't know whether it was my use of social media or my boyish charm and good looks, but within a few weeks, I had become one of the most requested speakers by campus groups all over the country. When I really started traveling for the campaign, giving several speeches a day, I decided to add a few campuses to my agenda, just to see what all the fuss was about.

I had barely been back on a college campus since I had graduated from the University of Pennsylvania in 2000. I had seen a campus only on the rare occasions when I had gone back to Wharton, where I would occasionally be invited to give speeches on business and my career in real estate. But then again, I had been talking mostly to the sane, well-adjusted portion of the student body. I'd had absolutely no idea what was lurking in the halls of the other buildings: the gender studies offices, the counseling centers, the microaggression prevention rooms.

Needless to say, I knew little of the way things worked on campus anymore, but I knew from friends and the news that they had changed a whole lot. According to stories, the kids were protesting anything they didn't agree with, refusing to read books that contained violence—which, in my opinion, excluded some great classics—and disinviting speakers they deemed "dangerous." I had no idea what I was in for, so I decided to enlist some help with my "youth outreach" operation.

A few months earlier, I had met a young guy named Charlie Kirk. We'd been introduced by an old college friend of mine. From what I could gather in those first brief conversations, Charlie was a bright young guy who was focused on all the right things. He'd founded his own political organization when he was only eighteen years old—Turning Point USA—which fought liberal bias and the discrimination against conservatives that was happening in colleges all over the country. Long before anyone saw that those things were a problem, Charlie did. And he was trying to do something about them.

Anything I encountered on a campus, Charlie had already seen it and knew exactly how to handle it. Over the years, Charlie had had everything from Coca-Cola to chairs thrown at him. More than once, as I'd be giving a speech and protestors would try to shout me down, Charlie would get his Turning Point USA supporters to shout "USA! USA! USA!" until they filled the auditorium and Antifa or the social justice warriors (SJWs) would lose their willpower. He also made sure that everyone on campus knew where the speeches would be held and ensured that all the events began on time and without a hitch. But Charlie was also instrumental in helping me understand the crisis that was building in our nation's colleges. Without him and the experience of seeing things play out and hearing stories from real students, I don't think I would be as alarmed as I am.

I don't think I was ever called a "Nazi" to my face, but I certainly heard the word more than once. These days, as Charlie and the rest of the Turning Point USA crowd explained, anyone the left doesn't agree with is a "Nazi." But I also heard other things that were just as troubling.

At one university, the protestors suggested that my *words* would "do violence" to marginalized communities on campus, such as people of color or members of the LGBTQ community. Apparently, those kids did not mean that word metaphorically. They really meant, with no hint of irony, that having to hear opinions they didn't agree with would actually be a violent act against them, the same way a punch in the face—or a blow from a bike lock—would be. And by the way, I would never say anything derogatory about people in the LGBTQ community or people of color, let alone try to do them harm.

But in today's climate, words have completely lost their meanings. When conservatives speak, it's called "violence." When liberals react to that speech by beating people up and throwing rocks through windows, it's called "self-defense." When a conservative says "America is a good country" or "God bless America," that's called hate speech. When a liberal says "all white people should be extinct," as Sarah Jeong from the *New York Times* said, that's called ironic protest. Suddenly, liberals classify whether something is a violent act based on how it makes them feel, not whether the person who committed the act—or, in most cases, spoke the words—actually intended them to be violent or controversial. Intent doesn't matter; feelings do.

To even begin to understand how we got here, it's important to zoom out and look at all the factors involved.

Although it goes back many years, the problem seems to have ramped up around 2010 or so, when a generation of kids who'd been raised with phones in their hands and participation trophies on their shelves first entered college. Their whole lives, those kids had been taught by their helicopter parents that feelings are the only things that matter and that they shouldn't have to be exposed to anything they don't like. Instead of playing outside and scraping their knees, those kids stayed on social media and got a 24/7 mainline of garbage and outrage beamed right into their brains.

It's no wonder they came out soft and unable to function.

Writing about the phenomenon in *The Atlantic*, Greg Lukianoff and Jonathan Haidt warned against the dangers of helicopter parents and social media. As they put it, "it's not hard to imagine why students arriving on campus today might be more desirous of protection and more hostile toward ideological opponents than in generations past. . . . Social media makes it extraordinarily easy to join crusades, express solidarity and outrage, and shun traitors." They also pointed out, correctly I think, that "social media has fundamentally shifted the balance of power in relationships between students and faculty; the latter increasingly fear what students might do to their reputations and careers by stirring up online mobs against them."

For me, that made sense. I can only imagine what my life as a college student would have been like if we had had Twitter and Facebook. Today, I wake up and thank God we didn't have social media or cameras on our phones back then. So do all of my friends. For me, life was a little different. During my freshman-year move-in day at Penn, I was the only student in my building who came alone to the dorm and unpacked my own stuff. After my mom's wine at Taco Bell incident, I was relieved to be 100 percent solo at Penn.

By that time, I had already done the whole move-in, say-goodbye routine about five times at boarding school. By the time I was a sophomore in high school, I could unload the car and have my bed made with military precision in about six minutes flat.

But for young people who've gone to college in the last few years, things are very different. All their lives, their parents went with them everywhere, and all their friends knew where they were at all times. They were living through some of the most volatile emotional years of their lives, and they had a massive audience at their fingertips. All they had to do was tweet, and the whole world would move for them. That's the kind of power you shouldn't have at any age.

Time and time again on the campaign trail, I saw their tactics in action. Even when I wasn't the target, I heard countless stories of speakers being disinvited from campus, conservative professors being "outed" by the online outrage mob, and college administrators—who are supposed to be the adults—acquiescing to crazy demands from the SJW crowd. The examples could fill a whole separate book, but here's one.

Just before Halloween in 2015, faculty members at Yale sent out an email telling students to avoid "offensive" costumes on Halloween. The email forbade students from wearing anything that included "culturally appropriative" elements, including sombreros, fake mustaches, and traditional Asian dresses. (If it was Harvard, would they have retroactively put Elizabeth Warren on notice?) A few days later, a lecturer named Erika Christakis wrote an email to students she supervised raising the question of whether the college should be telling students what they could and could not wear. She suggested that they figure it out for themselves—you know, like grown-ups do.

After all, who is the arbiter of what is considered "offensive"? Is something offensive just because a person who complains says so? Is there some kind of scale? No one seems to know.

Christakis seemed to have noticed that problem, and she did what she could to point it out. She was an adviser to all those students. It was her job to give them guidance on issues such as this.

"Talk to each other," she wrote. "Free speech and the ability to tolerate offense are the hallmarks of a free and open society." The email was very diplomatic, written in the spirit of conversation and debate. Obviously, the woman was not looking to start a fight.

But the mob got hold of it, and they gave her one. The email spread like brush fire all over Twitter and Facebook, and soon there was a whole mob of people trying to get Erika Christakis and her husband, Nicholas, both of whom live on the Yale campus, to resign. Just days later, in a scene that would become famous and go viral, a group of hundreds of students gathered outside their house. They wrote vile messages on their house in chalk and screamed at them. When Nicholas came out to speak with them, the mob demanded that he apologize. They accused him of "stripping people of their humanity" and "enabling violence." They demanded a "safe space" where—I'm guessing—there would be no offensive Halloween costumes. They also demanded that he apologize for his wife's email, which he refused to do.

In a particularly chilling moment, the lead crazy person got into his face and started screaming. "Who the fuck hired you?" she demanded. "You should step down! . . . It's not about creating an intellectual space! It is not! It's about creating a home here. . . . You should not sleep safely at night. You are disgusting!"

The faculty at Yale did nothing to help. Although some expressed sympathy in private, they were all too afraid to incur the wrath of the mob—which was made up of eighteen- and nineteen-year-old students—to speak out in support of Erika Christakis. Eventually she resigned from her position and her husband took a sabbatical. Once again, the mob won.

A professor of math education at the University of Illinois wrote a paper declaring that math —that's right, just good old *math*— was actually racist because it "operates as whiteness . . . and who is seen as part of the mathematical community is generally viewed as white."

Not long ago, 1,300 students at Oberlin College in Ohio signed a petition that would make a C the lowest grade that a student could receive in classes there. That was done, according to the letter, so that "no student would be made to feel less than 'average.'" Sort of defeats the mathematical notion of "average." But, remember: this is 2019, and math is racist. Another student demanded that before his class read *Antigone*, a classic Greek play that includes rape and violence, the professor should give "trigger warnings" so that no one would be "traumatized" by the violence in the play.

———

Everyone seems to have accepted the notion that college students need to be protected from ideas that make them uncomfortable. Instead of going to college to be challenged, they go to college to be coddled and sheltered from things they don't like.

And this isn't only an inference. The students have admitted it themselves. In a survey done in 2017, just after my father was elected and the fervor on campus was at its worst, 58 percent of college students said it was "important to be part of a campus community where I am not exposed to intolerant and offensive ideas." When you narrow the respondents down to the ones who identify as "liberal," the number goes up to 68 percent. In June of that year, a liberal professor named Lisa Feldman Barrett from Northeastern University published an op-ed in the *New York Times* titled "When Is Speech Violence?" Now, you might think, as I do, that the whole text of the article could have run about two words—"It isn't"—but Professor Barrett went on for about eight hundred. "If words can cause stress, and if prolonged stress can cause physical harm, then it seems that speech—at least certain types of speech—can be a form of violence," she wrote.

It's no wonder that students, with professors such as Barrett and publications that are willing to print their nonsense, act like babies in places that are all too willing to treat them that way. In fact, since the "great aWOKEning" came to college campuses around 2010, the number of administrators—whose sole responsibility is to coddle students and make sure they feel safe—has multiplied by a factor of five.

In the period between 1975 and 2008, the number of full-time faculty in the University of California system (of which Berkeley is the most famous member) barely increased at all, going from around 11,614 to 12,019. In terms of growth, that's actually on the low end. But the number of university administrators in the system spiraled out of control, from about 3,000 to 12,183. A massive percentage of the increase was "diversity officers," people whose job it is to make sure that students do not feel offended and that they aren't exposed to "microaggressions."

If you've never heard of these things, allow me to define "microaggression" for you. Coined by a professor at Harvard University in the late 1970s, the term refers to harmless questions and statements that, although pure or benign in intention, are offensive to members of certain minority groups, such as Asian Americans or African Americans. The list includes things such as "So where are you from?" or "You must do well in school." It also includes things such as "I like your hair" and "What kind of music do you like?" Apparently, these questions and statements make members of minority groups feel "other" and "excluded," and they reveal that the person asking the question or making the statement must be some kind of racist. I mean, think about it. Who hasn't done this, just wanting to start a conversation? When I was a kid, questions like these were just considered common courtesy. Like common sense, however, common courtesy is out the window. Maybe you're stuck in an elevator with someone, and you think a quick icebreaker might make the ride go faster. Well, not so fast, say the liberals. Next time you're in an elevator with someone of a different ethnic group, put your head down, shut up, and think about your white privilege.

Not only is term ridiculous, it's also based on a bad premise. It assumes that the intent of the speaker doesn't matter and labels things as "aggressions" that actually aren't aggressive at all. When you stop thinking that the intent of people matters, you take away all incentive to talk things out like adults. All of a sudden, you stop thinking that you can understand people by talking with them. As someone who talked with people for thousands of hours during the 2016 campaign, I know that this is incredibly dangerous. It also accepts the premise that speech is violence, making it seem perfectly fine that any violence you do in return for that speech is justified. It's no wonder that students have decided it's okay to throw rocks, turn over cars, and beat "Nazis" with flagpoles.

I mean, if speech really is violence and accusing someone of a crime counts the same as punching someone in the face, there are a whole bunch of reporters at CNN I'm sure my family and I would love to see brought up on charges. Do you think anyone would complain if we threw cuffs on Jim Acosta for all his "word violence" against me and my family? Maybe Chris Cuomo or Rachel Maddow?

Just a thought.

We've been treating college students as if they were fragile little babies for so long that they break down the second they hear something they don't agree with. This is the wrong way to think, and it should stop now.

———

If I've learned one thing about children—and human beings in general—it's that they can thrive only when they're challenged. Just as your muscles won't grow if you don't put them under the stress of weight lifting and your mind won't expand if you don't fill it with difficult thoughts, books, and arguments, people can't grow if they're not made uncomfortable, or at least challenged, sometimes.

According to an economist named Nassim Nicholas Taleb, there are three ways an object can be in the world: fragile; not fragile; or a third category, *antifragile*. When something is fragile, it breaks under stress and you can't use it anymore. A glass vase is fragile; so are light bulbs. When you expose them to the stress of hitting the ground, they break and become useless. Other things, such as steel and rocks, don't break no matter how much pressure you apply to them. On college campuses today, students are demanding to be treated as if they're fragile. They say that if they're exposed to too many bad ideas, they'll break and cease to function. But human beings are not fragile, they are antifragile.

Things in this third category actually become *stronger* the more pressure you apply to them. They can't survive without stress and tension. This is the way human beings are, especially as children. The more stress we endure—to a point, of course—the stronger we become. And if we live a life that is completely free of stress—say, stretched out in bed for a year watching television—our muscles break down and we become useless. This is the reason we get sick so much as children and then not as much as adults: we're building up immunities to things, getting used to living in the world. Since they were young, I've taken my kids up to our cabin so they can play outside in nature. I let my sons ride around the property on their quads, and if they fall, they've learned a lesson. I think it's good to let them make their own mistakes and get their own bruises.

Sometimes, of course, kids really do get hurt. A few years ago, for instance, my son Tristan took a hard fall on a family ski trip in Colorado and broke his leg pretty badly. We had to fly him back home to New York for surgery that require pins and plates to be put in his femur. But he recovered just fine, and he was right back on his skis the next year.

As a side note, the very first call I got when Tristan went into surgery was from Vice President Mike Pence—not a secretary, not the switchboard operator, but Mike Pence himself. The guy really is as nice as people say. This happens time and time again with Vice President Pence, whether the news is good or bad. But overall, I think a little mud is a good thing, especially for young people.

This is why we go to college when we're young. It's our time to try out different ideas, talk things out with people our own age, and be exposed to all kinds of things we won't see once we get out into the real world. For this to be effective, it has to include ideas that some people would consider "offensive." Otherwise, there's no opportunity for growth.

———

If you've been paying attention to this chapter, you might get the impression that all college campuses are horrible all the time—that they're all filled with SJW freaks who want to shut down all speech that doesn't make them feel safe. But visiting colleges wasn't all bad. In fact, we managed to have some fun.

Here's a good example.

As you might imagine, the last Saturday in October is a big weekend for college football, especially in the SEC and the ACC. On that Saturday, the Florida State Seminoles were hosting the Clemson Tigers in a night game. Charlie had worked out a short appearance for me in advance in a frat house on Florida State University's campus.

"It could get a little rowdy," he warned me.

How bad could it be? I wondered.

The event in the frat house was billed a "tailgate," but that description doesn't really do justice to what we walked into. Comparing it to the movie *Animal House* doesn't do it justice. I might have been a few years out of my frat boy element, but I quickly acclimated.

I had forgotten about how rowdy those parties could get. All of a sudden, I was back in the backyards and frat houses of my college years. I remembered all the kegs of beer, sleepless nights, and bad hangovers as though they'd happened only yesterday. Later, Charlie would tell me that there had been some 1,300 people there, and I don't doubt him for a moment. You couldn't move. Charlie and Tommy Hicks had to literally push me through a sea of students, most of whom had been drinking since early that morning. Obviously, clothing was optional.

I had been there only a few minutes when I realized that the people who had organized the little get-together expected me to give a speech. Though the house had a fairly large backyard, there wasn't a patch of grass or dirt or anything that resembled ground. Every inch of grass was covered by humans. Following Charlie, I felt as though I were swimming though the crowd. Luckily for us, the human tide seemed to be headed toward some picnic tables, which I thought would be as good a stage as any. I'm not going to complain about any of what happened to me that evening. Along with rooting for the Seminoles, I would say that nearly everybody there was rooting for Trump. Someone handed me a microphone attached to a small amplifier, like the ones you use for karaoke. As I got up on the table, the crowd reacted enthusiastically to me. Maybe a little too enthusiastically.

As I began to talk, the sea of Seminole fans started to close in. At the front of the human tidal wave was a group of coeds who had taken the clothing-optional suggestion to heart and started to climb up on the table. Now, I consider myself a pretty handsome guy (Hey, I'm a Trump. What'd you expect?), but I had never thought of myself as *girls-climbing-onto-a-picnic-table-to-get-at-me* handsome. But I was that night. Very quickly, we realized we had lost any semblance of control over the crowd. Leaving the way we came in, however, was not an option. For a moment, I thought I would meet an untimely end by being trampled to death by coeds. I guess there are worse ways to go. Luckily, Charlie noticed a fence at the back of the yard. Heads down as hands grabbed at us, we burrowed though the mass of flesh. I went over the fence like a recruit in Army Ranger School, though I think I lost a piece of my pant leg.

Back in the safety of the car, I turned to Charlie. "Imagine if they didn't like Trump?"

We would get our share of those. We did an event at one of the campuses of the University of Michigan. It was a very aggressive environment—750 or more protestors. When we arrived, the Michigan State Police came up to us and said that they couldn't guarantee our safety.

"Where's your security team?" one of the cops in charge asked.

"What security team?" I asked, looking at Charlie and Tommy. "It's just us."

Even some of the people with me said we should cancel. "Hell, no," I told them. "If we cancel, they win."

As it turned out, it was one of the best events we did. The energy was electric, with each side trying to drown out the other.

There were other times we got help when we didn't even ask for it. About a week before the election, we went to Ohio State University for another packed event. After I spoke, I went into the crowd to shake hands and take selfies with people. Maybe once in a while someone in that situation would make a smart remark to you, but for the most part the people were great. The crowd at OSU was particularly so. In the sea of Trump fans that day, however, I notice a guy standing by himself in the middle of the room. If I told you he was big, I wouldn't be accurately capturing the size of him.

He could blot out the sun. He stood there like an oak, not saying a word to anyone, just surveying the crowd. I had to find out what his story was before we left. I walked over to him.

"Hey, what's up?" I asked in a friendly tone.

"I'm just here so no bullshit happens," he said.

As it turned out, he was the center for the OSU football team.

Needless to say, Antifa was nowhere in sight.

OH-IO!

9.

ELECTION NIGHT

ON THE AFTERNOON of November 8, 2016, while Hillary's team was busy setting up their victory party, figuring out how not to shatter the glass ceiling of the Javits Center when they popped their champagne corks, I was in my office in Trump Tower with Tommy Hicks; Gentry Beach, another Texan, who was with us from the beginning; and Charlie Kirk. A longtime friend, Gentry and I had a lot in common. He'd also attended the University of Pennsylvania, my alma mater, and he was a guy's guy in every sense of the word. He worked his ass off. During the campaign, Gentry made phone calls night and day to raise cash, and he was phenomenal at it.

In those early days, the RNC was likely less than thrilled that Trump was their nominee. We needed guys who believed in my father and actually wanted to see him get elected, and Gentry was one.

Together, with a few others, we'd formed quite a team during the campaign. We did events and speeches as quickly as they rolled them out for us: six, seven a day towards the end. At midnight the night before, we were in New Hampshire with my father. We would have gone back to Michigan with him for one last rally that was held at 1:00 a.m. on Election Day, but I had to do TV hits that morning in New York. CNN, *Morning Joe*, Stephanopoulos, I did all of them on about two hours' sleep.

The polls (and we all know now how much they mattered) still had us down. Down significantly. Perhaps another campaign would have pushed back from the table, threw the napkin down, and said, "Well, we did our best. Let's see what happens."

But we weren't like other campaigns.

Instead, I was a caged animal: getting up from the small four-person table and pacing my office, all the while holding a cell phone to my ear, talking a mile a minute. As I did, Tommy and Gentry queued up the next conservative radio show host, having them ready for me as soon as I hung up on the current one. I put Charlie in charge of my social media, and he furiously typed as I dictated tweets. I had something like 50 million impressions, a number which is insane. I remember yelling at Sean Hannity, who was hosting his radio show. He had texted me that he was getting off the air.

"Get me on the next show!" I yelled into my phone. "We have to turn out the Panhandle! If you leave, get me on with your competition!"

I wasn't going to waste one second, or squander one opportunity to make a final pitch. It was like being in a battle for your life, and I wasn't going to stop fighting until there was nothing left to fight for.

We worked east to west, following the time zones until 7:00 or 8:00 p.m. EST. I believe I did forty-seven radio interviews in the span of several hours, which has to be some kind of record. I must have reached hundreds and hundreds of thousands of people. I said the words "Go vote" so many times, I swear, I can still hear myself saying those words when my office is quiet.

GET OUT AND VOTE! YOU GOTTA SHOW UP, TURN OUT. NOTHING ELSE MATTERS AS LONG AS YOU GET OUT AND VOTE. REMEMBER, IF YOU GET THERE AT 7:59 AND THE POLLS CLOSE AT 8, THEY STILL HAVE TO LET YOU VOTE! GET IN LINE! VOTE!!! VOOOOOOOOOTE!!!! NOW!!!!!

While I was in my office, Ivanka and Eric were in theirs, doing the same thing. I was running on pure adrenaline, testosterone, and about twelve Red Bulls. We weren't weeks or days out to election anymore. There were only hours left. We were coming to the end of one of the most brutal, hard-fought campaigns in the history of American politics, and we were much closer to winning than anyone (including some members of the Trump campaign, though most wouldn't admit it today) ever thought we would be. We never wanted to look back and think that we could have worked harder.

I wouldn't have been able to look my father in the eye if I had phoned it in the last day. I remembered one Saturday about three months earlier, being out in Bedminster with the whole family, Mike Pence, Reince Priebus, Steve Bannon, Kellyanne Conway, Chris Christie, and Brad Parscale—the whole Trump team. They were presenting to my Dad the schedule they'd come up with for the last ninety days of the campaign. I forget who was doing the talking, maybe Bannon, but it went something like this:

"Okay, you have an event this Saturday and then the rest of the day off. You have one on Sunday morning, but you'll be free that afternoon and the entire next day." I guess they thought they were doing him a favor by finding him days off, but I could see the reaction building in my dad's face. Ivanka, Eric, and I exchanged knowing looks. It wasn't a matter of *if* he would explode, just when.

"Enough!" he shouted. "There's only three months left to the election. I don't want any days off! If I lose, I'll have all the time off I need."

It was amazing to see. Two different levels of work ethic: those in politics, and my Dad's.

So, the idea of slowing down never entered my mind. Oh no. At this point, we could do 24/7 straight standing on our heads. We were going pedal to the medal.

———

At about 9:00 or 10:00 p.m. when I went down to the war room (election night campaign headquarters) on the 14th floor of Trump Tower, it felt like the whole world was holding its breath. Like watching the last batter hit a pop fly in the bottom of the ninth inning, except the ball stays in the air for five hours.

The energy in the war room was a kind of high-wire helpless expectancy. We were at the point of a campaign where there was nothing left to do but watch and get updates on turnout. My family and most of the campaign staff had congregated in front of the wall of six or so flat-screen televisions we'd set up. Even with the whole team it was intimate. We didn't have HRC's 1000-person campaign office. Like I've said, we were lean and mean. We had Fox News on, of course, with Megyn Kelly, but also the MSM. Every time I looked at my Twitter feed or at one of the liberal news networks, all I could see was the enemy. I know it sounds harsh, but there was no doubt they were against us. I heard journalists who were supposed to be objective reporters of the news talking about Hillary's path to victory, as if she was the only one that mattered in the race. As things began to tighten, it was "we" could still take down Donald Trump if X, Y, and Z happens. They might as well have been wearing *I'm-with-her* sweatshirts and cutting into a big sheet cake with Hillary's face on it.

To your face, however, these people would tell you they had no agenda, never took sides, and only reported the facts. Whenever someone called them out for their obvious liberal bias, they'd deny it. But now, here they were using their platforms on the most important night of the year to push propaganda for the Democrat Party and denigrate Donald Trump on live television. All pretense of objective journalism was abandoned. Instead, they showed who they really are—partisan hacks.

At one point, I glanced at my dad. Watching him in action during the campaign was certainly inspiring—to me and to everyone else on the staff. We had a front-row seat to see the most remarkable candidate in political history, one perfectly suited for the time, a first-time politician who shocked the political world. They had seen nothing like him before. His energy was unstoppable.

Though seasoned politicians insisted he came out of nowhere, I knew that not to be true. The energy that flows through my father is the same energy that flowed through my grandfather and great-grandfather before him. The 2016 Donald J. Trump for President campaign was a hundred years in the making, built on a foundation of American spirit, smarts, and grit.

Though it took me a while to realize, the same energy also flows through me. I've always looked up to my father and admired him more than anyone, but we seemed to have much different styles and approaches to life. Where he was brash and in-your-face, I was a little more reserved. Where he was at home amid the skyscrapers and kinetic energy of Manhattan, I was happy out in the woods or behind the wheel of my truck. But the campaign for president, and all the craziness that went along with it, changed all that.

It took me forty years and an unbelievably grueling race for the presidency for me, or anyone else for that matter, to realize that I'm much more like my father than I'd ever thought. It took getting backed into a corner for those traits to manifest. I felt the same responsibility to help my country that he did, and I got the same rush from sticking my neck out into the fight like him. After a few spats with liberals and the media, I learned that I had much more of his killer instinct than I thought, too. When we get hit, we hit back twice as hard. When we're backed into a corner, we come out swinging.

The first time I saw my father sit down all night was in the war room. He'd come down from the apartment when it started to become abundantly clear that Hillary Clinton was not going to sail to victory the way everybody had said she would. Watching him, I tried to find some sign that he was surprised by, or at least excited about, the fact that he might become president of the United States. But there was nothing. He just watched the screens like they were showing some old movie he'd seen twenty times before—cool, calm, and collected.

After the networks called Florida for us, DJT and the family headed upstairs with a few senior members of the campaign. Once we got upstairs, we stood around in my father's apartment with the whole family, including Ivanka and Jared. I thought about how much my sister and brother-in-law sacrificed for the campaign. From the start, Jared brought a sense of calm to a very unruly cast of characters. Meticulous, organized, and cool-headed, he was Michael Jordan to a whole team of Dennis Rodmans. Like the rest of us Trumps, he worked as hard as he could. No one seemed able to believe what was happening. On the way, we all remembered at once that my father hadn't allowed anyone to even contemplate writing a speech for that evening. Whether he won or lost, he was going to come up with his remarks just a few minutes before he had

At a rally in Cincinnati, Ohio, a supporter presented me with a pretty clever hat: TRUMP 2020 NO BULLSHIT. (Vincent Remini)

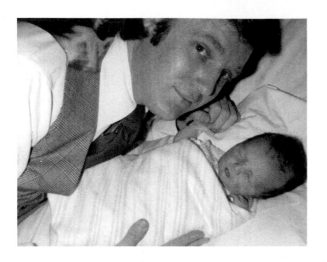

Above left: My father holding me as newborn. *Above right:* Early days—just shy of being one year old, with my mother, Ivana, in our apartment in New York City.

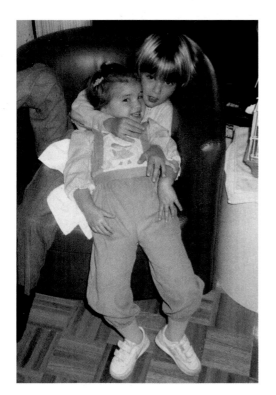

Above left: Me with little Ivanka. As an older brother, I always looked out for her and continue to do so to this day though she clearly doesn't need it. *Above right:* Eric, Ivanka, and I with Dad. We often visited him in the office during working hours as he worked to grow the company.

Above: In the Yankees dugout with dad and legendary Yankees manager Billy Martin. Dad would often take us to watch the games.

Above: When I graduated from the Hill School, I continued in the time-honored February tradition of jumping into the Dell, a pond on campus, with every other graduate. The tradition is much better when done voluntarily instead of being a wise guy 8th grader thrown in by seniors. Here I am soaking wet with Dad.

Above left: Visiting Florida State, we were welcomed at a frat party after the game. *Above right:* Kai, Tristan, and I on the back of a pickup truck at the Florida-Georgia football game. It was one of Kai's first public speaking engagements, and she had the crowd going. *Below:* At a tailgate party hosted by by legendary GA player and alum Kevin "Catfish" Jackson in honor of the big Georgia game.

Above left: Visiting the Navajo Indian reservation; they hadn't thought anyone would show. The room was standing room only. *Above right:* One of the last Navajo Code Talkers, a true World War II hero and strong supporter of Donald J. Trump.

Above left: In Trump Tower as we unfurled the campaign flag: Paige Scardigli, Kai Trump, Eric Trump, Kerry Woolard, Lynne Patton, Larry Glick, and I. *Above right:* On a swing in Arizona, Gentry Beach and I spotted a stalled vehicle at a busy intersection. It was over 100°F outside. The woman had no idea who we were as we helped push her vehicle off the road. Reporters tracked her down and wanted to know if it had all been staged. Obviously I would be incapable of doing anything decent.

Above left: Pictured here watching election night results with dad in the kitchen of his apartment in Trump Tower are Eric, me, Steve Bannon and Reince Preibus. (Dan Scavino)
Above right: An incredible moment in history. President-elect Trump accepting the concession call from Hillary Clinton. It's a screenshot of a video that I took at 2:37 a.m., a moment that forever changed the course of history.

Above: With my good friend, now cochair of the Republican National Committee, Tommy Hicks.

Above left: The entire Trump family on the steps of the Lincoln Memorial during the inaugural festivities. (Chris Kleponis-Pool/Getty Images) *Above right:* The President and Kai waving during an inauguration event. (Aaron P. Bernstein/Getty Images)
Below: Dad, Barron, First Lady Melania Trump, Donnie, Arabella, Kai, and Tristan having dinner at the White House during inauguration week.

Above left: Stepping off Air Force One in Washington after leaving Mar-a-Lago to attend Easter festivities at the White House. (Official White House photo) *Above right:* Tristan pretending to be on the phone while riding in the Beast during the inaugural parade. Perhaps he's negotiating with North Korea. *Below:* Donnie, Vanessa, Kai, and I in the Beast during the inaugural parade from the Capitol to the White House.

Above: With all of my children at the White House for the Easter egg roll. Spencer looks thrilled to be there. ***Below left:*** With my father, the President of the United States on *Air Force One.* (Official White House photo) ***Below right:*** Chloe wearing a US marine's cover. She befriended a marine who was stationed at Blair House during inaugural week. Even he couldn't keep up his stoic front around bubbly Chloe.

Above: Spencer and Donnie share my passion for the great outdoors. (Trig French)
Below left: Trekking down a mountain in the Yukon Territory of Canada with a caribou rack. It took several trips to retrieve all the meat. *Below right:* Donnie and I hunting for wild turkey in the vicinity of Lake Okeechobee, Florida. (David McCleaf)

Above: Donnie and I off the coast of Florida, hoping for a sizable mahi-mahi. *Below:* Ice fishing for rainbow trout with Chloe, Spencer, and Tristan in upstate New York.

Above: Kai with a great jack before we promptly released it. Hunters and fishermen are the best conservationists out there. *Below:* Kai, Donnie, and I, after they completed getting their scuba diving certification.

Above: Donnie and I sharing a duck blind in south Texas. *Below:* Having Kimberly with me at various events across the nation has been great! A very talented speaker, the crowds love her! (Trent Tidmore)

Above: Speaking at Turning Point USA in Washington, DC, one of the best youth groups in America, run by my friend Charlie Kirk. (Sergio Gor) *Below:* Jared, Ivanka, Tiffany, Kimberly, and I back at the White House after hearing President Trump deliver a spectacular State of the Union address. (Official White House photo)

Above: With Jared, Eric, and Dad prior to being hosted for dinner by Queen Elizabeth II in Buckingham Palace. ***Below:*** Dinner at Mar-a-Lago with Kimberly Guilfoyle, Sergio Gor, Tommy Hicks, Dad, and Charlie Kirk.

Above: Addressing the giant crowd of freedom-loving patriots at a Trump 2020 rally in Cincinnati, Ohio. I love meeting the thousands of people who show up to our campaign events. (Vincent Remini) *Below:* Politics has brought me and my father closer in a new way. For all of my life, I admired what he did for our family, now I appreciate all that he does for our great nation! (Official White House photo)

to deliver them. There was no reason to expend time or energy on speeches until there was a result. All of our focus was on the finish line; whatever came after would take care of itself.

———

By one in the morning, the only thing between my father and the presidency was Hillary's "firewall," which included Pennsylvania.

Along with some of the senior campaign staff, I watched the results on a tiny TV in the kitchen area of the apartment. Every time they zoomed into the fuzzy electoral map of Pennsylvania, I thought back to all the years I had spent there as a student in high school and college. I'd spent a quarter of my life in Pennsylvania. I thought of all the families I had met and all the sights I could see driving there—boarded-up factories, closed-down coal mines. The friends I made in the Rust Belt at the Hill School in Pottstown, and then afterward at the University of Pennsylvania, weren't the rich brats I knew who went to fancy private schools in Manhattan, and then on to Harvard or Yale. Many of the people I knew from Pennsylvania came from the parts of the state that had suffered the most. They were the ones who had seen the jobs go away in the 1990s as we shipped most of our manufacturing overseas—the ones who had seen their influence in national politics decline just about every year since I had been out of school. Until my father, all they knew was empty promises from politicians who really didn't care about them. These great Americans had a profound impact on my life at an early and formative time.

As I write this, the 2020 Democrat candidates, especially Joe Biden, are pandering to Pennsylvanians, pretending to understand the real pain they're feeling because they happened to be born there. What Joe won't tell you is that he lived in Pennsylvania only until he was ten. I spent nearly as much time there, and was old enough to actually remember it. Hillary had used the same playbook, and she'd left the state when she was even younger than Joe. And yet, she thought she was entitled to the votes of the blue-collar people from her "home" state. Every few years, people like Biden and Hillary spout the same lies about how they support working-class people, and then they pass legislation that benefits the elite political class and leaves everyone else behind. They don't care about working-class people or their jobs. They didn't care about people from places like Pottstown, Pennsylvania. If you look at the policies my father has enacted since taking office, from tax cuts to widespread deregulation, you can trace almost every one of them back to the voices that came from those small towns in Pennsylvania, Michigan, Ohio, and other states. Along with my father's signature, the executive orders and legislation written to enact those policies might as well have the names right at the bottom of everyone he'd met during the campaign.

At 2:00 a.m., they still hadn't called Pennsylvania. There was only 1 percent of the vote not accounted for in the state. Even if Hillary won every single vote, it still wouldn't be enough. Yet, the networks refused to call it for my father. What could have possibly been the reason for the delay? Could it have been ratings? Dangling a glimmer of hope to the left so they'd continue to watch even though in reality their candidate was finished? Couldn't be. No television networks would ever stoop that low, right?

Right.

They couldn't hold out forever. When the networks finally called the state and Hillary's path to the 270 electoral votes needed to win went up in smoke, just about every television set in New York City, San Francisco, and all the other sanctuary cities clicked off. When the people around me began to celebrate, however, a familiar feeling came over me.

I'd watched the left in action. On the campaign. On social media. With fake news. I knew that respect and convention meant nothing to them. That very morning, I was reminded how horrible they could be. With my two-year-old daughter Chloe in my arms and my daughter Kai holding my hand, I'd walked from work to vote at a local public school. On the way, I was called every four-letter word imaginable. You know, tolerant liberals screaming and cursing at me while I had four of my children in tow. To the left, I wasn't a father, and my kids weren't children. We weren't human beings. We were the enemy. If it was just me, I wouldn't have cared. It's happened so much to me, I wouldn't have given it a second thought. You start saying things like that to my kids, well, that's another matter altogether. I've used the hate the left has towards me as motivation. But this was something entirely different.

The vile anger on the left comes right from the top. The Clintons are one of the most corrupt and uncivil political machines in the history of our nation.

It was just another sign of their disdain for regular people, which would come back again when my father announced his reelection campaign in Orlando a few years later. Panning the camera over the long line waiting for my father to speak, the anchors would make fun of their flip flops and cargo shorts, wondering if that constituted "formal wear" in Florida. These were people who stood outside in thunderstorms for forty-eight hours. They weren't going to the prom. They were waiting to hear a politician speak. Half of them knew they weren't even going to get in, but they waited anyway. And then the media mocks them for being in casual, comfortable clothes out in the mud?

Please. Their hatred of anyone who doesn't live in New York City or subscribe to their radical ideas was disgusting to me.

Right before my eyes, the television anchors were telling me my father was the president-elect. But, if there was one thing I learned in the prior two years, it was that the Clintons were not about to roll over and die. Too much was at stake. More than even the presidency. A global network of power that they'd spent decades building was in peril.

I stood there in front of the television, in the place I'd grown up, with the people I cared about most in the world, and shook my head.

"No," I said, first to myself and then to the others in the kitchen. "No! They are not going to give in."

No matter what the results said, they would come up with some kind of trick to snatch the victory away. They would say the system had been rigged, that the voting machines were all wrong, that some of the ballots had been smudged and didn't count. "They'll come up with something," I said. "Just watch."

That entire night, I waited for the other shoe to drop. When John Podesta came out onstage at the Javits Center to announce that everyone would "regroup in the morning," he confirmed my suspicion. I knew it. He was buying them time, I thought. Even when I got to stand onstage at the Hilton Hotel with my father as he gave his acceptance speech, I was still strangely detached. In my heart, I felt the fight wasn't over. The feelings I had were surreal. I seemed to be more satisfied that Podesta had confirmed my suspicions than that we had won. I didn't like feeling cynical; it was ugly. But by then it was a conditioned response that I had learned over the prior two years.

———

Now, am I saying that I predicted then that the Democrats would cook up the Russian collusion hoax? Of course not. How could

I have thought that they were going to do something so incredible? That they would get liberals to believe a story so porous, so absurd, that if it were a movie script there wouldn't be a producer in Hollywood who would buy it? How could I believe that those same Hollywood producers, and just about every other liberal in the country, would swallow such a scam as though it were gospel truth? Still, I knew the fight wasn't over.

Of course, now we know the Democrats actually had begun laying the foundation of the Russia hoax months before the election. FISA warrants based on a phony dossier paid for by the Clintons gave the FBI license to spy on our campaign. Then, in January 2017, the media disinformation apparatus led by BuzzFeed began the dissemination of lies.

When I finally saw it begin to unfold, a strange sort of calm came over me. Oddly, there's a kind of comfort that comes when the bad thing you've been expecting to happen finally happens. Maybe because it's easier to fight your enemy when you can see what they're doing rather than waiting for the unknown. I wouldn't wish the cynicism I developed on anyone, but the whole process opened my eyes in a terrible and unfortunate way. Three years later, I think many more people have come to that same, tragic conclusion.

Meanwhile, it also took two months for me to realize the enormity of what my father had accomplished, and the weight of the job that he'd won. It was the day before the inauguration, and we were driving into Arlington National Cemetery, where he was to lay a wreath on the Tomb of the Unknown Soldier. I rarely get emotional, if ever. I guess you'd call me hyper-rational, stoic. Yet, as we drove past the rows of white grave markers, in the gravity of the moment, I had a deep sense of the importance of the presidency and a love of our country. I was never prouder of my father than when I watched as he stood before the tomb, his hand over his heart, while the Army bugler played "Taps."

In that moment, I also thought of all the attacks we'd already suffered as a family, and about all the sacrifices we'd have to make to help my father succeed—voluntarily giving up a huge chunk of our business and all international deals to avoid the appearance that we were "profiting off the office."

We're not talking about business with any foreign government agencies. This was based on the idea that we might be taken advantage of by a private business that would then have leverage on us. First of all, I don't think Trump Org has ever gotten duped by anyone and, second, the chances of something like that even being attempted are pretty remote. Frankly, it was a big sacrifice, costing us millions and millions of dollars annually, a huge book of business that I had personally built.

But it was a sacrifice we were more than happy and willing to make. Of course, we didn't get any credit whatsoever from the mainstream media, which now does not surprise me at all.

Still, we sidestepped the headache the liberal press would have given us if we didn't give up the business. Every deal we made would be twisted until they could find a serviceable lie. They would write that we were enriching ourselves; or that my father would use the presidency to somehow make money; or that he was under the thumb of some foreign government, a popular theme with the tinfoil hat gang and the MSM. We also had to give up a lot of domestic business because, as ridiculous as this sounds, we didn't want to run the risk of our domestic partners being branded racist, misogynistic, or any of the lies and labels the press had manufactured about my dad. Candidly, the additional scrutiny made even the most basic tasks virtually impossible. Yet it was, and continues to be, a small price to pay to watch America become great again and to regain our place as the rightful leader of the free world. No more Obama apology tours.

In one sense, the left and the liberal press effectively put me out of work. All that was left for me to do was spend my time campaigning for my father.

They might have been better off letting me just do my job.

The phonies came out of the woodwork after the election. I had thousands of emails on my phone by the next morning. All of them said practically the same thing: "We were with you from the start, buddy." Yeah, right. You haven't taken a call in 18 months, but now you're with us? Even worse. The same people who would text me telling me how much they loved our ideas would then be on Facebook deriding Trump the very next minute, probably looking for some "woke" points. You can't have it both ways, folks. But in politics everyone always tries.

I remembered back to my father's words in the elevator before he announced, "Now, we find out who our real friends are."

I don't think I made any truer friends than I did on the campaign. One of the reasons Tommy Hicks joined us, he told me, was because he was worried about some of the people we'd be around in politics. I told him I was pretty sure I'd be able to take care of myself, but the sheer audacity of some people was pretty staggering. On the night before the Inaugural, one donor called and asked if I could ask my father to appoint his friend's daughter to be the US Ambassador to Great Britain. "She's a reasonably successful investment banker," he added, as if that was enough to seal the deal. I'll get right on it, pal.

Plenty changed after my father took office, too, and much of that change was good for the American people. I guess I changed too. Politics had entered my bloodstream for all the good reasons. The opportunity was there for me to help forward my father's agenda, and help him accomplish his goals.

What didn't change was the attacks from the left. If anything, they only got worse. Let them take their best shot, I thought, because there was something else that hadn't changed.

The fight in us.

10.

A DEADLY FORM OF HATE

MY FATHER DIDN'T take a lot of time to make good on his campaign promises. On the first day he sat behind the Resolute desk, he began signing executive orders that covered everything from expediting environmental reviews that were slowing much-needed infrastructure projects to improving border security to slashing two regulations for every one a federal agency added. He also began to undo some of the most disastrous policies of Barack Obama's presidency.

The EO that caused the left to nearly implode was the one that banned mass immigration from countries that harbored radical Islamics. The ban was temporary, and it wouldn't have allowed spying on Muslims who live peacefully in this country, as the fake news would have had you believe. It was a preventive measure so that the secretary of state and homeland security secretary would have time to review the admissions process. Its purpose was to find ways of keeping people who hate the United States from coming into the country. I don't know about you, but to me it doesn't sound like a bad idea. It would have affected a tiny number of people.

It didn't take long for the liberal news media and the left to lose its collective mind over that one policy. Within just a few days, there were a dozen people on television every day, comparing my father to Adolf Hitler and that simple travel ban to the Holocaust. The left at large was doing the same thing they do on campuses: saying "Forget about facts, it's only the outrage you feel that matters."

THE WORLDWIDE WAR AGAINST CHRISTIANS

The bias against Christians on the part of the left and liberal lawmakers is bad, but at least liberals tend to just whine, while terrorists actually act on it. The same can't be said for the radical Islamic terrorists around the world. It's an empirical fact that radical Islam is waging a worldwide war against Christians, Jews, Hindus, and even Islam itself. According to Open Doors USA, a nonprofit organization that supports persecuted Christians around the world, each month 345 Christians are killed and 219 are imprisoned without trial because of their faith. "The primary cause of persecution is Islamic oppression," Open Doors stated. "This means, for millions of Christians—particularly those who grew up Muslim or were born into Muslim families—openly following Jesus can have painful consequences."

Yet according to the narrative pushed by the left in the United States, it is Muslims who are under attack and must be a protected class—one whose ideas we are prohibited from criticizing, even if we're not criticizing the people themselves. A victimhood complex has taken root in the American left, and it has done so while radical Islamic terrorism is on the rise. This has made it impossible to have anything resembling a real debate about radical Islam without being shut down or called a racist.

Democrats will tell you that being critical of radical Islam is the same as being critical of all Muslim people in the world. Obama ordered his entire administration to use the phrase "violent extremism" so as not to hurt the feelings of murderous cowards who strap suicide vests on pregnant women and sell children as sex slaves.

As cowardly as Obama's orthodoxy is, it gets even worse. You can almost understand, from a political point of view, the Democrats' reluctance not to call out these terrorists for what they are. They certainly don't want to piss off the left-wing media complex and the Hollywood propaganda machine. It is an act of unconscionable disgrace, however, for them to refuse to acknowledge the true identity of the victims of these attacks.

Last Easter in Sri Lanka, radical Islamic terrorists wearing suicide vests entered churches and other places where Christians were celebrating the holiday and detonated the devices. Some 250 people, mostly Christians, were blown to bits. Another 500 were wounded. When Barack Obama and Hillary Clinton finally got around to offering their condolences, they did so like this:

"The attacks on tourists and Easter worshippers in Sri Lanka are an attack on humanity," the former president tweeted.

"I'm praying for everyone affected by today's horrific attacks on Easter worshippers and travelers in Sri Lanka," the former First Lady remarked.

Easter worshippers?

Are they kidding?

What would they have called them if it had happened on December 25? Christmas carolers? Why don't they just slap the victims' families in the face?

Yet a month earlier in New Zealand, when a white extremist had shot fifty people in a mosque, they'd made sure you knew the victims were Muslim. "We grieve with you and the Muslim community," Obama had tweeted.

Not only is the liberal press complicit in this; it has made an art form out of covering for radical Islam.

Take the coverage of Omar Mateen, for instance. He's the monster who a couple of years back walked into the Pulse night-club in Orlando, Florida, and shot and killed forty-nine innocent people. He committed the act in the name of radical Islam. We know that because he told us so. In a call to 911, made as he was still shooting people, he swore allegiance to Abu Bakr al-Baghdadi, the leader of ISIS. You might remember that al-Baghdadi crawled out of his hole after the Sri Lanka attacks to praise the suicide bomb-ers and renew his vow to kill Christians. "The battle of Islam and its people against the cross and its people is a long battle," he said on the video he released.

As you can see, there's very little room for the interpretation of Mateen's motive.

Yet here's what the liberal media does: When someone commits an act of terror in the name of radical Islam, be it a bombing, a shooting, or a beheading, the press goes out of its way to call the perpetrators "sociopaths," "lone-wolf extrem-ists," and every other label for their behavior other than the one that is patently obvious or, as in the case of the Pulse nightclub shooter, what the terrorist himself tells us. When terrorists say they did something because they want to conquer infidels and establish a caliphate that covers the entire earth, the *New York Times* says, "Ignore that; they've probably had very hard lives." When Omar Mateen, the Pulse shooter, told us he had killed in the name of al-Baghdadi, the *Times* asked if he was a closeted gay man consumed by feelings of self-loathing and revenge. Instead of an editorial denouncing the ideology that had led to the attack in the first place, the *Washington Post* published one chastising officials for not seeing it coming.

This has been going on for as long as radical Islamic terrorists have been killing Americans.

Remember the Fort Hood shooter? The radical Islamic army major who shot and killed thirteen people at a military base? CNN labeled him only as an "army psychiatrist," with no mention of his religion or his extremist views, which had been documented in uncovered emails.

When some homegrown piece-of-shit militia group commits a terrorist act, however, the press will run out of ink calling its members Christians. Even its use of the phrase "white suprem-acist" is a lightly veiled pseudonym for "Christian." The double standard that exists in the media would be laughable in a less serious context. It's the Christians, they say, who bomb abortion clinics, but it's an army psychiatrist, not a radical Islamic, who murders more than a dozen people in cold blood. It's an evan-gelical who attacks gays, but it's a closet homosexual who kills dozens of people in a nightclub. It's a white nationalist Christian who attacks a mosque, but it's a man with a troubled mind who kills his coworkers in San Bernardino.

———

During the campaign, I sent out a tweet that had a photo of a bowl of rainbow-colored Skittles accompanied by the following text: "If I had a bowl of skittles and I told you just three would kill you. Would you take a handful? That's our Syrian refugee problem."

As metaphors go, I didn't think it was so terrible. Maybe not F. Scott Fitzgerald, but not bad for a guy with a business degree from Wharton, right? I was immediately labeled a soulless monster and, of course, a white supremacist (the left's go-to). You would have thought by the response from the left that I had murdered the Easter Bunny. It was an analogy that put our problem into perspective. Just numbers, folks.

Yet when Linda Sarsour, the head of the Arab American Association of New York, and cochair of the Women's March, declared a jihad against my father, there was not a whisper of protest. Unlike my bowl of Skittles, however, Sarsour's message to her followers was dangerous, and she knew it full well. Afterward, trying to soften her vengeful words, apologists for her tried to redefine jihad as a "spiritual struggle against vices."

In other words, the left can try to retrofit Americans' morals onto the barbaric, ancient idea of holy war to make themselves feel better, but they're only fooling the liberal audiences of the United States and Europe. For the rest of us who live in the real world, we know the truth when we hear it.

As it stands right now, the ideas contained in radical Islamic fundamentalism are completely at odds with the basic tenets of Western civilization. Still, anyone who dares utter this basic fact in public is decried as a racist, a participant in "hate speech," or worse.

Now before people in the fake-news media take me out of context and too carried away, let me be crystal clear: I am not talking about the vast majority of Muslim people around the world

If we aren't free to criticize radical Islam on its merits and to speak freely about what's wrong with people who subscribe to it blindly and do bad things in its name, we are not living up to the ideals of free expression set out by our founding documents. We've been told for so long, usually in the aftermath of some monstrous

Islamist attack on the civilized world, that Islam is a religion of peace, but we must also acknowledge that there is a radical element that would kill you, me, and even the trans hippie who's eating a vegan kale salad right now. Even most Muslims know this. Early in my father's candidacy, right after the San Bernardino terrorist attack, DJT called for a complete shutdown of the country's borders to Muslims, the same as he would do later in office. About midnight that night, I got a call telling me I would appear on one of the morning shows at six the next morning to talk about the ban. When I asked for talking points, they said, "You're on your own." As I've mentioned, we were a lean, mean team. The next morning, I hailed a livery cab. I saw the driver look at me in the rearview mirror and could see the recognition in his expression. He was Middle Eastern, and I thought, "Oh, shit, here it comes." Instead of giving me a piece of his mind, however, he leaned back over the seat and said, "I've heard your father's comments. I think he's one hundred percent right.

"I know it's the ones who are preaching hate, oppressing women, killing people who ruin it for us all," he continued. "Even the ones like this man [the San Bernardino shooter] who came to the United States legally are ruining it. They have to find a way to stop them. I don't blame him for banning everyone until they do."

The vast majority of Muslims feel the same, because they're the targets of radical Islam, too.

During the 2016 presidential campaign and its run-up, my father used the phrase "radical Islamic terrorist" in at least sixty tweets, and in most of them he called out Obama and Hillary for not using it. Despite the tidal wave of outrage from the left, it was the first time I know of that a politician had the courage to say what a whole lot of Americans believe.

Why do liberals go out of their way to apologize for or excuse radical Islam while at the same time they condemn Christians, masculinity, family values, and the American way of life? You can't have it both ways!

Maybe you disagree with my dad and the Americans who support him. If you do, guess what? You're allowed to. Last I looked, disagreement not only is our constitutional right, it was encouraged by our founders. By definition, however, a disagreement has two sides. If one side engages in a full-out war of misinformation, hurtful invectives, and physical violence toward the other, it's not a disagreement.

It's called hate.

THE WAR AGAINST CHRISTIANS IN THE UNITED STATES

Wouldn't it be great if there were an institution in the United States dedicated to fact-checking every word that comes from the mouths of Democrat politicians and their so-called public intellectuals? An organization whose job it would be to report on things that people say with some accuracy? Sadly, the liberal press has abdicated its role as the purveyor of truth in the United States and has become an activist organization for the American left. It has bought and sold the idea that there is a culture war going on—between the oppressed and the oppressors, the colonizers and the victims, the evil capitalist pigs and the innocent gender studies majors of the world. This might not be so bad if it weren't for the disastrous, real-world effects these ideas can have.

Nowhere is this upside-down thinking by the left more evident than in the way Christians are treated in our country today.

In August 2018, the Senate Judiciary Committee was supposed to review the qualifications of Judge Amy Coney Barrett for a seat on the US Court of Appeals for the Seventh Circuit. You'll notice I said "supposed to," because that was not exactly what ended up happening.

Judge Barrett is a shining example of what a justice should be: always tough but fair and very concerned with looking out for those who have the least protection under the law. At the time of her nomination, she was a professor at Notre Dame Law School and a mother of four lovely children. My father had chosen her after months of deliberation because he believed she was the most qualified candidate.

There were those who said he had chosen Judge Barrett solely because she was a woman, an olive branch to the crazed left-wing feminists in Congress. (Remember: if you're a conservative, you get no woke points for being a female. In fact, you get docked a few woke points for being a traitor.) I don't think that had anything to do with it. My father has hired women for major roles for about as long as Joe Biden has been rubbing their shoulders and letting out hot breath onto their necks—which is to say, *a very long time.*

But it is worth noting that during the nomination process, the National Women's Law Center—an organization whose motto is "Expanding the possibilities for women and girls since 1972"—came out *against* Judge Barrett, saying she was a threat to "civil, constitutional, and reproductive rights." The organization is actually interested in expanding possibilities for only some women. It's no different from the American Civil Liberties Union, which stopped fighting for the civil liberties of *all* Americans a long time ago. Now, they just cherry-pick the woke ones.

It was Judge Barrett's religion, however, that the Senate committee targeted. Democrats on the committee blasted her for her "dogmatic" belief in Catholicism. Barrett is a law professor at the University of Notre Dame, a Catholic university. How dare she believe in her faith! Senator Dianne Feinstein, the committee's ranking Democrat, scolded her for doing just that.

"When you read your speeches, the conclusion one draws is that the dogma lives loudly within you," Feinstein said of Barrett's writings regarding the professional obligations of Catholic practitioners. "And that's of concern when you come to big issues that large numbers of people have fought for for years in this country." The writings she referred to expressed the professional obligations of Catholic law practitioners.

One of the people who came to Barrett's defense was the president of Notre Dame. In a letter to the senator, the Reverend John I. Jenkins reminded Feinstein of the role religion had played in our nation's beginning. "Indeed, it lived loudly in the hearts of those who founded our nation as one where citizens could practice their faith freely and without apology."

Judge Barrett's experience wasn't a one-off by any measure. In November 2018, senators Kamala Harris of California and Mazie Hirono from Hawaii suggested that Brian Buescher, my father's nominee for the US district court in Nebraska, be disqualified because he belonged to the Knights of Columbus. The Knights of Columbus? What's next to disqualify someone? Membership in the American Automobile Association? The Book of the Month Club? The Cub Scouts? Come on! The Knights of Columbus has been doing charitable works for 136 years. What in God's name would membership in it be disqualifying of anything?

Then there was the confirmation of Trevor McFadden to the district court in DC. During his confirmation hearings, Sheldon Whitehouse, a Democrat senator from Rhode Island, grilled Judge McFadden about statements made by his pastor about same-sex marriage. Hey, Sheldon, you remember anything about separation of church and state?

It scares me, however, that the kind of anti-Christian bias shown to Judge Barrett and the others has become so common in this country that we barely notice when US senators engage in it. The left in this country has completely forgotten the Judeo-Christian values on which the United States was founded. Democrats forget that the only reason we have a country in the first place is because a bunch of people got onto a ship and sailed here from England so they could practice their religion freely. Then, when it came time to write their laws, they looked to the Ten Commandments for guidance.

Separation of church and state in this country means that the government can't tell people what faith they can practice. It doesn't stop people from making laws based on their religious beliefs.

But let's pretend for a moment that we lived in a world that had not yet been turned entirely upside down. Let's say that I, a white Christian male, sat on a committee that reviewed prospective justices. Let's say I was questioning a young Muslim woman who wanted to be a judge (or a senator or a PTA president) about her religious beliefs. How far down that line of inquiry do you think I would be able to go before the riots began? Five seconds? Maybe ten if the C-SPAN connection was slow? Do you think Dianne Feinstein would ever ask a Muslim nominee to a court if he or she believed in Sharia law? Or if he or she would discriminate against those who drink? Give me a break! No one, for instance, has asked Ilhan Omar in a public forum whether or not she married her brother to commit immigration fraud. Of course, that's off-limits.

And what do you think would happen if I told this imaginary Muslim woman that I was "deeply uncomfortable" because I thought the "dogma" of Islam "lived loudly" within her? Yeah, it wouldn't have been pretty.

Unlike the fake grandstanding we hear from Senate Democrats, the Simon Wiesenthal Center in Los Angeles is one of the great examples of those who take a real stand against intolerance. Wiesenthal tracked down and brought to justice Nazi war criminals from around the world. Today the center serves to educate the next generation when horrors of humanity are ignored. My friends Carol and Larry Mizel chair the center, which ensures that all those who visit never forget the horrors of the Holocaust. Incidentally, Carol was one of the first to endorse and actively support my father.

At the time, the fact that we had any support in the Jewish community was baffling to many pundits. But it shouldn't have been. He made promises to them, and he kept every single one. He campaigned on appointing conservative judges, and he's delivered in a spectacular way. He campaigned on restoring fairness in trade and he's taken the Chinese and other nations head on. Similarly, he promised to move the United States Embassy to Jerusalem, something which multiple presidents including George Bush, Bill Clinton, Other Bush, and even Barak Obama also promised to do but never delivered. Barack Obama made no secret of his disdain for Israeli leadership, so perhaps we shouldn't be surprised in his lack of support to move the embassy. My father, however, has always been and will always be a friend to Israel.

Let's take a step back and see how this simple move has been delayed for years. In 1995, Congress passed overwhelmingly the Jerusalem Embassy Act which called for the United States to relocate our embassy from Tel Aviv to Jerusalem. The law allowed for the White House to sign a waiver to delay the move if it wanted. Presidents Clinton, Bush, and Obama all chose to delay the move for a total of almost twenty-three years!

That's the difference between my dad and Obama, Bush, and Clinton. When he makes a promise, he follows through. One of his top priorities was to move the embassy to Jerusalem, so he got right to it with our friend and great Ambassador David Friedman to start planning for the move.

The media went wild. Political pundits lost their minds. Even some politicians who had voted for the very law started questioning the wisdom of the move. All these geniuses proclaimed that the move would result in an all-out war between the Israelis and the Palestinians, a new intifada. Everywhere you looked someone was condemning the move, from world leaders to the Pope who called for the "Status Quo" to be respected. Even the Chinese urged caution. Give me a break. The United Nations, which rarely makes an effort to condemn anything, convened the Security Council, which promptly and almost unanimously voted to condemn the United States over the move. The United States ultimately vetoed the resolution. Even jihadi and terrorist groups weighed in and called for armed struggles against the move.

Pundits in the United States declared it irresponsible, reckless, and hurtful to the peace process! Remember, every single time this law has come up for a vote in the Senate, over 90 percent of the Senate has supported it. Sometimes, it's passed with literally zero opposition. And yet, when President Trump tried to do what everyone really wanted, people were absolutely triggered!

And how much of the doom and gloom happened when my father followed through on his promise? Practically none. Casualties were minimal, smaller acts have caused much larger violence and death in the Middle East. Millions of people did not die as many in the media claimed would be the result. In Bethlehem they turned the lights off on the Christmas tree. There were some protests outside the Middle East but they quickly disappeared.

What happened to the inevitable intifada? What happened to the war that never materialized? What happened to the start of World War III that the often wrong but never in doubt "experts" claimed would result from this move?

Courage takes action, and my father is never afraid to act. He believed it was the right thing to do. The state of Israel gets to decide where their capital is, and the United States should support the only democracy in the Middle East. You see, the United States is a leader, and others follow us. It's called leadership—something Obama sorely lacked. It's time for America to take its rightful place as the leader of the free world once again.

11.

MISS GENDERED

EVER SINCE THE DAY I gave my first campaign speech in support of my father, there's been a fair amount of speculation as to where my own political career might take me. For instance: Would I resign from the The Trump Organization and go on the road indefinitely? Take a permanent position on my father's campaign? Maybe run for office myself one day? Well, here, right now, at long last, I would like to put all those rumors to rest. I will not be seeking political office. In fact, I won't be continuing in politics at all. I have my sights on something much bigger.

Effective immediately, I am going to concentrate all my efforts on becoming the greatest, most powerful player in the nine-to-twelve-year-old division of my local girls' softball league.

Now, look, I know what all you transphobic bigots are thinking. *Don! You're not a girl! You're forty-one years old! You can't do that!*

Well, dear reader, that's where you're wrong. In this new alternate reality of the left, crazy old ideas such as "age" and "gender" and "sanity" don't matter anymore. It is no longer anyone's business what sex you were assigned at birth; all that matters is how you feel. If I wake up one day feeling like a thirteen-year-old girl named Susan (which would come as a pretty big surprise to my girlfriend, Kimberly), then you are required—by law in some countries—to call me that. And if I, speaking as little Susan, decide that I want to start absolutely crushing home runs over the center-field fence in my daughter's slow-pitch softball league, you are required to let me suit up in my pink pinstripes and get out onto the field. If you don't, you'll be "misgendering" me.

And misgendering people can get you into a lot of hot water.

Just ask Kate Scottow, a woman who lives in Hertfordshire, England. In February 2019, she was arrested by local police for "harassing" a transgender woman (which means a man who identifies as a woman). You see, she referred to her as a "he" on Twitter. (I know, I know. This can get confusing.) Police showed up at Scottow's apartment and arrested her in front of her autistic ten-year-old daughter and her twenty-month-old infant son. In court, the prosecutor accused Scottow of engaging in a "campaign of targeted harassment" against the transgender activist, all because she refused to call the activist by her preferred pronoun.

This is how far the left's nonsense has spread. Not only will you be shunned from public life for pushing against its radical agenda, you could actually face jail time for it.

Now, for those of you who haven't heard about all this transgender news, let me see if I can catch you up.

According to liberals today, many of whom reside in their mom's basements or their university dorm rooms, babies are born with a biological sex, but they are not born with a "gender identity." Male babies—excuse me, babies with a Y chromosome—are not necessarily boys, just as babies with two X chromosomes (formerly known as female babies) are not necessarily girls. It's only when they get old enough to decide for themselves whether they're a boy or a girl—I guess when they choose to play with either G.I. Joe or G.I. Jane—that the gender is decided. In the meantime, they grow up gender neutral.

Sometimes they don't have to pick a gender at all. That's called being "nonbinary." If someone is nonbinary, you have to refer to that person with whatever names and pronouns they ask you to. Judging by some of the forms I've seen lately—in doctors' offices, school offices, and so on—these pronouns can be anything from "they/theirs" to "ze" or "zim" or "zer" (zer?). Last time I checked, there were about twenty-eight different options in total, and I'm sure that's grown a lot since. Also, you don't need to undergo any sort of gender reassignment surgery or hormone therapy to change your gender anymore. All you have to do is declare that you are another gender, and people have to accept it.

It used to be that terms like this applied only to people who had undergone surgery to change their sex from male to female or the other way around, which at least made some kind of sense. But today that's no longer the case. Men can be women if they say they are, and women can be men if they say they are.

This gets even crazier when you're talking about people who consider themselves to be "genderfluid," meaning people who believe that they can assume a different gender every day—or every minute or every few seconds. Believe it or not, these people exist. Just google it, and you'll see. They'll be Billy one minute and switch to Betty the next. According to the new rules of the left, all they have to do is say it—or *feel* it—and it automatically becomes true. You can't say a word against them.

So if you call a person Betty when s/he is feeling like Billy, what happens? Do you get charged with a hate crime? What if that person *feels* as though you committed a hate crime? Because remember:

These days, all that really matters is feelings. Facts, evidence, and logic have gone out the window. Once you accept the fact that feelings matter more than facts, it doesn't matter whether you're dealing with religion, race, or kids' basketball games. You're in trouble.

Now, I am a "live and let live kind" of guy and truly don't care what you identify as. As far as I'm concerned, you can identify yourself any way you want. Whatever makes you happy. Just don't send me to jail if I get it wrong.

I do have a problem, however, when some individuals take advantage of the situation and try to game the system. So if you're a male athlete in college and you're getting your ass handed to you by all the other big, strong males in your division, you might have a way out! All you have to do is declare that you're a woman, and suddenly your competition gets smaller and less muscular. It's like magic!

Now, you might be wondering *Don, how often does this really happen?* The answer is "More often than you might imagine." There are a bunch of mediocre male athletes who have suddenly decided that they've "been women their whole lives" when they found out it might boost their chances of winning a medal or getting some free press, or perhaps getting an athletic scholarship.

For example, take CeCe Telfer, a track and field athlete who competed as a man until she was about nineteen years old. Telfer was born a boy, went through puberty as one, and emerged a fine specimen of manhood. In the years she competed as a man in the NCAA, running for Franklin Pierce University in New Hampshire, she was ranked somewhere in the 200s—a respectable position for any athlete who's worked hard. CeCe's hard work earned her a college scholarship, a spot on the team, and accolades from all over the country. But it wasn't enough. During her third year at Franklin Pierce, CeCe announced that he was actually a woman and wanted to switch from the men's team to the women's team. She did not undergo any kind of surgery to make the change, nor did she provide any evidence that she had "always been a woman," as she claimed. All she had to do, under some new NCAA rules put into place during the Obama administration, was undergo something called "testosterone suppression therapy" for one year.

Over the course of her high school and college careers, CeCe had been working out hard, and it showed. She had a man's body and a man's muscles—which, as a matter of science, are nearly twice as durable and powerful as those of the average female. Even though she was average in the men's division, she was still biologically equipped to run harder, faster, and longer than just about any woman in the world.

That's not sexist. It's just a fact.

Not surprisingly, when CeCe began competing against other women—meaning women who had been women their entire lives, who had worked their asses off to become the best in their division—she smoked the competition. It wasn't even close. And why wouldn't she? For all intents and purposes, she was a man (and a strong one at that) wearing women's clothes. Before long, she was the single fastest woman in the NCAA. The transgender community celebrated.

I thought it was ridiculous, to say the least, so I tweeted about it. Over the article announcing that a biological male was now the fastest woman in the NCAA, I wrote this message:

> Yet another grave injustice to so many young women who trained their entire lives to achieve excellence. Identify however you want, to each his own, but this is too far and unfair to so many.

I had been on Twitter long enough to know that when you post something like that, there's going to be blowback. (When I post anything, there's blowback, especially when that thing takes on contemporary wokeness.) But to my surprise, the world was pretty calm about that one. Even the nuttier members of the social justice warrior left were on my side. "Cannot believe I'm saying this," wrote one leftist activist, "but I think I'm with Donald Trump Jr. on this one." I guess there really *are* some things we can all agree on.

Even Martina Navratilova, the legendary tennis player who grew up not too far from my grandparents' village in Czechoslovakia, weighed in. Here's a woman who had worked her entire life to become one of the greatest of all time. To her, the idea that we were going to allow men who couldn't hack it in their own division to start competing against women was "cheating." The blowback she got was major (and she has since walked back her hard line on the subject after a full-frontal assault by the SJW left), but it was still nothing compared to what I get for an average tweet about politics. It seems that, by and large, the public is in agreement about this.

When we allow mediocre men to compete in women's sports, we do a disservice to all the hardworking young women who have fought to get where they are. I sometimes wonder where the feminists are on this issue. They sure don't speak out much, to be honest.

I harbor no ill will toward CeCe Telfer, and I wish her well in all other areas of her life. But she needs to understand that it's not fair to push women around because you need to win. They have rights, too, and those rights include the right to a level playing field.

In the cases of some young women, excellence in a sport can be the difference between going to the college of their dreams and not going at all. Often, the parents of female athletes who go to college would not be able to afford the tuition if it weren't for athletic scholarships. And there's no way to get help with tuition like that unless you're one of the top female athletes in the country. Sometimes dropping one place in the rankings—say, because a faster woman named Bill showed up and started winning all the races you used to win—can cost a young woman her first-place ranking and eliminate her chances of getting a scholarship. This is not fair, and it shouldn't be allowed to continue.

But it does continue, as shown recently at the University of Connecticut, where two male students competing as women blew away the real women student athletes in several track and field races.

As I write this, three female athletes in Connecticut have filed a complaint with the US Department of Education's Office for Civil Rights. As one of their legal counselors put it, "Women fought long and hard to earn the equal athletic opportunities that Title IX provides. Allowing boys to compete in girls' sports reverses nearly 50 years of advances for women under this law. We shouldn't force these young women to be spectators in their own sports."

I couldn't have said it better myself. I wish those girls all the best. For the sake of my own daughters, who are shaping up to be pretty good golfers and basketball players, I hope they can compete under fair circumstances. My daughter Kai, who's twelve, can really smoke me playing one-on-one. Maybe she has the potential to be amazing. Then again, maybe I'm just terrible at basketball. Maybe both.

From track and field to volleyball to weight lifting, trans athletes are smashing women's hard-earned records. Now, before all the liberal elite go screaming murder, let me reiterate: I don't care what outfit you wear or whether you choose to identify as gay, lesbian, or trans. What I care about is redefining fair practices, such as allowing men to compete as women in sports. It's funny, you never hear about trans men (women) dominating men's divisions. I'll wait for that to happen before I start rooting for trans women (men) who compete in the women's divisions.

Cheating hardworking young girls out of their scholarships is bad, but it's far from the worst symptom of this recent social trend. At least when you're talking about track and field, there's no physical touching allowed. No one's going to get hurt because a man in women's clothes runs past her at top speed on the track.

But when it comes to contact sports, there's more than just our sense of fairness and lost scholarships on the line. This is where it becomes a safety issue. I don't think anyone was totally comfortable, for instance, when a mediocre mixed martial arts fighter named Fallon Fox decided he was going to transition to a woman. This wasn't just a man who wanted to run races in lanes next to women. This was a man who was losing bouts to other men, so he decided he wanted to beat up women instead. In one of his last fights, against a woman named Tamikka Brents—who held on for a very long time, considering the circumstances—Fox used his big hands to beat Brents into an early technical knockout. Hours after the match, doctors discovered that Brents's skull had been fractured. There is no universe in which that should be acceptable, nor is there anyone who can argue that it was a fair fight!

———

Outside the sports world, this trans trend goes from the bad to worse. Take, for instance, Bobby McCullough and Lesley Fleishman, a couple in Brooklyn who became internet famous in 2019 for raising their child without a gender. As McCullough told *New York* magazine in one of many profiles that were written about him and his gender-neutral baby—which the article called a "theyby"—he warned the hospital staff on the day his baby was born that they were not, under any circumstances, to refer to the baby's anatomy. He went on to say that he wanted to prevent his baby from "being gendered in that intense moment." Apparently, McCullough and Fleishman thought that just the mere mention of the baby's biological sex would screw up theyby's ability to choose their own gender. Oh, man. This gets nuttier by the minute.

And these people are not alone! Though I'm shocked, SHOCKED, that the gender-neutral craze caught on in Hollywood, there are at least a half-dozen stars who are reportedly raising gender-neutral children.

Look, as I said, do what makes you happy. If you want to name your child after a blender, teach him or her the tuba, or hold off on assigning a gender for a while, go right ahead. She/he/they/zim/zer is your kid. No one should be able to tell you what to do. Least of all the government! But there's a point at which this behavior stops being funny or eccentric and starts impacting your child.

Or starts becoming ridiculous, such as transgender "teaching tools" for children. Devised by transgender activists, these tools include the Genderbread Person and the Gender Unicorn. (The unicorn came about because of complaints that the Genderbread Person looked too much like a man.) These tools teach children that when it comes to gender, there are plenty of options to choose from. Just some of the options include: genderqueer, nonbinary, pangender, androgyne, neutrois, gender variant, cyborg, two spirit, glitterbutch, genderfluid, trigender, and genderless.

Apparently, according to the tools, children can think they're male, have the biological sex of a woman, dress like a man, be sexually attracted to women but romantically attracted to men, or any combination or percentage thereof. "Gender isn't binary," read the instructions for the tools. "In many cases, it's both. A bit of this, a dash of that." Again, I don't care what you do, but when you start to insert the wrong genders into sports, it's no longer just impacting you.

When it starts to get harmful, in my opinion, is right around the time some of the crazy parents begin going to "gender specialists," who wear white coats and stethoscopes, to discuss whether or not their little theybies should begin the process of transitioning genders in a medical way. In some cases, parents whose children express tendencies of genders other than their own—boys who like to play with dolls, for example, or girls who like little toy army men—are told by these specialists that hormone therapy to suppress puberty, and/or a full-on surgical transition, might be the only way forward.

———

The social justice warriors' assault on basic sensibilities has spiraled out of control. After the all-gender bathrooms debate—when the left demanded that confused old men in dresses be allowed into the same restrooms as little girls—it was pronouns. After pronouns, it was men playing on female sports teams. If things keep going the way they are, don't be surprised if in a few years, you see a bill on the House floor—likely with "Ocasio-Cortez" and "Tlaib" written somewhere on it—that forbids all parents to assign their babies gender identities at birth. And don't be surprised when it gets passed. Like every other crazy idea that the left has had—from the Green New Deal and free college to prison voting and unlimited abortions—this one will come from the far left and then creep slowly but surely toward the center. It'll start with one of the crazy people, the avowed socialists and Marxists. Then it'll find its way to the more centrist Democrats, who know they need the crazy vote to get elected. Then, before you know it, it'll be brought up during the Democrat primaries in front of the whole country on national television. This is how the left lost its mind in the first place, and it's not going to stop anytime soon. Just watch and see.

If you want to ask people to refer to you with the pronoun "they" instead of "he" or "she," go right ahead. Most people wouldn't have a problem with that if you asked nicely. But I have a problem when you start threatening consequences if I don't call you "they" instead of "he" or "she"—especially when those consequences involve the full force of government.

I also have a problem when people start saying, as some researchers have been saying over the past few months, that trans people are being discriminated against because straight people don't want to date them. I'm a live-and-let-live type of guy. I'm fine with people transitioning, using different pronouns, and referring to themselves with whatever names they see fit. But men shouldn't be branded transphobic, homophobic, or bigoted just because they're not lining up to date women with beards and penises.

For too long, we have allowed the laws of our nation to be written by its most aggrieved, least stable citizens. We've pandered to ideas that have no basis in reality because we know that the people who came up with those ideas will turn the social justice mob on us if we don't.

———

I guess I should probably get back to telling you about my impending Little League softball career. Then again, maybe I'll try junior women's golf instead. Nah, better not. There's already one Trump in junior women's golf: my daughter Kai. For my dignity's sake, I should stick to softball. Kai would kick my ass on the golf course and on the basketball court. Legitimately.

12.

THE ENEMY OF THE PEOPLE?

BACK DURING the previous administration, when former president Obama took a trip to England for a state visit, he was met with a relatively small but vocal protest that flew a diapered baby Obama balloon over the streets of London . . . Yeah, right. Like that would have happened in a million years. If it had, the liberal Twittersphere would have blown up. Sparks would have flown from keyboards in newsrooms around the country as writers pounded out outraged headlines. Liberal pundits' heads would have exploded on television screens.

So, it's no surprise that when a similar balloon caricature of the current president flew over London, the press expressed the same shock . . . About Donald Trump? Not a chance in the world. Instead, we had a photo or video of the balloon on the front page of nearly every liberal newspaper and leading every newscast, all accompanied by some snarky elitist-liberal attempt at humor. It didn't come as a surprise. I didn't expect the press in England to be any fairer than the media here—my father's poll numbers in England aren't so hot. But guess what? Neither were George Washington's. You know why? Because he fought for America.

I don't really care how my dad polls in other countries, and neither should you. I don't give a damn about balloons, either. The liberal press can write their little jokes until they run out of ink, for all I care. What I do care about, however, is the hypocrisy that is pervasive in the mainstream media. When a balloon depicting London's liberal mayor, Sadiq Khan, in a bikini flew over London, the United Kingdom's *Metro* newspaper ran a headline warning that "Flying the Sadiq Khan balloon is not an exercise of free speech—it is a party for bigots."

So, a Sadiq Khan balloon is bigoted, but a Donald Trump one is a big joke? You want to know a real joke? How about Barack Obama's nomination for a Nobel Peace Prize just eleven days after he took office. Eleven days! What in God's name could he have done in eleven days to warrant one of the most prestigious awards in the world? Well, the nomination was just an aberration, right? The judges were just swept up in the whole Obama hysteria, and they would never present him the award, right? Well, they did, just eight months into his presidency. And how did Obama live up to that lofty distinction? By increasing troop levels in Afghanistan to seven times that of George W. Bush, by overseeing a dramatic increase in drone strikes, and by being responsible for the death and injury of tens of thousands of people in wars across the Middle East. So, of course, he belongs with other Nobel Peace Prize winners such as Mother Teresa and Nelson Mandela.

———

The thing is, it wasn't always like this. Before my father was a candidate, his relationship with the press was pretty good. He was friendly with all the network anchors and many of the major columnists. Reporters knew they could call him at any time, day or night, and get an excellent quote for the story they were working on. Flattering profiles of him ran when we'd open a new building, golf course, or resort.

It wasn't a total love affair. The media has never been entirely fair, especially the press in New York. There were always moments when someone, usually a young reporter trying to make a name for him or herself, would take a cheap shot at him. Back in the '90s, when Dad had financial problems and when he and my mom were getting divorced, it seemed all his friends in the press turned on him. One of the reasons I wanted to get out of New York City and go to the Hill School in Pennsylvania was to get away from the cruel, nonstop coverage of my parents' split.

From the moment *The Apprentice* became a mega-hit (which is to say from the very first episode), however, the press pretty much gave DJT the star treatment. Even when my father announced he was running for president, the MSM was eager to cover him. Of course, the media—and the entire political world—didn't take him seriously at first and believed his campaign would be a bust. Still, they knew DJT would be good copy. It's all about ratings and click-bait today. It's not about news.

In a sense, you couldn't blame the press for being skeptical. He'd been toying with the notion of running for president for a while. The first time the idea came up, at least in a public sense, was when Oprah asked him in an interview back in 1988 if he was going to run. Google that interview, and you'll be surprised. In all this time, over thirty years, my father's views on trade, America's standing in the world, and other countries paying their fair share haven't changed one bit. You could take that spot on *Oprah* and play it at a MAGA rally, and the crowd would go wild.

The first time he announced his intention to run was in 1999 on Chris Matthews's show, which was broadcast from the Irvine Auditorium at the University of Pennsylvania. I remember it well. At the time, I was attending the Wharton School and was in the audience. A large percentage of the audience that day were Wharton students. When Matthews asked my father if he was going to run and my father said, "I am indeed," the room exploded in applause. After the cheers died down, he looked at Matthews and said, "Perhaps." He then said he would only run if he had a chance to win the nomination. Vintage DJT.

The timing wasn't right for him. He looked into running a couple of more times, in 2004 and 2008. With each time, however, my father got more fed up. His anger towards the incompetence of our leaders grew; he knew he couldn't stay on the sidelines anymore. If the country were going to change direction, he'd have to be on the field. In 2015, he saw his opportunity.

———

It was no surprise that DJT's announcement drew a lot of coverage; the escalator ride is now an iconic moment. In hindsight, however, that day marks the beginning of something other than the campaign. In a sense, it was the beginning of the end of any credibility the liberal media still possessed.

As I've mentioned, his announcement speech started the fake narrative of my father being racist. If the press gave him any fair coverage at all at first (very little) it wasn't because they liked him as a candidate. They thought he could knock off the more viable Republican candidates to ensure a victory for Hillary. When DJT raced to the top of the polls and stayed there for months, the common belief in the mainstream media was that sooner or later the air would leak out of his campaign. When, in venue after venue and stadium after stadium, my dad spoke to wildly enthusiastic capacity crowds, the liberal press first shrugged it off, calling it celebrity worship that wouldn't last. When he locked down the number of delegates necessary for the nomination, however, things got serious with the press and the propaganda and lies began to flood the liberal media. As always, however, the libs overplayed their hand. They thought that DJT would be the easiest for Hillary to beat. In their bubbles, removed from what was happening in the country, they ended up sealing Clinton's political fate.

———

For me, fake news was an eye-opening experience. I was never a news junkie. I read the *New York Post* at home, and the *Times* and the *Wall Street Journal* at work. By the time I was on *The Apprentice*, I was getting all my news through social media. Though my news intake and awareness increased with social, I still hadn't fully realized how one-sided reporting could be. It was while I was on the campaign, however, when I began to see the bias, the lying, the self-importance of the liberal press. I would watch Ivy League–educated news anchors sit back and feel offended on behalf of people they've never met. Watch as they acted all righteous and angry from behind the anchor's chair while not having a clue about what mattered to Americans. Out in the small towns of the United States, and talking to people who come from the affected communities, I saw how vast the disconnect was between the media and the people they supposedly covered.

Out on the campaign, I also saw the number of ways the mainstream media manipulates the news. One of the first things the press did to try and stop my father was giving up even the pretense of sourcing stories. "Anonymous sources," "high ranking official," "someone close to the Trump campaign," all might sound impressive and make it seem that reporters were doing their jobs fairly, but what it actually meant was the reporter was making it up.

Another favorite tactic of the liberal media is creative editing. I can't tell you how many times I've watched a piece on the news with a clip of my father saying something controversial and then realizing that I was with him when he was supposed to have said it. I find myself saying to the television, "Wait a minute. I was at that speech. When did he say that?" Then I realize they've done it again. They've taken something that my father said in jest and cut the piece to a soundbite, editing out all the laughter and context. A good editor can turn a noncontroversial statement or moment into an international crisis. They take a partial sentence from minute twenty-three of a forty-five-minute speech, and a word or two from minute thirty-five, splice them together, and voilà! Instant controversy. That it's all taken out of context doesn't matter at all to them.

First, I'll give you an example of a stupid way the press does this, then a serious one. At the end of his first year in office, my father went to Japan to visit Prime Minister Shinzō Abe. Right before a working lunch in the Akasaka Palace in Tokyo, the two leaders stopped at a koi pond. The video of the moment that went viral and ran on every liberal news outlet shows my father dumping a whole box of fish food into the water. *New York* magazine's headline read: "Trump Under Fire for Improper Fish-Feeding Technique." The entire video, which CNN ran much later, shows Prime Minister Abe dumping his whole box in a moment before. DJT had a quizzical expression on his face, but he didn't want to embarrass his host so he did exactly what Abe did.

Maybe the most infamous manipulation of my father's words came after the Charlottesville riot. First, let me say, I think the hate crime committed by the neo-Nazi sympathizer—running his car into a crowd of protestors, killing a young woman, and injuring thirty-five others—was a despicable act of a coward. He's going to be in jail for the rest of his life, and that's where he belongs. But almost from the moment the incident happened, the press was trying to somehow blame it on my dad. It didn't matter if they had to lie or not. Donald Trump had to be at fault.

They got their chance when my father held a press conference at Trump Tower about week after the incident. The media that day was in a lather, shouting questions at my dad, trying to get him to say something they could use against him. When they couldn't (DJT is a cool customer in the most heated press situations), they made it up. So inflammatory was the lie, it led the news cycle for weeks. In fact, it is still told over and over by the liberal press to fuel the bigger lie that my father is a racist. The press reported that my dad had described neo-Nazis as "very fine people." Nothing could have been farther from the truth, and yet those words were repeated an infinite number of times in the media. The short video clip of the news conference that was played incessantly showed him saying there were very fine people "on both sides." Viewers of the clip, already biased by liberal news channels and newspapers, naturally assumed he was talking about neo-Nazis. But he wasn't. If you watch the whole press conference, you would see that my father was talking about a different set of protestors. Not the neo-Nazis or Antifa, not the conflict that exploded in bloody carnage, but the protest about the statue of Robert E. Lee. Some people wanted the statue taken down; some wanted it to stay and have the park in which it stood renamed after the Confederate general. And guess what? There were fine people on both sides of that protest.

Now it wasn't as if my father was vague. He was the opposite. His words were absolutely clear.

"I'm not talking about the neo-Nazis and the white national-ists," he said. "They should be condemned totally."

So, in what universe does *they should be condemned totally* become *very fine people*? In the echo chamber of lies that is the liberal media. Leading Democrat contenders are still campaigning on the totally fictitious part of the story in order to hurt Trump. And you know who's calling them out? That's right, absolutely no one.

———

By the time of the Republican National Convention, the press had already turned their sights on us, his children. I wasn't shocked. By then, I knew that any sense of fair play and dignity, if there were any in the first place, had gone out the window.

Maybe the worst of it, at least in the beginning, was how they treated my sister. Before my father ran for president, Ivanka was the darling of those glossy magazines such as *Vogue*, *Harper's Bazaar*, and *Vanity Fair*. Even the *New York Times* ran complimentary pieces about her. As my father's chances to be elected improved, those same glossies and newspapers started publishing hit pieces on her. Ivanka is one of the nicest, most brilliant people I know, and I'm not saying that because I'm her brother. She is. And yet, one reporter for *Cosmopolitan* was so rude, Ivanka got up and left in the middle of the interview.

Though Ivanka might have been the first target, the press wasted no time going after all of us. Right after the convention, *GQ* ran an article titled "Donald Trump's Family Is Just as Bad as Donald Trump." Why take shots at us one at a time when you can lump us all together? But it also showed us how much the left feared us as a collective fighting force for our father.

One of the fake narratives the press created about us was that we are all spoiled rich kids.

As the child of one of our country's wealthiest men, I was placed squarely in the top 1 percent of our society from birth. As much as the press seemed to want me to be ashamed of that or apologize for it, I'm not and I won't. As the son of a rich white man, I know I'm not allowed to have an opinion, let alone voice it these days. I do recognize I've been blessed, but I was blessed with parents who taught me a work ethic and the value of a dollar. I knew that my father would never give me a dime that I hadn't worked for and earned myself. The liberal press will tell you that I got into Wharton because my father's donations to the school, but they won't tell you about how hard I worked for the grades to get in on my own. The press portrayed me as a rich brat from one of the wealthiest zip codes in the country, but they won't tell you how I spent every summer in communist Czechoslovakia when I was a kid or the manual labor I did growing up for my father (I remember my father saying, "If you're going to build a building, you better know how to dig a foundation") or that I spend weeks sleeping on the couches of my hunting buddies, or about the twelve-hour days I worked at Trump Org. And, it didn't take long for them to start calling me a white supremacist. When they run out of lies about us Trumps, that's their default.

The press also committed sins of omission. How many of you know, for example, that my sister Tiffany is in Georgetown University Law school? I bet it's not a lot of you. The media portrayed Tiffany's relationship to Ivanka, Eric, and me as estranged. There is no estrangement. First of all, I'm sixteen years older than Tiffany, and she grew up on the West Coast, so we just didn't have the interaction I had with my other siblings. Once she came east, however, and began working with us on the campaign, she became part of the fighting force I mentioned above. Tiffany is a wonderful, funny, intelligent woman and, as they do with Ivanka, the way the press continues to treat her is unconscionable.

———

November 8, 2016, was, without question, the worst day in the history of liberal journalism. The mainstream media was in both shock and mourning. Honestly, it was as if someone died or had been assassinated. Lefty pundits such as Martha Raddatz, the moderator of the second debate who was supposed to be unbiased, cried on air as the reality of the results sank in.

Then, in July of 2018, when Raddatz tweeted out a hateful column about my father and the press, I tweeted this right back at her:

@DonaldTrumpJr
Your crying on live tv on election night probably has nothing to do with the extreme bias exhibited daily by the liberal media, but in case it did why the hell would any rational person trust the media these days? Give me a break.

But the media wouldn't feel sorry for itself for long. Oh no. They weren't about to let the American people choose their own president.

It's common knowledge now that the phony Steele dossier had been lying around newsrooms for months before BuzzFeed "broke the story" in early January 2017. Christopher Steele, as you remember, is the ex-British spy who was hired by the Clinton campaign, through an opposition research firm called Fusion GPS, to dig up dirt on my father. Steele assembled an unprecedented collection of lies that even the *New York Times* said was likely Russian disinformation. It was lying around for months because it was too fake for even the fake news to publish. Once my father was elected, however, the media, working in concert with the deep state elements of the FBI and the Department of Justice, saw Steele's work of fiction in a whole new light. Still in shock and willing to believe anything that would change the nightmare of November 8, the rank and file of the left was a market for the taking. All the media needed to publish Steele's trash was something that would give it just the slightest appearance of credibility. Enter James Comey, the fired and since disgraced FBI director, who handed the mainstream media that credibility on a silver platter.

———

James Comey knew the dossier was a fuse to a time bomb which he had hoped would consume my father's presidency. That none of it was true didn't matter to him. All he had to do was hand the phony dossier to the president-elect during an official visit and then leak the visit to the press. Presto chango! In that moment on January 7, 2016, the dossier went from a pile of garbage to a document in an official intelligence briefing.

From then on, the media and the upper echelons of the FBI and DOJ joined forces to essentially overthrow our government.

The FBI had already used the phony dossier to obtain a FISA warrant to spy on Carter Page, who was a volunteer on the campaign for about six minutes. With its now-infamous Crossfire Hurricane investigation, the feds had already been spying on the Trump campaign for months. Neither of those investigations or any other investigation proved any collusion between the Trump campaign and Russia. But for the MSM, the dossier was the granddaddy of all unverified sources. If it weren't for the phony Steele dossier, there wouldn't have been a Russia investigation by Robert Mueller, and there wouldn't be the biggest fake news story about me.

On June 27, 2018, CNN broke a story that Michael Cohen, the imprisoned lawyer who had once worked for my father, was going to testify that he was present at a meeting where I told my father of the infamous Trump Tower meeting—in advance. I'm sure you remember, that was the meeting that supposedly exposed me as a Russian spy. The story, which had none other than Carl Bernstein of Watergate fame sharing the byline, blew up the internet. It was a bombshell, and the smoking gun the left had been praying for. It substantiated every Russian collusion story that came before it.

Most importantly for the left, CNN's story gave Robert Mueller the ammunition to take down the president. Finally, the social justice warriors of the world could stop complaining about Trump and go back to complaining about whatever they'd complained about before—probably how persecuted they felt. At long last, the left had gotten what they'd prayed for. Except for one little problem. Well, actually, a couple of little problems.

Now I'm not a journalist, thank God. But if I were, I think I would take any information I received from a convicted liar with a grain of salt. Not only is Michael Cohen a world-class liar, he was also facing sentencing at the time. He would have given up his rabbi to stay out of jail. So that's number one. Number two, the reporters had only one source, and that source wanted to remain anonymous. I don't know, but I probably wouldn't put my Carl Bernstein on top of the story which had only one anonymous source, especially when I knew the source was Lanny Davis.

Davis was Cohen's lawyer. He was also a longtime Clinton pal and a political operative. Oh, and one more thing: He's not that smart.

In the midst of all the hysteria the story caused, Lanny Davis went on Anderson Cooper's show and said that CNN's information was wrong and that his client was not at a meeting with my dad and me talking about Russian dirt on Hillary. He contradicted his own information! On the network where he had given the information!

If that wasn't dumb enough, he also denied that he ever talked to CNN about it.

If it were only CNN that knew that Davis was the source of the story, they might have been able to cover it all up. But they weren't the only news outlet that knew. The *Washington Post* was running its own stories and using Lanny Davis as the source. Needless to say, Davis's disclosure caused a bit of a meltdown at the newspaper. In the world of fake news, you never tell anyone you're lying, especially on TV!

Time and time again, the liberal press manufactured stories about me to take my father down. Another of their big whoppers was that I knew about the WikiLeaks dump beforehand. If you remember that little nugget, I was supposed to have prior information about a huge trove of documents on Hillary that WikiLeaks was going to publish. The story, again on CNN, was based on information from an email I supposedly received six days before the dump. The anonymous source on the story was likely Adam Schiff, the chair of the House Intelligence Committee, commonly referred to as Adam #FullofSchiff or #BullSchiff. The leaked email implicating me, he told the news station, was marked September 4. That would have indeed meant that I knew about the WikiLeaks dump before it happened on September 10. Except September 4 wasn't the correct date of the email. The 14 was the correct one, four days after the whole world knew about the WikiLeaks dump. Someone conveniently left out the number one. It was also an unopened email, so I never saw it. But that matters not when trying to overturn the duly elected POTUS.

Again, CNN told us it was the biggest story of the year. Again, the story blew up the internet. Again, it was total bullshit. To add insult to injury, CNN never retracted the story. Instead, the network "updated" the bullshit story they ran. They also published a small explanation of the "mistake," in which they claimed the sources for the story had been vetted by their "in-house fact-checking team": better known as the Three Blind Mice.

CNN issued a statement retracting the story at the beginning of December 2017, when my father was the president-elect. It was complete nonsense, and didn't admit any wrongdoing at all, but at least it was something. It had been a banner bad week for fake news. A few days before, ABC News fired their star correspondent, Brian Ross, after he reported that Michael Flynn was going to testify that my father told him to contact the Russians during the campaign. The story was a complete lie. Even after ABC realized it was a lie, they left a tweet up about the story that was shared 25,000 times before the network deleted it. I find it funny that it always seems a fake news story stays up for days after it's proven false, and if there's a retraction, it's at 3:00 a.m. on a Saturday. Remember, it's all about clickbait.

Then there was NPR's big water pistol, er, "smoking gun." They reported that I had lied to Congress about the timing of a Trump Tower deal in Moscow. According to the story, Cohen said that he sat in on a meeting during the campaign where I told my dad about meeting with Russian officials about Trump Tower Moscow. The reason this was big news was because I'd told the Senate committee that the deal had disappeared before my father announced his candidacy. If the information had been correct, not only would the president's son (that would be me) be facing a jail sentence, but it would add jet fuel to the Russian collusion hoax. Pretty bad, right? Except the information wasn't correct. In fact, it was dead wrong. Reporters at NPR were in such a rush to try to nail me, they didn't see that I had told the Senate committee about two prospective projects in Moscow. The one they thought happened in 2016 had dissolved before my father ran for president. Michael Cohen put together the other one. NPR knew it was wrong ten minutes after they posted the story, but then left it up for nine hours while the rest of the news world piled on. It was too good to bother to fact-check. All they had to do was read a few more lines of my testimony. But they couldn't be bothered. They just wanted to dunk on me. But it was another catastrophic fail. At least NPR tried and issued a correction. A half-hearted one, but it was more than CNN bothers to do. All the cable news network does is lie, get caught, and then blame someone else.

———

Look, I do understand why people believe the lies the liberal press peddles. It's hard to see past the media's hysteria surrounding first my father's candidacy and then his presidency. Even on a subconscious level, the constant barrage of how Trump hates immigrants, women, and minorities (and how they all hate him back) has to have an effect. It even has one on me. When all you hear is nonsense, it's the nonsense you begin to believe. But somewhere along the line, there has to be accountability in the media.

In May 2019, Adam Schiff cosponsored a resolution calling for the US government to reaffirm its support of press freedom. "I'm proud to introduce this resolution recognizing the importance of press freedom around the world, and affirming the need for US leadership to promote a free and fair press," Schiff said.

I couldn't agree more, especially the "fair press" part of "Bull Schiff's" statement. The mainstream media is still free to write and report what they want, and no one is going to stop them. They haven't, however, been fair to my father since his decision to run for president. The mainstream media is still free to write and report what they want, and no one is going to stop them. They haven't, however, been fair to my father since his decision to run for president, or any conservative other than the ones who try so desperately to be loved by the media so they turn on my father. There's Mitt Romney, for instance. How quickly that weakling forgot what the press did to him during his failed run for president. But unlike Trump, he was too weak to fight back, and that's why he lost. The media got the scalp they were looking for.

DJT is 100 percent right when he calls the *New York Times* "failing." The entirety of the print news business has been circling the drain for some time. Since the advent of the internet, newspapers no longer have a sustainable business model. Two things can happen to a failing business: Either it curls up into a ball and goes quietly, or it develops a survive-at-any-cost mentality. Even when it costs your ethics and standards. Today, for reporters to keep their jobs at major newspapers, it's almost mandatory for them to have a Twitter following. To have a Twitter following, you have to be opinionated. I know all about this. Reporters' Twitter followings expect them to be on their side, and reporters happily comply. They have to feed the beast, and the beast is hungry all the time.

There are others in the liberal media whose only concerns are air time and brand building.

I'm going to take a big chance here with my base by telling you this: I have a friendly relationship with Al Sharpton. I see him every couple of weeks at the Grand Havana Room, a cigar club I belong to. He's a fixture there, and we've chatted casually every time we've run into each other for years. As a funny aside, I was in the club having a cigar about a week after the election with a couple of good buddies. Rudy Giuliani was with some people at a table next to us, and Al was at one across the room. At one point he got up and walked past me to go to the men's room.

"Al!" I yell out. "What are you doing here?"

"You know I'm always here, Junior" he answered.

"But what are you doing here *now*?" I said. "I thought you said you were moving to Canada if Trump won?"

The room burst out in laughter. Even Al had to chuckle.

We call each other "frenemies." He'd been an acquanitance of my father's for over thirty years and even called me when he needed a broker and reference for a place to live. For Al, and many like him, the Donald J. Trump presidency is a gold mine for brand building.

Now, like most things, not every single solitary reporter in the liberal press is biased or has an agenda. Some actually go out and try to report the news fairly. For top-tier reporters, however, being fair is not in the job description. Still, I try to be friendly to the reporters I interact with. And some try to be friendly back.

Maybe no other statement by my father is a more significant trigger to the MSM than when he says the press is the enemy of the people. It actually sounds terrible. But if you look at their actions over the past three years, how could a reasonable person come to a different conclusion? Inevitably, when he says those words some editorial writer for the *Times* or CNN, maybe Thomas Friedman or Jim Acosta, will bring up the importance of the free press to democracy. They'll remind us of the First Amendment, quote Thomas Jefferson, and regale us with fond memories of the days of Woodward, Bernstein, and Watergate.

Fake news is about as patriotic as a flag burning. The *Washington Post*'s slogan is "Democracy dies in darkness" even if we peddle BS for three years. Give me a break. Fake News.

———

In early June 2019, my father traveled to the United Kingdom for a state visit. It was during that trip when protestors flew the Trump balloon. My father brought his adult children and their spouses to meet the queen, which caused a furor in the liberal press. How dare he bring his family!

Aside from that stupid complaint, and a few other equally stupid complaints, the trip was great in just about every way. My father and the queen got on well and we had plenty of fun.

At one point during the visit, DJT and the family took a little side trip to Doonbeg, a charming little town in the west of Ireland. Back around 2008, during the Irish economic crisis, we became interested in a property along the sea in County Clare. The setting there, with the dunes and the spray of the wild Atlantic, is breathtaking. We spent millions updating the existing facilities and building cottages and a spa. Today, it's one of the most beautiful properties we have. We also employ about 300 locals. Given that the entire population of Doonbeg is about 740, it's a pretty sure bet that we are the biggest employer in town.

It was Brendan Murphy, who's in charge of our real estate sales in Ireland, and Joe Russell, our GM at Trump Doonbeg (as the locals call it), who asked us to stop by the pubs and say hello to the locals, who've been great throughout the time we've been going. We were happy to do so.

The people of Doonbeg were wonderful to us. The pubs, all five of them, were packed to the rafters. It got to be around midnight, but parents allowed their children to stay up late just to meet us. At Tubridy's Bar and Restaurant, Tommy Turbridy, a legendary Irish footballer, raised his pint in a toast: "On behalf of the people of Doonbeg and the county of Clare, a big Céad Míle Fáilte to the Trump family," he said. It means "a thousand welcomes" in Irish. At some point, a reporter called out to him and asked if it was safe to say that ninety percent of the people in Doonbeg supported Trump.

"No," he said, with a sly smile. "It's a hundred percent of them."

The local parish priest, Father Joe Haugh, told a reporter, "There's a special place in heaven for the Trumps."

There's nothing like Irish hospitality.

We thought it only right to buy a round of drinks in each of the pubs. Caroline Kennedy (no, not that one!), the owner of the Igoe Inn pub, asked if we'd go behind the bar and "pull the pints," as they say. It brought me back to my days in Colorado.

The next day, *The Daily Beast*, or the "the Daily Least" as I like to call them, and the British press, which always looks for the negative angle, posted stories that we'd run out on our tab and stuck poor Caroline Kennedy with the bill. We hadn't. If the reporter who wrote the story had bothered to check, they would have known that we had prearranged to have the bill sent to us. But why do your job when you can make up a story that's going to get a lot more attention than the truth? So that's what they did. They imagined Eric and me as part of the entitled rich who couldn't care less about the livelihoods of the working class.

Out of all the lies the press has written about me, you would think that running out on a bar tab wouldn't even make the list. But since I was a bartender in Aspen who worked for tips, I know that not paying your bar tab is just about the lowest thing a patron can do. I say *just about the lowest*, because the lowest thing you can do is accuse someone of running out on a tab who hasn't.

———

In my lifetime, the press has gone from Walter Cronkite, "the most trusted man in America," to Jim Acosta and Fake News. It's a shame. Soon, social media will be the main deliverer of news, and that's only going to make it worse for people looking for the truth.

13.

SHADOW BANNED

HOW THE LIBERALS' GRIP ON SOCIAL MEDIA CAN RUIN YOUR LIFE

FROM THE MINUTE he won the election, there were people wondering whether my father would give up the social media platform that had helped him sail to victory. "You won," one headline on the site Mashable read. "You can stop tweeting now!" Even some people on the right questioned whether he would keep sending out 140- or 280-character barbs from the Oval Office. They believed it would be somehow trivial or beneath the dignity of the office. My father had even hinted at it himself at a rally in Harrisburg, Pennsylvania, just a few days before the election.

"Don't worry," he said. "I'll give it up after I'm president."

I don't know whether he was kidding about it then, but I do know—as all of you probably do, too—that he did no such thing. Why would he? I just spent an entire chapter going over the massive mainstream media machine that wakes up every morning with the intent of destroying my father. They use every last drop of their resources to spread lies about him, embarrass him in public, and impede his agenda with Democrat propaganda and talking points. Is my father just supposed to sit back and take that? Of course not. Twitter is the only way he has of reaching out to the American people, and he'd be a fool not to do it at every opportunity. Next to traveling around the country to talk to real working-class people and listen to their concerns, interacting with them on Twitter is the best way for my father to stay in touch with voters.

Sure, the platform can be an absolute dumpster fire. Most of the time, for me at least, scrolling through my feed involves sorting through death threats, a whole encyclopedia of swear words, and comparisons of me to everything from excrement to an extraterrestrial before I can get to my news stories. But it wasn't always that way.

———

Believe it or not, there was a time when social media was fun. I think it was probably around the tail end of the second (and final, I hope) Bush presidency, when the flip phone was the coolest thing around and my friend Kid Rock's "All Summer Long" played all summer long. My father was still the host of a little show called *The Apprentice*, and I would sit to his right in the boardroom every week. It was a tough job, but somebody had to do it. Don't get me wrong, without the television show my father might have never gone into politics.

Every once in a while, when I knew there was something engaging or funny coming on an episode of the show, I would send out something called a "tweet" about it. Those "tweets," people told me, would go out into the world via the internet, and hundreds— maybe even *thousands!*—of people might see them. They were like newspaper ads you didn't have to pay for. I figured it was a great deal, at least on my end, and I started sending out a few of those "tweet" things every week. My father, never one to turn down free press, also started messing around with the platform. He used it to promote his buildings, announce his cable news appearances, even to rag on the haters and losers who went up against him in public. Inevitably, it led to politics, the subject that dominates so much of social—or not-so-social—media today.

Take interactions like this one, for example. On February 7, 2013, my father tweeted a criticism of President Obama:

@DonaldJTrump
Obama can kill Americans at will with drones but waterboarding is not allowed—only in America!

Then one of the many liberals on the internet who was attacking him in the comments section wrote, "If you hate America so much, you should run for president and fix things."

My father sent back: "Be careful!"

Obviously, they weren't careful. They kept hitting him and hitting him, making him more and more fed up, until eventually he would have no choice but to run. See, liberals? You should have stayed quiet!

Soon his Twitter account became like an extension of our dinner table, only with the whole world was invited. I watched my father's follower count rise slowly, while mine did, too. He built up his online following as he did one of his skyscrapers: one brick—or shiny glass panel—at a time. By the time he got into politics seriously around 2012, @realDonaldTrump had an audience of about 4 million, nearly double the size of the *New York Times'* readership. By 2016, he had 6 million followers, and I had just over a million. My father and I had never seen anything like it. Long before Twitter existed, DJT had been a master of brand and promotion, but this was different. He could speak to the world immediately. And the world took notice. If you don't believe me, just look at the explosion of populist candidates around the world after he was elected. You think he had something to do with that?

Fast-forward to today, and I can't go a couple of hours without taking a peek at my Twitter timeline. As vile as the comments can get (and believe me, they can get pretty vile), I can't help it. Every morning when I'm in the car on the way to work, I take the pulse of the world via my social media feeds, just so I know what's coming and how I can prepare for it. I'm sure that most people who are on Twitter do exactly the same thing. For the heads of companies such as Twitter and Facebook, this is probably a dream come true. They have made it so that millions of people all over the world cannot live without their products. In business terms, that's like being the guy who owns the rights to water and oxygen or being a pantsuit salesman near Hillary Clinton's house.

But for us, the people who actually use the platforms, it's not such good news. For us, Twitter and Facebook have become addictions that are almost as bad as any of the other ones you hear about—things like alcohol, drugs, or food. They hit the same receptors in the brain and drive us crazy in exactly the same ways. Only instead of being addicted to molecules such as alcohol or nicotine, we're addicted to being outraged. One thing Twitter can do better than any other platform that's ever existed is create outrage, most of which is faux outrage or, as I like to call it, fauxtrage. It can learn what makes you angrier than anything, find a million things like that every day, and then show them all to you nonstop. As a guy who has as large a segment of haters as I have, I know this better than anyone.

Even if I tweet something that's relatively benign—say, a Merry Christmas message, the Twitter mob will find a way to attack me for it. I swear, these people are better than any intelligence agency in the world at bringing up old tweets and twisting them around to ruin somebody's life. Just look at what happened recently to the conservative political commentator Tucker Carlson, who years ago used to call in to a shock jock radio show. Liberals took his words out of context and applied them to today's norms and frame of reference. The same thing has happened to me on the *Opie and Anthony* radio show. One minute we're talking about men-only golf clubs, and the next I'm one of the biggest male chauvinists around. It was the *OPIE AND ANTHONY* show! We were all joking! However, joking is no longer allowed—at least not if you're a conservative. Only liberals get to turn around and say they were joking when they get called out.

Look, I've been chastised online by conservatives too. I once defended Chelsea Clinton after she was attacked on Twitter for speaking out about anti-Semitism following the Christchurch, New Zealand, mosque shootings. But not all craziness is created equal. Conservatives may be stuffy sometimes, and they're as quick to become outraged as anyone else (especially on social media), but they're nothing compared to the fit-throwing freaks on the American left.

These are usually young people, so they've been living with social media practically since they were in the womb, and they usually use Twitter, Instagram, or Snapchat as their main point of contact with the world around them. Even Facebook, which was brand new just a few years ago, is too old for them. Trust me: do that for long enough, and you'll end up a psychopath. It's no wonder that the incoming class of freshman Democrats was able to whip up such strong support among millennials. People such as Ilhan Omar and AOC have been speaking the strange insider language of Twitter and Instagram practically as long as they've been alive, which is like about twelve years. When they send out tweets attacking me or any other conservative using words such as "canceled" or "hella problematic" or "microaggression," they know exactly what messages they're sending to the online mob. Like cyberterrorists, they are well schooled in the arts of igniting mass anger and gaslighting, and they know how to weaponize Twitter.

These people have a playbook, and it works like this: When someone you don't like does a thing that you think is evil—let's say, for example, that John Smith, the director of a major motion picture, has failed to cast enough trans people of color in his movie—you come up with a "hashtag" about him. For instance: #JohnSmithSexistPig. Or #WhitePrivilegeJohnSmithDie.

The next step is to send out a few thousand tweets about John Smith with the hashtag you created. The volume of tweets makes Twitter think that lots of people, not just you, care about the issue. You're hacking the algorithm to create outrage. Then, once the tweets are all out there, your crazy SJW buddies can search your hashtag and send out their own tweets about John Smith. Before long, you'll have John Smith "trending." That means that all those who open Twitter will see that this poor guy's name has popped up. And when they click on his name, they'll get a list of about ten thousand tweets saying what a horrible person he is.

By that point, someone will have probably combed through every tweet John Smith has sent since 2008 and found a sexist joke or two, maybe a few off-color comments from when he was thirteen. They will get thrown into the mix. By noon that day, the *New York Times* will have written a story about the incident as if the world actually cares, and then CNN and MSNBC will take it from there. The op-ed page at HuffPost will call for John Smith to be fired and replaced with a nonbinary trans person (or something), and then whatever film studio was funding the movie will be forced to cave under the pressure and fire the guy. After being fired for something so controversial, he'll never get another job as a director again. That's called being "canceled." If you're a social justice warrior online, getting someone "canceled" is just about the best thing you can do. It's like hitting a home run, but for people who don't know the difference between a baseball bat and a bowling pin.

If you think I'm exaggerating, consider Roseanne Barr. If you remember, she sent out a tweet that the mob found offensive and because of the SJW backlash has now lost her hugely successful television show, had her name dragged through the mud, and will probably never appear on television again—all because of a late-night nonsense tweet that barely anyone could understand. And, yes, it was a stupid tweet. (I have to say "stupid" because if someone doesn't immediately and repeatedly disavow, he can be dragged in as complicit, even if he had no idea.) If it hadn't been for the coordinated efforts of a crazed online mob, that tweet would have stayed buried in the twenty-tweet-long thread it had come in and we all could have forgotten about it. But she's conservative and was on television being pro-Trump. In Hollywood, that's a capital crime.

The same goes for Kevin Hart, who made a few allegedly homophobic jokes during a stand-up comedy special that came out just under a decade ago. For years, no one had cared about those jokes. Comedy used to be funny because we were able to poke fun at things we held dear. Then, once it was announced that Hart was going to host the Oscars, the Hollywood SJW mob started cranking out the outrage tweets like crazy. They followed the playbook that I've described above to a T. Within days, Hart had succumbed to the online mob and agreed to step away from the gig. Every day brings a new list of people who've been shut down by the online outrage mob, and every day the mob has to stretch itself further and further to get people worked up. It has to create new rules for what's considered offensive, new ways for people to break those rules, and even stranger punishments for when they do. It must be exhausting. But if they're going to survive, it's necessary. You just can't sustain that level of outrage without expending an enormous amount of energy to come up with things to be outraged about.

Sometimes, of course, the stuff just comes out of thin air, which is what usually happens to me. I can't tell you how many times I've had people come at me with screenshots of things I've never said, jokes I've never made, or pictures of me doing things I've never done.

When the left runs out of real things to be mad about, it's all too happy to run with the fake stuff. If you need another example of that, put this book down and go google "BuzzFeed dossier." See how much of what you read is true.

Though it's tempting to say that this addiction to outrage is just another both-sides issue, in which the right and the left are equally culpable, that clearly isn't the case. You just don't see conservatives—even the younger ones who know how social media work—using the same organized mob tactics used by left-wing SJWs. (This might be because most of us have jobs and don't have time to sit around hashtagging all day.) But it's also because at its very core, conservatism is striving toward something. We believe in freedom of speech for everyone, not just the people we agree with. Beyond that, it's really just the same stuff we've been talking about for years: free markets, capitalism, Judeo-Christian values, and personal responsibility. Whenever conservatives get into an online scrap with someone, it's usually to defend one of the things I just mentioned. We either win or lose that fight, and when the fight is over, we're pretty good about letting it go.

The Democrats, on the other hand, don't really have that kind of animating principle. There are no bedrock values in the far-left social justice warrior movement. When you ask its adherents what they believe, they'll usually say something like "equality for every-one" (which, in liberal speak, translates to "equality for me but not for thee"), but they can never tell you what that looks like or how to pay for it. They believe in a fictional place where everyone has exactly the same amount of money and we've all morphed into one androgynous gender identity. That place is sort of like the Soviet Union in the 1960s, only on Mars. All they really know is that the world isn't fair and that someone—preferably someone white, male, and conservative—needs to be punished for it. They want everyone in the world to be as angry and miserable as they are. But they aren't working toward anything, and they don't know how to build things. Left with nothing tangible, liberals get more radical, hate more people, and keep lowering the bar for what's considered "offensive."

Take, for example, this tweet from Randa Jarrar, a college professor at California State University, Fresno, who posted this just after former first lady Barbara Bush died (her account is now private):

Barbara Bush was a generous and smart and amazing racist who, along with her husband, raised a war criminal. Fuck outta here with your nice words.

Guess what Jarrar teaches? Creative writing. Perfect!

Now, I'm not saying Twitter is inherently a bad thing. With-out Twitter, Instagram, and Facebook, we might very well have ended up with Hillary Clinton as president of the United States. During the 2016 election, the mainstream media were so slanted in one direction, so hell bent on twisting my father's words and making him out to be the worst person who's ever lived, that there was really nowhere else for him to go *but* Twitter. If it hadn't been for the direct person-to-person communication that social media provided, my father might never have been able to break through the mainstream media and the Hollywood propaganda machine and reach as many voters as he needed to reach. So we should give these platforms their due, at the very least.

But as soon as my father was elected, the tide turned. Twitter and Facebook decided to use all their power against him and any conservatives who support him. Now, we as a country have allowed Twitter, Facebook, and other tech giants, whose staffs are almost entirely liberal, to censor the opinions of conservatives without consequence. These days it isn't just wild mobs of Twitter users who coordinate to take down conservatives; it's the heads of the social media companies themselves. They ban the accounts of conservatives for fraudulent charges of hate speech, hide our posts via algorithms that no one understands, and write their terms and conditions to excuse the casual racism and violence of the left. In this day and age, when social media are the new public square, this "shadow banning" amounts to a complete suppression of freedom of speech. It can't be allowed to continue.

I wish it weren't this way, where nearly all our public discourse happens on social media platforms. I really do. But sadly, that's where we've ended up. When news breaks, Twitter is the first place I go to get real-time updates. When I have an opinion that I want to get out into the world and I don't want the spinmasters at CNN or the *New York Times* to chop it up and rearrange it first, I post it on Twitter. There's a reason why, when the *Times* thought it had caught me red-handed trying to fix the election with Russia, I posted all my emails (which, according to Robert Mueller and anyone else whose eyes are connected to their brains, completely exonerate me) on Twitter. Once they were posted, no one could alter them. Everything went right from me to my followers, and no one else got in on the transaction.

At least that was how I thought it worked.

I am now aware that with every day that goes by, Twitter and Instagram are removing more and more of my posts from people's timelines. They're doing the same thing to other people who speak out in support of conservative values. People who have liked or shared my posts have been reporting sudden problems with their accounts or temporary lockouts from their devices. People have even been suspended for things they tweeted years ago but that have only recently been highlighted.

Here's an example from my own Instagram account. As you will see, I followed the infamous Jussie Smollett story pretty closely on social. When CBS first reported that Jussie had actually paid his "attackers" (who supposedly wore MAGA hats) to attack him, I posted this:

@DonaldTrumpJr
Shocked, I really thought MAGA folks (who are all over downtown Chicago) were waiting with a rope/bottle of bleach to ambush a [rich] guy at 2am in minus 4 degrees because those are conditions where all people go out for Subway rather than order Seamless. Seemed so real.

Instagram took the post down, citing violations and saying I was "putting people in danger." I mean, seriously. Go look it up. Was anyone put in danger by that? When it was thought that Jussie's attackers were real, Instagram didn't touch the most vile, crazy, violent protests in his favor. But one conservative voice reposts a news story *from the mainstream media* that the attack was faked, and it removes the post.

I was one of the first ones to call out shadow banning. About two years ago, I was looking at my analytics and I noticed something weird. I'd been posting with my usual frequency, and receiving my usual impressions, maybe 35 million impressions for the time period, and my new follower account registered zero. That's impossible. You can't have that many millions of impressions and have no new followers. So, after the usual spew of hate crap: "Nobody's looking at your feed anymore!", I put up a post calling-out Instagram for manipulating the account. Within a week, I was magically back up to where I was, about twelve thousand new followers. Amazing how that can happen, right?

So, fast-forward to the Smollett post. After I reposted it, and called them out for taking it down, I received an outpouring of thousands of comments and DMs, some even showing videos, of how Instagram was interfering with my following. Some weren't allowed to like my posts or my father's. The little heart would light-up, and then it would flash back off. Some commented, "Hey Don, I had to follow you three times this week and I never unfollowed you." With others, it was, "Don, I was blocked-out of my account for twenty-four hours for liking one of your feeds." What made it even crazier was, it didn't have to be a political tweet! It could've been a photo of my kids with my dad! So, it was then that I realized the scale of Instagram's interference censorship, and could only imagine what they were doing to my father. Take a minute and think about this: if they can do it to me with millions of followers, if they can do it to the PRESIDENT OF THE UNITED STATES!!!, do you think you're safe from their biased influence? I didn't think so. And, you know something, I can't think of a single time of this happening to a liberal. Not once.

After the damage was done, Instagram said it was a mistake. Funny how these mistakes happen only to conservative posts.

———

I would like to believe that this is all a bunch of misunderstandings. After all, Twitter is relatively new, especially in company years. It's been around only since 2006. In the old days, it wasn't uncommon for a big tech company—say, Apple or Microsoft—to have a few hiccups along its road to success. Let's remember that Apple almost went bankrupt two or three times before anyone ever knew what an iPhone was. If I didn't know what I know, I would be happy to extend the same benefit of the doubt to Twitter and Facebook. But when you look around at the employees who work at these big tech platforms or you consider the fact that just about everyone who's had problems with censorship has been conservative, it becomes clear that this is no accident or technological hiccup. It is a deliberate attempt by hipster liberals in Silicon Valley to shut down the voices that hardworking Americans want to hear.

When it's the liberals who engage in what the left likes to call "hate speech," that's all well and good. But when conservatives do it, they're labeled hateful people and banned for life. Take, for example, the case of Sarah Jeong, an Asian American woman who was hired by the op-ed pages of the *New York Times* to write about technology. Jeong is an avowed liberal and SJW who made her career calling out racism—real and imagined—and oppression in the tech industry. She was a professional complainer who got a job at the perfect place. Then someone found these tweets, which Jeong had written over many months in 2014:

Oh man it's kind of sick how much joy I get out of being cruel to old white men.

Are white people genetically predisposed to burn faster in the sun, thus logically being only fit to live underground like groveling goblins?

#CancelWhitePeople

White people marking up the internet with their opinions like dogs pissing on fire hydrants.

Now, if you're a normal person, those tweets might sound racist to you. At first glance, Ms. Jeong might seem like a textbook racist. All the ingredients are there. Needless cruelty? Check. Indicting an entire group for the actions of a few members of that group? Check. Stunning ignorance and lack of empathy? Double check.

The liberals who run Twitter, however, didn't seem to think there was anything wrong with the posts. In fact, they took Jeong at her word when she said she had been only engaging in "satire" and "mimick[ing] the language of [her] harassers." So a journalist is now a comedian, but an actual comedian like Kevin Hart is not? Okay, got it! Apparently, racist statements are racist only when they're made by certain people against certain other people—usually with those in the first group being conservatives and those in the second group being liberals. Twitter decided that because Sarah Jeong was a liberal who'd just been hired by the *New York Times*, the mother ship of all brain-dead liberals, she would get a free pass. Would the newspaper have done that for a conservative? No way!

They were not so kind to my friend conservative commentator Candace Owens, who decided to do a little experiment after Twitter demonstrated that it was okay with casual racism on its platform. Just a few hours after Twitter cleared Jeong—and was apologized for by the *Times*, which declined to fire her even as more racist tweets were being unearthed—Owens reposted some of Jeong's most racist tweets word for word, with one small change.

Read them again, and see what you think.

> Oh man it's kind of sick how much joy I get out of being cruel to old Jewish men.

> Are Jewish people genetically predisposed to burn faster in the sun, thus logically being only fit to live underground like groveling goblins?

> #CancelJewishPeople

> Jewish people marking up the internet with their opinions like dogs pissing on fire hydrants.

Within a few hours, the mob that keeps constant watch over Candace Owens's Twitter account had reported those tweets to headquarters, where they were deemed too offensive to be seen. If you go looking for them now, you'll get a message saying that they violated Twitter's terms of service and can't be displayed. Just for reposting those tweets with one small edit, Owens was banned from Twitter—something that never happened to the woman who wrote them in the first place.

It would be bad enough if this were some kind of isolated incident. But it's not. It happens all the time, and it's getting more and more brazen. For instance, as Ted Cruz tweeted a while back, how come @RealJamesWoods gets banned and the actor Jim Carrey, one of whose paintings depicts Attorney General William Barr drowning in a sea of vomit, doesn't? Last year, Facebook banned Jesse Kelly, a conservative talk show host, but kept Linda Sarsour after she declared a jihad against my father. Twitter lets Antifa keep its many accounts (even though violence is literally in its mission statement), but it bans alt-right organizations all the time. It even banned the conservative activist David Horowitz and didn't give a reason. I can't think of a liberal who's been banned.

For example, consider Kathy Griffin. Somewhere in the archives, I've got photos of her with Donald Trump before he ran for president, and she's laughing it up as though they're best friends. Then my father gets elected, and she holds up a fake severed head resembling him in a photo shoot. So much for friendship! You would think that doing something like that to the president of the United States would be a career ender, right? Not in the universe we live in. A year after she posted the photo, she boasted to a liberal television show that her hateful gag had helped her career.

Look, I'm fine with free speech. Do whatever you want, say whatever you want. But the double standard is astounding. If a conservative did what Kathy Griffin did, he or she would certainly never work again.

This biased censorship also shows up on YouTube, which is owned by Google. Take for instance, the plight of poor Carlos Maza. As a writer for the lefty online news site Vox, Maza is kind of a social justice policeman, scouring the web for content that upsets his fragile self-image. Not too long ago, he set his sights on the conservative vlogger and comedian Steven Crowder. Among other things, Crowder had called Maza a "lispy queer." Okay, it's offensive, but Crowder is an R-rated political shock jock. That's his schtick. And Maza is a public person who is all about building his online presence. You think his motive might have included something more than just defending his being gay?

Maza complained to YouTube, which at first refused to censor Crowder, stating that the vlogger was not urging his followers to harass the Vox writer and that his comedic commentary was not threatening. Maza wasn't about to give up, though. He began shaming the gay employees of the world's largest video service for allowing such a travesty to happen. Here's what he posted to the employees: "YouTube has decided to side with the people who made our lives miserable in high school. It's decided to use the platform you've helped create in order to arm bigots and bullies with massive megaphones. Why do you stick around? What are you going to do about it?"

Hey, Carlos! I got news for you. If everyone tried to even the score from high school, we wouldn't have time for anything else. Personally, I would be spending my whole day trying to get back at the seniors at the Hill School who kicked my ass when I got there as a smart-ass kid from NYC. Since Maza was targeting tech staff (who are as fragile as they are liberal), however, the strategy worked. YouTube immediately demonetized Crowder's channel; in other words, they took away his ability to make money from advertisements. Following Maza's tantrum, YouTube then changed its censorship rules: "Even if a creator's content doesn't violate our community guidelines, we will take a look at the broader context and impact, and if their behavior is egregious and harms the broader community, we may take action." It also promised a servicewide review of other channels, and YouTube CEO Susan Wojcicki later personally apologized to the LGBTQ community.

In other words, if what you say hurts the left's feelings, pack your bags. As far as the online giants are concerned, the right is always wrong.

———

In a survey conducted by Quillette, Professor Richard Hanania (of Columbia University, of all places) found that out of the twenty-two prominent political commentators who had been banned from Twitter during the period 2005 to 2017, a whopping twenty-one of them were supporters of my father. If we extrapolate from those few people to the wider internet, this could mean that over 95 percent of the time, when Twitter decides to ban someone, it's for expressing a conservative opinion and usually for supporting Donald Trump. This is not only wrong; it's so transparent that only a moron—or a social media platform that knows it has the full protection of the media and the political establishment—would ever try it. This seems like a deplatforming attempt, a trial run for 2020. These companies want to minimize the impact that someone like Trump can have so that the movement will never gain traction.

If you're one of my older readers and the whole Twitter thing baffles you, don't feel bad. You're not alone. Even Twitter doesn't know what Twitter is. Facebook doesn't know what *it* is, either. Just this year, testifying in front of the House Committee on Energy and Commerce, Mark Zuckerberg, Facebook's founder and CEO, tried to tell the world that Facebook is just a technology company that doesn't intervene at all in the messages that are posted on its platform. I would bet a lot of money that his little speech was suggested by Facebook's lawyers, because if it were true—which it's not—Facebook and Twitter would enjoy some pretty cushy protections.

This is because of something called the Communications Decency Act, which was passed in 1996, in the days of the dial-up modem and long before everyone had computers in their homes, let alone belonged to social media networks. According to a section of this law, websites cannot be held accountable for content that's posted on their platforms. They're just supposed to sit back and watch the shit show happen. This is why when you scroll down to a comments section on YouTube or Facebook, you often see some pretty hateful stuff. As long as a website doesn't take any steps to curate or change the content, it's protected by this law, and it can't be held accountable for anything its users say.

But once a website starts to make decisions about what it's going to allow and not allow on its platform, it goes from a "platform" to a "publisher," at least in the eyes of the law. Once Twitter, Facebook, and Instagram start to ban people or remove content, they're no longer just interested observers of content who sit back and let their users run the show. They're publishers just like the *New York Times* or the *Washington Post*. Clearly, this is what they're doing. They've admitted it themselves.

Last summer, Jack Dorsey, one of the founders of Twitter (probably fresh off some weird meditation trip to the desert somewhere), appeared before lawmakers to explain his company's practices. During one hearing, Senator Ted Cruz pointed out that Twitter and Facebook now have power that is much greater than that of any other company that has ever existed in the United States, and that's including the ones that have been broken up by antitrust laws. According to the rules of the free market, you need to have competition. Otherwise, the company that controls the whole thing becomes lazy, corrupt, or worse. This is what is happening right now with big tech companies such as Twitter, Facebook, and Google. Because they're so big and because they're almost 100 percent liberal, they have the power to tilt the national conversation to the left and literally block the voices on the right.

In the end, Jack Dorsey admitted that Twitter had blocked its
users from accessing about 600,000 accounts. An extremely disproportionate number of these accounts, he said, belonged to conservatives. Some of them even belonged to the very members of Congress
who were questioning him that day. Twitter, Facebook, and Google
have become modern-day monopolies. The internet was created
at the expense of the taxpayer. Monopolies on search engines or
social media should not be enabled or tolerated by our government. Yes, we should reduce entry barriers for others to compete,
but it will take something phenomenal to overtake Google. Forget
about Russia trying to influence the US election with the measly
$100,000 it spent on ads; how about the real influencers, the multi-
billion-dollar companies such as Facebook and Google, that block
and silence the voices of conservatives?

Considering how the deck is stacked, what my father, and I
to a lesser extent, have accomplished on Twitter is remarkable. Ev
Williams, another cofounder of the social media giant, recently
called my dad a "genius" and a "master of the platform." He's right;
he is. But just imagine how powerful our Twitter accounts would be
if the playing field were level. And level for everyone, including you.

Think about it. If they can minimize the president of the United
States—or at least try—what can they do to you? Recently, an expert
on the subject estimated that somewhere between 2.5 million and
10 million voters had been swayed to Hillary by Big Tech's tactics
during the election. There goes the popular vote! Make no mistake.
They did it before, and they're going to do it again. As long as the
outrage machine is still operating, it's never going to stop.

14.

THE LATE-NIGHT KING OF COMEDY WITH JUSSIE SMOLLETT AND THE FAUXTRAGE ORCHESTRA

IT SEEMED that Jussie had picked the wrong night to go out for a footlong.

It was two in the morning on January 29, 2019, the single coldest night of what had already been one of the coldest winters on record. Not the sort of night you'd expect to encounter a lot of pedestrians. Yet this young, gay, black actor was heading home on foot to his apartment in a fashionable section of Chicago. He'd gone out to an all-night Subway restaurant for a sandwich. (A lot of rich young actors go to Subway at 2:00 a.m. in −4° F weather instead of ordering Seamless. Nothing to see here, folks.)

According to the account he would later give the police, Jussie was on the phone with his manager when he heard someone screaming at him in the distance. He turned to see two large

white men staring at him. Then he realized—*gasp!*—that they were
wearing red Make America Great Again hats!

The two men started walking toward him, hate in their eyes,
yelling racial epithets and gay insults. One of them carried a length
of clothesline. The other had a white bottle marked "bleach."

"Hey!" one of them yelled. "Is that him?"

"Faggot, *Empire* n***er!"

Now, if you've never tuned in, allow me to explain: The show
Empire is a kind of soap opera about hip-hop that is popular with a
black audience. Jussie Smollett plays a young, up-and-coming singer
with lots of relationship problems. Even if those two crazy rednecks
did exist, I don't think they'd have recognized him from the show, let
alone made him their target. Jussie wasn't exactly the star of the show.
Also, I doubt these supposed white supremacists were tuning in.

But according to Smollett, when they got close enough, those
two *Empire*-viewing, Trump-loving racists started beating him with
their fists, kicking him with their boots, and trying to fit the rope,
which they had pre-tied in the shape of a noose, around his neck.
One guy poured bleach from the white bottle onto his body. The
other punched him in the face, shattering his sunglasses (because
what completely sane, definitely-not-on-drugs young actor doesn't
wear designer shades when he goes out at 2:00 a.m.?). Then, before
the two crazed maniacs got their last punches in and left Smollett
bleeding and bleach soaked in the street, one of them shouted at
him, "This is MAGA country, n***er!"

Satisfied with their violent hate crime, the men then disappeared into the subzero air of Chicago.

———

It was quite a story. When Jussie went public with it, which
happened almost immediately, the outpouring of support from

the left was overwhelming. Every liberal hate-watch group in the country came out to demand that something be done. A legion of social justice warriors, armed with their keyboards and hashtags, stormed the internet. So many outraged tweets came from Hollywood that the lights in Tinseltown dimmed.

Just hours after the news broke, Kamala Harris, a Democrat contender for president, whose campaign Jussie had supported, called the attack a "modern day lynching." Cory Booker did the same thing, using precisely the same language—almost as if they had been reading from the same script. It seemed as though every liberal in the country wanted to use the attack as an example of something larger: the racism that's inescapable in the United States and the casual hatred and bigotry that, in their opinion, had propelled Donald Trump to the White House—in other words, the DNC's talking points. Within a few hours of the attack, the hashtag #JusticeForJussie was trending.

The rush to judgment was so swift, so overwhelming, that no one from the left seemed to care one bit about the details Jussie had given. Every elite liberal was positive that Trump supporters would do something like that. And every elite liberal was quick to blame my father for it.

———

From the moment I heard Jussie's tale, I knew there was a good chance that it was bullshit.

I mean, Subway? At two in the morning? When it's −4° outside? And he's wearing a sweater and sunglasses? Please. Who takes a vicious beating, holding his cell phone to his ear the whole time, and manages not to drop his sandwich in the process? Who would keep a flimsy noose around his neck for forty-five minutes after the attack?

And the attackers? Who would be dumb enough to wear a MAGA hat that time of the morning in Chicago? Come on! They would have been shot in two seconds! And why would they target Jussie Smollett anyway?

But the kicker was their saying "This is MAGA country!"

I've been to all fifty states and talked to hundreds of thousands of Trump supporters, and not once in all that time, from all those people, have I heard the phrase "MAGA country."

You know what Trump supporters call MAGA country?

They call it America!

So I decided to retweet some folks who were raising questions about the details of the supposed attack, questions that any reasonable person would ask. They weren't lunatic figures on the fringes of the alt-right. They were respected commentators who had the good sense to ask questions when nobody else would: Candace Owens and the actor Terrence K. Williams (both black, by the way).

Within hours, I was met with a backlash so big that Jussie Smollett was no longer the story; I was. Later that night, a news story titled "Is Donald Trump Jr. Promoting a Jussie Smollett Conspiracy Theory?" was careening around the internet, followed by a torrent of comments accusing me of—you guessed it—being a racist. My Twitter mentions exploded.

I would like to say I was surprised at the overreaction, but I really wasn't. Overreacting is the left's favorite pastime. Being OUTRAGED is what they do. They're always so SHOCKED! Still, the hypocrisy grated on me. I hadn't said anything racist about Jussie Smollett. And there was nothing racist about doubting his story. I was simply pointing out how his story defied all logic. But all of a sudden, I was an evil racist just for asking the questions.

When it comes to the left and its rigid adherence to orthodoxy, even asking questions can be too much. If the questions stray too far from its narrative, they don't want to hear them.

Just as the triggered SJW editors were pushing "publish" on the stories targeting me, new details were emerging about the attack—details that that began to punch holes in Jussie's story. It was information that any real journalist might have been interested in. But those people weren't real journalists (most journalists aren't real anymore), so they didn't care. The new details didn't fit the hate-attack narrative they wanted so much to be true. All they wanted to do was keep feeding the liberal outrage machine.

So the Chicago Police Department had to do their reporting for them. It released new details on February 1, which leftist news organizations repeated only with the most extreme reluctance. According to their report, during the search for the two crazy white MAGA racists, Chicago police had found no such people. But they had recovered some footage from a security camera that showed two large men walking away from what appeared to be the scene of the crime. The chief communications officer for the Chicago police told his Twitter followers that the cops were very interested in questioning those two men and asked everyone to be on the lookout for them.

The next night, Jussie played a concert that had been scheduled before the attack. Between songs, he took the microphone and launched into a weird, half-sung-word-poetry kind of speech, telling the crowd that he had been "one hundred percent factual and consistent on every level." You know, the sort of thing you say when you're totally innocent and have nothing to hide. Smollett also noted that people had been saying "some stuff" about him that was "absolutely not true."

Then, on Valentine's Day, the pair of crazy white racists every-one had been looking for turned up at the police department of their own volition. At last there was a breakthrough! Only those two gentlemen weren't crazy, they weren't fans of Donald Trump, and they had not attacked Jussie Smollett. Not in any real sense, anyway.

Oh, and they weren't white.

The men who came forward were two brothers from Nige-ria named Olabinjo and Abimbola Osundairo. Each one was just over six feet tall and pretty well built. One was an amateur boxer. Soon police would learn that they worked on the show *Empire* as extras and had allegedly sold illegal drugs to Jussie, arranging the sales via text message. According to police, Smollett had offered them $3,500 to stage the attack and paid them with a check for said amount, upon which he had affixed his signature and the date. In the memo line, he had written "personal training sessions." Police also discovered footage of the brothers buying bleach, a clothes-line, black face masks, and red baseball caps.

Now, I don't think I'm cut out for the staged-hate-crime business. But if I were, I really don't think I would pay my "attackers" with a personal check. (I also probably wouldn't hire two black guys to stage an antiblack hate crime. But, hey, that's just me.) But Jussie did. Thanks to that small piece of evidence—with the signature, the weird memo line, and the matching date—public opinion finally started to shift away from Smollett. On February 20, he was charged with disorderly conduct and filing a false police report. He turned himself in, stood before a judge, and paid $10,000 bail to the city of Chicago.

Of course, Twitter was filled with repentant Hollywood stars and Democrat politicians apologizing for rushing to judgment.

Yeah, right . . . Presidential hopefuls and social justice warriors were off to find the next fauxtrage.

Some of them twisted themselves into pretzels trying to moonwalk back their initial reactions. Here's what Kamala Harris had to say:

I'm very, um, concerned about obviously, the initial, um, allegation that he made about what might have happened.

Clear as a bell, Kamala.

It's a little different from the succinct "THIS IS A MODERN DAY LYNCHING" she had first posted.

"Strange that no one in Hollywood or the Main Stream Media seems to want #JusticeForJussie anymore. Wonder what changed?" I tweeted.

———

Predictably, the left had nothing to say. As the facts kept coming, it kept getting quieter (funny how that tends to happen).

In some sick way, the Smollett attack—when people believed it—was the best thing that had ever happened to liberals. For two years, they had been telling the world that Donald Trump had made our country more racist, more divisive, and more dangerous for minorities, and they'd been saying it without a shred of evidence. It was one of those things that—I don't know—just felt true, man. But that attack, with its gratuitous violence and horrible B-movie dialogue, gave them all the evidence they needed. It was like Christmas all over again, a gift too good to be true.

You see, in the prevailing view of the left, this whole country is a sick, evil white supremacist plot gone wrong. The left likes to think we didn't like Barack Obama because of his race. In fact, we didn't like him because of his economic stance, globalist views, and gun-grabbing, big-government, liberal policies—the list is never ending—but race wasn't our issue with Barry.

They believe our founding fathers were nothing but murderous colonizers who eliminated the Native Americans, enslaved African Americans, and set up the country so that all ethnic and racial minorities would be oppressed for eternity. Anyone who's proud to be an American is racist. From the leftist historian Howard Zinn up to AOC, people on the left believe that history has been a battle between good people and evil people, oppressors and oppressed, colonizers and victims. This is a binary system. There is no gray area between the two types of people. No nuances. You can be either an oppressor or an oppressed. And if you're a white man, you're almost always the former.

Here's the thing: Democrats have built an entire platform around victimhood and oppression. Radical liberals believe that the more labels you have—lesbian, bi, trans, gay, black, Hispanic, etc.— the more "woke" points you have. And the more you've suffered and been oppressed, the more you are worth in the eyes of the modern Democrat Party. More important, you cannot gain an understanding of what it's like to be black, transgender, or gay by talking to people, reading, or doing your own research on the subject. In fact, it's racist of you even to try.

So when a minority or a person of color says he or she feels as though something has happened to him or her—whether it's a microaggression or a full-on act of racial hatred such as the one Smollett described—you are required by the wacky bylaws of leftism to believe that person. If you don't, you're a racist.

———

Jussie took advantage of that flaw in reasoning, and liberals hit the jackpot with all the victim boxes that he checked. How could they pass on the chance? You can imagine Hollywood already planning a movie, Harvard offering him a professorship, and *Time* magazine putting him on its cover!

If something doesn't change very soon, it won't be long before someone tries to do it again. You can't decide how smart or worthy of praise people are based on how much they've suffered or been oppressed by the system (or how much their ancestors or people who are like them have suffered and been oppressed) and not expect there to be consequences.

I've always said that if you took all the labels that liberals hold in such high esteem and combined them into one person, you would have the ultimate Democrat candidate for president—a nonbinary minority who identifies as a dolphin, maybe. And although nobody has managed to check all those boxes, our friend Jussie Smollett came pretty damn close. He was OppressionTron 2.0: a gay, black, sensitive man who worked in Hollywood and supported Kamala Harris, the first black female candidate for president. Plus he was an activist with a huge social media platform!

Jackpot! His woke score was off the charts.

Because of their obsession with identity politics, liberals were on Jussie's side from the beginning. Nothing could have swayed them from their defense of him. And even as some peeled off and joined the real world as the Smollett saga continued, he still had a few strident defenders—far too many, in my opinion, even for these polarized times. DeRay Mckesson, a supporter of the Black Lives Matter movement and the host of a podcast for Crooked Media, seemed only to be concerned about what the Chicago police were doing wrong.

In the eyes of radical liberals like Mckesson, cops are nothing but evil people who only murder young black teenagers. Anytime cops enter the picture, they're immediately labeled the bad guys.

No amount of research or evidence to the contrary can change their minds.

Another ride-or-die supporter of Smollett, apparently, was Cook County state's attorney and Hillary pal Kim Foxx. As documents would later reveal, Foxx worked out a backroom deal that would set Jussie free, absolving him of blame and allowing him to avoid the years of jail time he might face if the case ever went to trial. All he would have to do was forfeit his $10,000 bail to the city of Chicago—essentially a bribe for his freedom, if you ask me. That deal went into action on March 26, 2019, when Smollett strode into a courthouse in Chicago and stepped up to the microphone, reiterating that he was still not changing his story.

"I would have not been my mother's son," he said, "if I was capable of one drop of what I was accused of."

We hear a lot about white privilege in this country today. Well, I haven't heard anyone give a name to whatever happened to Jussie, but I'm waiting.

Whatever you want to call it, it's a miscarriage of justice. Just hours after the decision was made, Rahm Emanuel, the mayor of Chicago and former chief of staff to Barack Obama, held a press conference. "This is without a doubt a whitewash of justice, and sends a clear message that if you're in a position of influence and power, you'll get treated one way, [while] other people will be treated another way," he said. "There is no accountability in the system. It is wrong—full stop."

Donald Trump Jr.
@DonaldJTrumpJr
Never thought I'd agree 100% with RAHM Emanuel.

If Rahm Emanuel, who served in the very administration that

brought this kind of hysterical identity politics into the mainstream, was that upset about Smollett, you know it had to be pretty bad! Believe me, Rahm knows a thing or two about pulling strings, so if he thought it was bad, it was BAD.

No matter what he does, how often he breaks the law, or how much he lies, Smollett will never be held accountable by the mob. If you're looking for an example of systemic privilege, don't look at middle-class white people. Look at Smollett, who broke the law, got nailed in court, and still, at least at this writing, does not have to pay for the crime he committed.

That is privilege.

——————

The Smollett stunt wasn't an isolated incident. Not by a long shot. The left has been pulling this kind of crap ever since the campaign. Just after my father was elected, the Southern Poverty Law Center, the lefty watchdog group, published a report titled "Ten Days After: Harassment and Intimidation in the Aftermath of the Election." The first example it used in the report was the Hopewell Missionary Baptist Church in Greenville, Mississippi, which had been torched and vandalized a week before the election. Firefighters found the words "Vote Trump" spray painted on a wall in the burnt-out hull of the church.

"The incident was just a harbinger of what has become a national outbreak of hate, as white supremacists celebrate Donald Trump's victory," the report stated.

Two weeks later, a member of the church was arrested for arson that was not "politically motivated," according to the police. He had spray painted "Vote Trump" to throw police off the scent.

There was no outbreak of hate, only an outbreak of phony hate crimes.

———

Andy Ngo, the editor at Quillette I mentioned earlier, has written often about fake hate crimes against the LGBTQ community in Portland, including one that supposedly happened in the aftermath of the Jussie Smollett case. The Portland incident caused widespread panic in the trans and gay communities there and spurred a rash of other supposed attacks. The first so-called attack happened on February 10, 2019, to a trans woman named Sophia Gabrielle Stanford, who claimed she was the victim of a "brutal and aggressively blatant hate crime." A GoFundMe page was posted as a "Trauma fund for our girl." The page described the attack in detail: Stanford had been hit in the head from behind with a baseball bat, had been found unconscious in the street by a "good Samaritan," and had been transported to the hospital for a CAT scan and treatment for her wounds.

According to Ngo, however, the Portland police have a completely different story. The responding officer found Stanford lying in the street drunk and wrote in his report that he believed she'd fallen to the ground and hit her head.

The GoFundMe page went viral, raised thousands of dollars, and added fuel to the growing number of alleged hate crimes against gays and trans people in the area. The local newspaper fanned the flames, apparently without checking with the police. The Democrat mayor of the town tweeted that the reported crimes "were deeply disturbing" and invited the trans and gay communities to join him in a town hall meeting to listen "to victims and leaders." Activist leaders sent out "attack warnings" and told the community to carry Mace. The progressive city of Portland was gripped in panic.

One of the so-called attacks that happened in the wake of Stanford's pushed SJWs to the next level.

Jenny Bruso, who describes herself as a "fat-queer activist," claimed in a Facebook post that two white men had pulled up next to her and her partner, Brie Jones, at a busy intersection and thrown a full beer can at them that had hit Jones in the face. The post included a photo of Jones with a small scar and a red cheek. In the heated atmosphere, the post went viral. Bruso said they had reported the attack to police, but the cops told Ngo they had no record of it. When he contacted Bruso to inquire about the attack, she refused to talk to him and took the post down. It was too late, however, to stop the momentum of outrage.

SJWs began posting photographs of the "attackers," members of the Proud Boys group who had been in a brawl with Antifa activists the year before. "These are the faces of the attackers that have been terrorizing the queer/trans community lately. If you see any of these faces in public, hit them with a brick, because the police don't do anything to stop it," read one viral Instagram post. Unverified rumors littered social media, including one accusing one of the Proud Boys of murder.

One of the men targeted as an attacker was thirty-five-year-old Robert Zerfing. According to Ngo, Zerfing had renounced his membership with the Proud Boys long before his photo was posted. By "doxing," the process of finding documents on the web and publishing them, searchers found Zerfing's address and posted it online. A text he received from one activist read, "4 hate crimes in the last week you were involved in. Paybacks a bitch mother f—ker." He's received numerous death threats.

According to organizers involved in the gay and trans communities in Portland, there were at least fifteen hate crime attacks in the aftermath of the one Stanford alleged. According to Ngo, the police do not have a record of any of them.

On the national level, the left has used erroneous information like Portland's to fuel the phony narrative that hate crime have been soaring since my father was elected president. In story after story about this worrisome trend, they point to the FBI's 2017 Hate Crime Statistics report. According to the report, the number of hate crimes in the United States was at its highest since Barack Obama was elected eleven years ago, an increase of nearly a thousand crimes from the year before. What that number doesn't tell you, however, is that almost a thousand new law enforcement agencies contributed statistics to the report. In other words, the instances of hate crimes aren't rising. They're just finding ways to bump up the number artificially.

Not too long ago, the *Wall Street Journal* published an op-ed that quoted Wilfred Reilly, a political science professor at the historically black Kentucky State University. According to Mr. Reilly, who's written a book called *Hate Crime Hoax: How the Left Is Selling a Fake Race War*, the report is deeply flawed. "To be responsible for the entire surge, each agency [of the 1,000] would have to report exactly one hate crime," he told the *Epoch Times*. "I believe with reason—given the average agency has reported between 0.44 and 0.63 hate crimes annually in recent years, and that high-crime agencies are more likely to withhold data from the FBI in the first place—that almost all of the surge is due to this technical change in reporting rates."

Reilly also says that as many as 10 percent of the hate crimes reported to the FBI in 2017 turned out to be fake. That's seven hundred fake hate crimes!

The more the media spin stories like Jussie's to the public, the more the left, starving for anything to fuel their hatred, believes that hate crime is rampant, leading to more erroneous reports of hate crimes and fake hate crimes. Around and around it goes.

It's not as if fake hate crimes are victimless. They increase distrust and hysteria in communities, add gasoline to an already flaming political divide, instill hate into people who previously had none, and distract police from doing their jobs, which includes saving lives. Here's just a percentage of what Smollett cost his city. Chicago police put twenty-four detectives on the case. They worked one thousand hours, not including overtime. They executed fifty search warrants and watched dozens of hours of surveillance tape. Now, it's not as though the cops in Chicago have nothing else to do. During that January, one of the coldest on record, twenty people were murdered. The angry Eddie Johnson, the superintendent of the Chicago Police Department, called Smollett's alleged stunt "shameful."

"I just wish the families of gun violence in this city got this much attention," he said, "because that's who really deserves [it]."

———

The left in this country has become so radical, so intent on proving that cops and Republicans are evil while people of color and members of the LGBT community can do no wrong, that it is refusing to accept what is right in front of them. To be a member of the Democrat Party in 2019, you have to deny evidence of all kinds. As George Orwell wrote in *1984*, "The party told you to reject the evidence of your eyes and ears. It was their final, most essential command."

Of course, the Democrats would be nothing without the mainstream media, their all-purpose PR operation. The media are the vehicle through which all the identity-politics craziness gets out onto the airwaves. The Jussie Smollett case was a prime example. On February 24, after the whole thing had been revealed as a hoax, Jonathan Capehart, a columnist for the *Washington Post* who suffers from a serious case of Trump Derangement Syndrome, went on MSNBC and argued that, yes, although Jussie had faked the whole thing, it was Donald Trump's fault that everyone had fallen for it. I'm not making that up. "The president actually stokes the atmosphere of menace and insecurity that millions of Americans feel across this country," he said, not joking at all. "There are people in this country who every day feel that their very existence—their own security is at stake. And so, you know, the president's superpac, right-wingers, far right, conservatives who are using the Jussie Smollett situation to rhetorically bash people who are afraid for their own existence and their own lives . . . is really despicable."

So hold on. Jussie creates a fake hate crime and tries to blame my father for it, and it's . . . my father's fault?

Look, I don't know what part of the universe the guy lives in, but down here in the United States, things just aren't that bleak anymore. By almost every measure imaginable, life for people who claim to "feel that their very existence is at stake" has only gotten better over the past fifty years. Their quality of life has improved. High school graduation rates for racial minorities have soared. Unemployment among African Americans is at its lowest levels in the history of this country. DJT has implemented prison reform and pushed through opportunity zone legislation to help those he apparently discriminates against. And there are no bands of insane racists roving the streets looking for minorities to beat up. There certainly aren't racist Trump supporters looking to assault people just for being who they are. But it is better for Democrats, whose entire platform relies on calling the other side of the aisle a bunch of racists, if voters *believe* that the world is a scary and racist place.

Those people are so triggered by the current president that they will believe anything.

———

In an ideal world, as laid out by Dr. Martin Luther King Jr., people would be judged based on the content of their character, not the color of their skin. Operating on that belief, we managed to pass the most sweeping civil rights legislation in the history of the world, improve conditions for all races, and begin to heal the divide between black and white people in this country. Now people who claim to share Dr. King's vision of the world are asking us to go backward, to pay more attention to the color of everyone's skin and less attention to the content of their character. They're claiming that knowledge can come only from being born a certain color or with a particular sexual orientation and that no one can understand anyone else just by sitting down and talking to them. This takes away what makes us human, and we need to move away from it.

Accepting Jussie Smollett's view of the world, where getting beaten up by racists makes you cool—or could perhaps add more pay to your already lucrative acting salary—and the whole world is just one big scary place where evil racists go on the prowl for innocent victims, would be a huge step backward for society. Some days, I worry that we have already taken a big backward step. Think, for example, about how easy it would have been for Smollett to get away with perpetrating his little hoax. All he would have had to do was clean it up a little bit, maybe lose the noose and the bleach or do some better planning before the event, and people would have bought it. What concerns me about the case isn't that a liberal is getting away with a crime. (As I write this, the city of Chicago is in the process of appointing a special prosecutor who might take care of that.) What concerns me is that the whole liberal world was more than willing to take Smollett at his word despite the mountain of evidence to the contrary.

Liberals have become so deluded in their hatred of my father that they'll latch onto any story that makes him look bad, even a story as phony as Jussie Smollett's. But the kind of hatred that Smollett was trying to create has no basis in reality. That's why he had to pay people to act it out.

So, Jussie, I'd like to personally thank you for bringing this all to light and for this indirect contribution to Trump 2020. Jussie, you're the best, and, as it's been said, I hope you're not beating yourself up over it—AGAIN!

15.

JOE CHINA

ABOUT THREE YEARS AFTER I had the discussion with Rusty, the union carpenter in Wisconsin, Joe Biden visited a union job site a few miles down the road as part of the kickoff of his 2020 presidential primary campaign. Apparently, he had stopped into a Delaware union hall one time in, like, 1984 to use the bathroom, and now he was acting as though the organized labor vote should be all his. Truth is, he has no claim on the union vote. None at all. He makes a big deal about growing up in the blue-collar town of Scranton, but from what I heard, he didn't have it all that hard. His father ran a car dealership in Delaware and before that had owned an airport and crop-dusting service on Long Island. He was also an executive in a chemical company during the war. Joe went to prep school, just as I did. He's had his fingernails manicured since he was elected to the US Senate, and that was back when Nixon was president. I'm not saying he isn't good with his hands; he's just not fond of using them for work. Judging from the legislation he's supported—NAFTA and the Trans-Pacific Partnership (TPP) agreement—it doesn't seem as though he's all that found of work-ers, either.

But his kind of arrogance, purporting to be a regular Joe while actively working against labor, shouldn't be surprising to you. In fact, it's perfectly consistent with the Democrat platform. Despite what they've done (or haven't done) politically over the past two decades and the disastrous policies they've enacted, politicians on the left seem to think they're entitled to votes based on who they are. *We're the Democrat Party*, they'll say. *Vote for anyone else, and you're for the one percent or a racist!*

If you think I'm exaggerating, just look at what happens to any woman or ethnic minority who dares to stray from the Democrat Party and its liberal agenda. They're excommunicated, burned as a witch. When Kanye West put on a MAGA hat and went to the White House, he was attacked as though he had just thrown a bag of kittens into the ocean. People were boycotting his concerts, burn-ing his records (which they had already paid for), and going after any artists who had the audacity to work with him. When Candace Owens, the black female political commentator with whom I've done events many times, decided to testify in front of Congress about how harmful political correctness can be to young black women, she was labeled a Nazi and threats were made on her life. An op-ed piece in the *Philadelphia Inquirer* compared her to a house slave. Last April, Candace was eating breakfast with Charlie Kirk in a local Philly diner when a mob from Antifa, the militant left-wing organization, surrounded them, screaming obscenities and throwing bottles at them.

With tactics like that, it's no wonder Democrats don't have to do any real voter outreach—or enact any real policies—to keep people pulling the levers for whatever wacky liberal wins their primary. Everyone is so afraid to be labeled racist or sexist that they'll vote for anyone with a D next to his or her name. It doesn't seem to matter that they're voting against their own self-interest. Over the past few years, largely thanks to the culture of outrage and public shaming, Democrats have been allowed to have it both ways. They buddy up with the economic enemies of the United States on Monday, making it easier for us to ship high-paying jobs overseas to countries that pay their workers a fraction of our wages, and then by Friday, they're out giving speeches to union leaders, saying they actually give a shit about the American worker. All of them, from Elizabeth Warren and Hillary Clinton to John Kerry and Barack Obama, are as two-faced as they come.

Joe Biden's duplicity, however, takes the cake. Before he was going on and on about foreign interference in the 2016 election, threatening to take my father out behind the high school gym and beat him up, "Joey Hands" was making a number of state visits to China, all on the taxpayers' dime, to cut what seem to be more than a few shady deals. In December 2013, he went there on an official visit on *Air Force Two*, allegedly to settle some disputes about territory in the East China Sea. To help out with that, he took along his son Hunter, the noted military scholar and—wait, no, that can't be right. Oh, here we go. He took along his son Hunter, a guy who had been thrown out of the Naval Reserve for cocaine use and was trying to start up a private equity firm with a buddy, John Kerry's stepson and ketchup heir Christopher Heinz. During the trip, Hunter and Heinz sat in on meetings with the US-China Business Council, where the vice president struck a pretty friendly tone with the leadership. According to press reports, ten days later, Hunter's new hedge fund signed a billion-dollar deal with the Bank of China, which is owned by the Chinese government. That deal was expanded to $1.5 billion a little while later. So, let me see if I got this straight. Three journeymen investors, including the sitting Vice President's son, are able to get a $1.5 billion deal with the Chinese government the first time they try. That's one, comma, five, zero zero zero zero zero zero zero zero. Some of the best businesspeople in the world, all with great track records, have tried and failed for years to get their hands on that money. I guess the Bidens had something special to offer. As Steve Hilton of Fox News discovered, the company had posted pictures of the meeting on its Chinese-language website but not on the English-language version of the site. Clearly, they had something to hide. Imagine if their names had been Trump instead of Biden. Think about it. What would happen if I went to China and came back with 1.5 dollars, let alone 1.5 billion? Think anyone would ignore that? That's what I thought.

I've never heard any story—not even a fake one—that comes close to Biden's. Here we have two sons of the swampiest swamp creatures the swamp has ever seen, Kerry's and Biden's "swamp babies," hitching a ride on Daddy's plane and cutting deals during official state business. If there were any money to be made, all 330 million citizens of the United States should write letters and demand stock in Hunter Biden's company. After all, they're the ones who paid for the deal that got it going.

Now, if you're thinking that Joe Biden's son having business interests in China doesn't change the way Biden would deal with our adversary as president, consider this: The Chinese government plays a much different role in that country's economy than our federal government does in the US economy. Banks in China are not private businesses. They are owned by the government. So when you do business with a Chinese bank, you are doing business with the Chinese government. There's simply no way around it. And when you do business with the Chinese government, you are signing on to its terms, not ours.

Make no mistake: China is what happens when you run an economy based on the tenets of communism, socialism, and favoritism. It's the worst of crony capitalism. The welfare of the state is all that matters, and the workers exist only to make sure the state has enough money. The state decides who is awarded lucrative businesses. If it weren't for political opposition in the United States, the left would be pulling us further and further into a system just like that one.

Biden's chummy relationship with China dates back at least as far as the Clinton administration. In the closing months of the Clinton White House, Congress granted China "permanent normal trade relations" (PNTR) status. Biden supported the measure and in doing so completely underestimated the future of our trade relations with China. On the floor of the Senate, Biden said he saw no reason to think that trade deals with China would hurt US manufacturing. Nor did he see China as a competitor of ours. He said that China had an economy "about the size of the Netherlands."

It was that kind of thinking that put us behind the eight ball with a $400 billion–plus trade deficit with China and why my father is doing all he can to rectify it.

Of course, a guy as savvy as Biden would realize the error of his ways, right? Well, here's what he said during a campaign event in Iowa City in May 2019: "China is going to eat our lunch? Come on, man. They're not competition for us!" Tell that to the hundreds of thousands of people who lost their jobs to cheap labor and horrible trade deals with China.

Now, for Joe and his family, I'm sure this is true. After all, you can't be in competition with an entity that you're doing billion-dollar deals with. But for the rest of the United States, I would say that China is going to be a major competitor in the years to come. This doesn't mean that its economy is stronger or that we can't beat it. It does mean that China does not operate on a level playing field and that this creates several disadvantages for us. For example, the Chinese government is able to spy on its citizens with a kind of accuracy that Josef Stalin could only dream about.

Now about Hunter. I've been in the political eye for just a little over four years. During that time, I have been accused of colluding with Russian spies, trading on my father's position for hundreds of millions of dollars' worth of business deals, and sympathizing with white supremacists. The only thing I haven't been accused of by the liberal press is global warming, but I'm sure that's coming. Even though all of the aforementioned accusations are stone-cold lies, I almost understand why I'm such a target for the left. I'm Donald Trump's son, and by virtue of that alone, I'm on the left's most wanted list. Add that I'm a hunter, a shooter, and someone who doesn't abide by political correctness, and the target on my back gets bigger. Then add my Twitter account, and it's no wonder I've become the left's public enemy number two behind my dad. What baffles me, however, is how someone like Hunter Biden gets a pass from the press. Only recently has Hunter garnered any newspaper ink or mention on cable news for the stunts he's pulled. For the entire time he was the vice president's son, Hunter operated without any scrutiny at all. And boy, oh boy, did he operate. Here's a highlight reel of his biggest hits.

In 2009, after closing a swampy lobbying firm in Washington, Hunter Biden opened a venture capital and investment firm called Rosemont Seneca Partners with Heinz and two other partners. Five years later, square in the middle of Obama's second term, they set up shop in China. They named the company Bohai Harvest RST. The "Bohai" represented the Chinese stake in the company, the "RS" stood for Rosemont Seneca, and the "T" stood for the Thornton Group. A consultancy firm in Massachusetts, it was run by James Bulger, the son of longtime Massachusetts Senate president Billy Bulger and nephew of James "Whitey" Bulger, the infamous Boston gangster. Isn't that nice?

In his book *Secret Empires: How the American Political Class Hides Corruption and Enriches Family and Friends*, Peter Schweizer described the curious timing of a 2013 trip to China the vice president made with his son and daughter:

> Vice President Biden, Hunter Biden and [Hunter's daughter] Finnegan arrived to a red carpet and a delegation of Chinese officials. Greeted by Chinese children carrying flowers, the delegation was then whisked to a meeting with Vice President Li Yuanchao and talks with President Xi Jinping.

According to Schweizer, that trip coincided with the deal between the Bank of China and Rosemont Seneca that formed Bohai Harvest RST.

"In short, the Chinese government was literally funding a business that it co-owned along with the sons of two of America's most powerful decision makers," Schweizer wrote.

Bad, right? It gets worse. One of Bohai Harvest's investment partners in China was the Aviation Industry Corporation of China (AVIC). Just the year before, according to the *Wall Street Journal*, AVIC had stolen technologies dealing with our stealth fighter for the Chinese version. Can you imagine anything remotely close to that happening during my father's presidency? We'd have a special counsel appointed faster than you could say "Adam #FullofSchiff."

"My frustration is not that the solid reporting on Trump has been too tough, but that the reporting on the Obama administration has been way too soft or in some cases nonexistent," Schweizer wrote.

But if you think China was bad for Joe and Hunter, things really got interesting a few years later in Ukraine. On March 16, 2016, Joe Biden flew to Kiev on a mission. In his sights was Ukrainian prosecutor general Viktor Shokin, who was so corrupt that the vice president of the United States had to fly to Ukraine to take matters into his own hands. In no uncertain terms, Biden told the Ukrainian government to fire Shokin or the United States would withhold $1 billion in loan guarantees. One billion is a lot of money, and the threat worked. The prosecutor general was voted out by the Ukrainian parliament soon after.

Now, on the surface, it would seem that Biden was like a new sheriff in town, riding to the rescue. The only thing he was missing was a stallion and a white cowboy hat. Like a lot of things about Biden, however, what's on the surface has very little to do with what's going on in secret.

About the time of Joe's visit to Kiev, Shokin had reopened an investigation into a Ukrainian energy company called Burisma Holdings. On the board of Burisma Holdings, getting paid upward of $50,000 a month, was one Hunter Biden. Hunter, who even the failing *New York Times* had to admit had no prior experience in energy, had just been discharged from the navy reserve for a cocaine-related offense, and had been given the job solely for his connections in Washington. "Hunter Biden and his American business partners were part of a broad effort by Burisma to bring in well-connected Democrats during a period when the company was facing investigations backed not just by domestic Ukrainian forces but by officials in the Obama administration," the *Times* stated. In other words, Hunter was enlisting high-profile Democrats and the swamp creatures who surround them to shield his company from scrutiny by the US government! By any measure, it was a pretty bold move by the vice president's son and one that sent the Washington rumor mill into overdrive. Everybody in the Obama administration had to know what he was doing. Everyone except dear old Dad, who claimed that he had found out about his son's involvement in Burisma only when he had read about it in the newspaper. Now, my father calls the former vice president "Sleepy Joe" for good reason. But he'd have to have been in a coma not to know what his own son was doing in Ukraine. And I'm not even talking about the lines!

————

I began this section by telling you that I've learned a thing or two about politics. Here's another thing I've learned: The hypocrisy on the left has no limits, and the Mueller Report might be the best example of this. Victor Davis Hanson, who wrote *The Case for Trump*, summed up nicely the double standard Mueller applied to Democrats in a piece he wrote for *National Review*: "The problem with the Mueller investigation, and with former intelligence officials such as Brennan, Clapper, Comey, and McCabe, is pious hypocrisy. Those who have lectured America on Trump's unproven crimes have written books and appeared on TV to publicize their own superior virtue. Yet they themselves have engaged in all sorts of unethical and illegal behavior." And when their lies are exposed, they just cook up new ones. When it's not collusion, it's obstruction. Then, when it's not that, it's something else. It's a constant cover-up, and it always leads to nothing.

When it comes to being sanctimonious, Democrats literally wrote the book, and Joe Biden is a prime example. One of the best things about my father's presidency, however, is how he's exposed the deception under which Washington operates. Still, people such as Comey, Clapper, Brennan, and Biden continue to get away with criminal behavior because the left refuses to see what is now plainly evident. So we have to fight fire with fire. If liberals get to investigate, so should we. As Peter Schweizer wrote in an op-ed for the *New York Post*: "If a two-year investigation of President Trump, Russia and the Trump family was justified to ensure the president isn't compromised, an investigation into Joe Biden, China, Ukraine and the Biden family is imperative."

I can hear the left now: "You can't investigate Joe Biden; he's running for president!"

Yeah, right. Nobody running for president ever gets investigated.

———

As the election approaches, there are some things you probably won't be able to avoid. First, there will be the inevitable "town hall" events during which Democrats will try to tap into some of the off-the-cuff magic that got my father into the White House in 2016, rolling up their sleeves and putting one foot on a stool while they do their best *Gee, that's a good point* faces. There will also be a thousand photo ops with blue-collar workers, all screen-tested by the campaign staffs for diversity and camera-readiness. These will probably end with the candidate promising to "keep jobs in America" and "look after the working class." If you're lucky, the candidate might even be wearing a cute little hard hat.

Please know that no matter how uplifting they may seem, the photos are all bullshit, especially if Joe or Bernie is wearing the hard hat.

16.

THE OPPOSITION

AN INCONVENIENT TRUTH: THE DEMOCRAT CANDIDATES ARE OUT OF TOUCH, OUT OF THEIR MINDS, AND FRANKLY DON'T GIVE A DAMN ABOUT THE AVERAGE AMERICAN.

IN ASSESSING THE 2020 Democrats hoping to run against my father, I have to be careful. It's very easy for me to become sarcastic.

Lord knows, the last thing today's political debate needs is more sarcasm from me. I mean, what purpose would it serve for me to call Vice President Biden "Joey Hands"? Or make fun of Crazy Bernie—oops, Senator Sanders—again? Or refer to the senator from Massachusetts as a fabled Native American princess from the 1600s? There is no reason to add fuel to the fire, especially in today's political atmosphere. Anyone who does so is provoking just for the sake of provocation.

Besides, if I make fun of Senator Sanders, he might throw one of his famous crippled-granny right hooks my way.

But before I get to the circus, er, candidates, I'd like to say a word or two about today's political process.

With the exception of the last presidential election, over the past few decades the elite political class has made sure that real people who communicate to voters in understandable ways can't make it through the primary process and the general election. Instead, they have closed off that path to just about everyone except for a few airbrushed, camera-ready candidates. Those people spit out the right slogans; have big, absolutely unattainable ideas; and bend to the will of the establishment. Both political parties are guilty of this. By the time my father threw his red MAGA hat into the ring, we had been padding the corners of our public discourse for so long, pandering to the most sensitive people among us, that—never mind the Democrats—the Republican Party, the party of Abraham Lincoln, Ronald Reagan, and decent, hardworking people everywhere, was only a fading shadow of its former greatness.

I've said it a few times already in this book, but it bears repeating: Donald J. Trump single-handedly pulled American conservatism back from the brink of extinction, and he did it by ignoring *every single rule* of American politics. He didn't pose for the typical candidate photographs or use establishment-approved phrasing in his speeches; he definitely didn't adhere to the usual norms of practiced dialogue. He made his own rules and beat the system by breaking the old ones.

Even so, it's still a hard fight. After all, how do you run against free college, free health care, free housing, and free everything else? Sadly, it doesn't matter that there is absolutely zero chance of liberals delivering on their insane promises, because today, the sound of the promises is all that matters. And in case you haven't thought about it, the phrase "Yeah, but that costs money" isn't exactly a killer campaign slogan. Remember, this is the party that wants to drop $93 trillion on farting cows.

If Democrats want to have any chance of defeating my dad in 2020—and, to be honest, I think they have very little—they're going to have to learn to play by his rules. That means no focus groups or debate answers that have been rehearsed a thousand times (or given to bad candidates ahead of time), no resorting to accusations of racism every time they can't answer a question, and definitely no pretending to be for the American worker when you're planning to raise taxes, increase spending, and ship American jobs overseas. No promising free stuff that they definitely can't deliver, either. Instead, they're going to have to nominate someone who's smart and authentic and has the support of the people. In other words, someone just like my dad. In the absence of that, they run the same risk of becoming completely irrelevant, just as the Republican establishment did.

Why am I telling them this, you ask. Because I believe in the American political system and I want it to survive for the future of my children—and theirs. My father's election proved a lot of things. One of the biggest is that given an even chance, the American people know what they're doing.

THE DEMOCRAT HOPEFULS

By the time you read this, I'm sure that the field of Democrat presidential hopefuls, which was about 412 at one point, will have gotten smaller. Most of them have no chance of winning anyway. They're just looking for some free and much-needed PR help for their otherwise nonexistent profiles. As I write this, some have already dropped out and are running for lesser offices such as US senator, governor, high school class secretary, etc. Kirsten Gillibrand has already hoisted the white flag and said she'd be willing to be the Democrat nominee's running mate. She'd do anything for a leg up, like the time she tried to hit me up for a donation by telling me how much she loved the second amendment—true story. When I heard that, it got me thinking about VP candidates for Joe Biden. If he becomes his party's nominee, it's a pretty good bet he will be thinking out of the box, making a daring choice that will add a little mystery and romance—er, excitement—to his campaign. I'd really like to hear from you about this. So for Joe's sake, whataya say we give him a hand? Please tweet your ideas to @DonaldTrumpJr #BidenRunningMate and let's see what we come up with.

Joe Biden. Since we're speaking of the former vice president, let's start our analysis of the Democrats with him. For months, Joe's go-to line on the stump has been "Government has failed you." Now, call me crazy, but I'm not sure a guy who's done nothing but—hold on, let me check my notes here—oh, yeah . . . *be in government* for the last fifty years should be complaining about how horrible the government has been, do you? I actually agree with Gropey on this one, but if I were him, this probably wouldn't be my lead. If things were really that bad, shouldn't he have done something to fix it by now? What you see here is an aging Democrat who is so close—I mean *so* close—to actually being self-aware. He knows government sucks. He knows he's been in government for the last fifty years. He just hasn't quite put those two things together yet. Oh, well. There's still time for him to figure it out. Not much time, but still.

Speaking of which, the other problem with Joe is that he's completely out of touch. I mean, he's like yesterday's candidate. In fact, dress him up in a teal-colored pantsuit, and you'll swear it's 2016 all over again. Next to Crooked Hillary herself, Biden is the most corrupt establishment candidate ever to take a lobbyist's checks, and he's got an unbelievable amount of power with the swamp creatures of Washington. Give him the chance to go back to the White House, and the place will be crawling with reptiles quicker than a campaign volunteer can say, "Please, Mr. Vice President, no." And that's not even considering the big-money donors who'll come rolling into DC like an eighteen-wheeler caravan or the Chinese, who have him and his son Hunter bought and paid for. Let's not forget the fact that Hunter Biden has shady ties to China that no one seems to be able to explain to anyone, and got kicked out of the Naval Reserve for testing positive for cocaine, among other shady stuff, enjoys almost complete immunity from the mainstream media. Now look, I quit drinking for a reason. I understand that some people have problems with addiction. But this isn't about addiction. I've said it before, but it's worth mentioning again: What do you think would happen if I, Donald Trump Jr., tested positive for cocaine? Do you think CNN would go live and say, "There's probably a rational explanation for all this, let's hear the guy out"? Probably not.

Luckily, Biden would be the easiest candidate for my father to take apart. Think about it. If Kamala Harris can hand the guy a smackdown, what do you think DJT will do to him? Poor Joe doesn't have the brainpower to go up against my father—and I mean that literally. His people excuse his gaffs and flubs as just "Joe being Joe," but, I don't know, it seems to me he's suffering from more than just senior moments.

Odds against being the nominee: 2 to 1.

Bernie Sanders. Reason not to vote for him: this quote from the 1980s:

> It's funny, sometimes American journalists talk about how bad a country is because people are lining up for food. That

is a good thing! In other countries, people don't line up for food. The rich get the food and the poor starve to death.

Bernie Sanders has spent his whole life pushing for a system that has never worked in the history of Western civilization—one that has made hundreds of millions of people poor and destitute—and now he's doing it with millions of dollars in the bank and three luxury homes to his name. For a guy who hates capitalism so much, he's actually done pretty well in the system. Think about it: he found a niche market, developed a product—which I'll call "delusion"—and then he sold the hell out of that product in his market. The guy is the ultimate Commie Capitalist.

Odds against being the nominee: 5 to 1.

Elizabeth Warren. Back in June 2018, when Kimberly Guilfoyle, my girlfriend, was a host on *The Five* on Fox, she and the other hosts took a 23andMe DNA test. They did it in response to the Warren heritage controversy. If you haven't seen her—and if you haven't, you must have been locked in a fallout shelter somewhere—Kimberly is beautiful, a perfect combination of dark Irish and Puerto Rican princess. When her test came back, those ancestries dominated her results. There was, however, a little surprise. When I heard about the results, I immediately opened my Twitter account and proposed a wager with Senator Warren: ten grand to her favorite Native American charity if she could prove she was more Native American than my girlfriend. We never heard back from her. Too bad. It would've been the easiest $10,000 donation I ever made. Kimberly is 6.1 percent Native American. And Pocahontas? Well, she's got essentially no percent.

Shortly afterward, I took Kimberly to the annual Fourth of July party at the White House, along with our friends Sergio Gor, Andy Surabian and Arthur Schwartz.

I wanted to go because I could join my father in thanking the troops and their families who would be gathered on the lawn of the White House. I always enjoy speaking with our troops, real Americans who have given so much and have sometimes been forgotten in the perpetual wars of the Middle East. Some of the biggest hero's I have met over the last 4 years include the bravest soldiers who fought for this nation, patriots like John Wayne Walding, Rob O'Neill and Marcus Luttrell. After shaking hands and posing for photos, we found ourselves in the diplomatic room inside the White House, enjoying a quite moment and some air conditioning from the blistering heat, we were soon joined by President Trump and the First lady.

Not surprisingly, in a room full of politicos—the topic soon turned to politics, including the looming Supreme Court nomination. Not one to keep quite about big news, Kimberly decided to share with the room that she had just gotten back her DNA results which turned out to show she was not just that Irish and Puerto Rican, but also 6.1% Native American, part African and even part Ashkanazi Jewish.

My father listened attentively and we soon changed topics, but it was only a few days later that he was campaigning for Matt Rosendale in Montana and also challenged Elizabeth Warren to a DNA test! Not one to be outdone, he significantly increased the ante—to one million dollars. If she took the DNA test and proved she was part Native American, my father would donate that money to a charity of her choice.

So what's the big deal about her DNA lie? Well, first, besides looking really stupid promoting herself as a minority, it's a despicable thing to do. She said the subject hadn't come up when she applied for a job at Harvard. Really? Then why, I wonder, did the university boast that it had a Native American professor? It went as far as describing her as a person of color in the *Fordham Law Review*. Wonder how they explained the blond hair?

Look, ask yourself this: If Warren has no problem being a fake American Indian, why would she have a problem faking anything else: her diplomas, grades, age, the list can go on forever. And what about the people who applied for the Harvard job and didn't get it because they told the truth? To this day, she denies that she got any benefit from doing so. In my opinion, that makes what she did much worse.

It's bad enough that she's an admitted liar without a conscience, but she's also as smug as you can be about it. Even her so-called apology at a presidential forum lately was little more than a campaign stop.

In the last presidential election, voters despised the way Hillary talked down to them. She came across as though she felt she was better than the people whose votes she wanted. Elizabeth Warren is ten times worse; at least Hillary wasn't literally a Harvard professor. Warren talks to people as if they're the dumb kids in her class. Yes, she has some actual policy plans, at least compared to the rest of the Democrats, but she might as well be talking about nuclear fission. And when she tries to put on the "regular Jane" routine, what happens? Well, if you haven't seen it, google "Warren beer video." Her "impromptu" announcement speech on Instagram is hilarious. I've seen better acting in grammar school plays. By the way, Elizabeth, why'd you take the label off the beer? They wouldn't give you product placement money?

As I've said often throughout this book, I'm not a political strategist. I don't aspire to be one, either. But still, I have to wonder who on the Warren campaign thought it would be a good idea to take the DNA test results proving she was maybe 1/1024th Native American and spin it as a victory. But I do know that whoever's idea it was, Warren herself had to approve it. At best, this shows a serious lack of judgment. At worst, it shows total incompetence.

Still, at least at this writing, there's an outside chance that Warren will be the Democratic nominee. The way the Democratic Party is lurching toward socialism, I wouldn't be surprised.

Odds against being the nominee: 5 to 1.

Kamala Harris. Up to now, she's grabbed the spotlight in the debates exactly once, when she accused Joe Biden of being a supporter of racists (which I have, too, often) and against busing to desegregate public schools back in the 1970s. I'll give her this, she set up Biden perfectly. If you remember, she told a story about a little girl in California who rode one of the first desegregation buses. When she dropped the hammer with the line "That little girl was me," Joe's reaction was priceless—as though someone had just told him his zipper had been open for the last thirty years. Unlike Elizabeth Warren's inauthentic beer video, Harris's words came across as an earnest, off-the-cuff attack against someone who had really hurt her feelings. But it wasn't. According to people inside the campaign, the Harris team worked on scripting those few sentences for months, making sure the optics and the delivery were pitch perfect. That whole speech was about as sincere as a singing e-card.

What isn't funny is her record as California's attorney general. She supported her state's draconian "three strikes" law, which, according to the Justice Policy Institute, sent black people to jail at a rate twelve times as high as whites. Many of those people were nonviolent, even petty criminals. A whole generation of black men and women were sent to jail while Kamala Harris was in charge.

Meanwhile, it's my father who's getting criminal justice reform passed. In December 2018, he signed the First Step Act, which rolls back harsh drug sentencing and allows for alternatives to prison such as treatment for opioid addicts and work-release programs. The bill passed Congress with overwhelmingly bipartisan support. That's how you change things in Washington.

Odds against being the nominee: 15 to 1.

Mayor Pete. Look, I have nothing against Mayor Pete. He seems like a genuinely nice guy, but the optics are all wrong. He's just done nothing to merit this kind of job. Even his own constituents have no idea what he's done. Also, that *no-jacket* thing? What's going on there? On my friend Representative Jim Jordan, the no-jacket, shirtsleeve look works. Jim comes across as just what he is, a no-bullshit straight shooter, because that's just what he is. But on Pete, it makes him look lost, as though his mom forgot to put his pudding in his lunch box. Pete's just not ready for prime time yet. Maybe in a couple of cycles, but not now. Besides, he's got enough going on in the small city he runs. If he can't manage the police and the racial discord in South Bend, Indiana, how the heck is he supposed to run the country? His town is rated a whopping 301st among the United States' largest cities. If you can't run a city that's not even in the top three hundred, how are you going to run the world's largest economy? He's the second-to-worst mayor in the United States. Who's the worst? Keep reading and you'll find out.

Odds against being the nominee: 25 to 1.

Beto O'Rourke. Reasons to not vote for him: Irish guy who uses a Hispanic first name for effect. Waves his arms around too much. Fading badly. Wrote short stories about running over kids with his car. Was arrested for trespassing. Tried to leave the scene of a drunk-driving wreck that he caused, according to officers who were on the scene. Thinks he's Batman.

Okay, so maybe not the last one. But did you really need anything else after the murder fantasy about children? I didn't even think you'd read the next ones.

Odds against being the nominee: 25 to 1.

Cory Booker. I don't think Senator Booker has much of a chance, but I'll give you a good reason not to vote for him anyway: he has an imaginary friend. Not kidding. Look it up. On stump speeches and other occasions, he's fond of telling people about a guy named T-Bone whom he met when he first moved to Newark. At the time, Booker was attending Yale Law School. That's after he went to Stanford, of course, and after having grown up on the tough streets of Harrington Park, New Jersey. Not. Harrington Park is one of the nicest suburbs in the state. Anyway, T-Bone, according to the senator, is a "drug lord." Call me crazy, but I don't think they use the term "drug lord" in the Clinton Hill neighborhood of Newark. T-Bone, Booker tells his audience, once promised to "bust a cap in his ass," which sounds like dialogue from the 1991 movie *New Jack City*. Look, it's as simple as this: Booker almost certainly made T-Bone up. He created him, I guess, to burnish his "street cred." After all, when you grow up in a town where the biggest crime is low-foam cappuccino, you need all the street cred you can get. But don't feel sorry for the senator from New Jersey. There might be big things ahead for him. I'm thinking a TV series: *T-Bone and Booker*. Got a ring to it, right?

Odds against being the nominee: 30 to 1.

Amy "Minnesota Nice" Klobuchar. Like Booker, Beto, and Mayor Pete, the senator from Minnesota is an also-ran, so I won't give her much ink. But I do have a word of advice for anyone who goes to work for her: Duck.

Odds against being the nominee: 50 to 1.

The Field. I'm not going to go through every candidate because I love the outdoors and I don't want to see trees go to waste. So in the interest of conservation, I'll just put them into one big pile, which I'll call, let's see . . . Oh, I've got it! I'll just use their polling numbers! You've heard of the 1 percent? Drumroll, please . . . let's give a big conservative welcome to the *none percent!* SteveBullockJulián-CastroJohnDelaneyMichaelBennetTulsiGabbardWayneMessam-TimRyanJoeSestakTomSteyerMarianneWilliamsonAndrewYang.

If you've been following the Democratic presidential primary race closely—and I don't know why you would—you might have noticed someone missing from my name mash. That's because I wanted to save the best for last.

Bill de Blasio. Worst. Mayor. Ever.

One of de Blasio's first public events as New York City mayor came on Groundhog Day 2014. All he had to do was go to a zoo on Staten Island, meet the groundhog (whose name was Chuck), tell the people whether or not Chuck had seen his shadow, and go home. Easy, right? Not if you're Bill de Blasio. When the zookeeper handed the animal to him, the mayor promptly dropped it on its head. Because de Blasio is about twelve feet tall, the fall was fatal. I'm not kidding; a veterinarian had to put the animal down a week later. So the first thing he did as mayor of New York was kill a groundhog. And things only got worse from there.

The police in New York City absolutely hate the guy, and I don't blame them one bit. He has done nothing but undermine them and make it impossible for them to do their jobs. He told his biracial son to be afraid of cops! When a police officer named Miosotis Familia, a mother of three, was shot in the head by a cop-hating parolee, instead of going to the vigil in the precinct, de Blasio took a trip to Germany. Just recently, New York cops have been targeted by people who throw buckets of water on them. Under any other mayor, those people would have been charged for assaulting a police officer. But not under this mayor. Police officers, who put their lives on the line every day, are publicly humiliated, and de Blasio shrugs his shoulders.

By every single metric he's a failing mayor. His school system consistently ranks as one of the worst in the country. Recently, he contemplated doing away with classes for gifted children. So he wants to put the next Einstein in with the *Welcome Back, Kotter* kids? Smart, Bill, really smart!

Along with being a terrible mayor, de Blasio is a very bad politician. So while cops are being assaulted, serious crimes such as murder and rape are spiking, and his constituents live in rat-infested public housing, where do you think the mayor is? In Iowa having a corn dog. According to the *New York Post*, de Blasio worked from City Hall for a grand total of seven hours in the month of May 2019, earning an effective salary of $3,080 an hour. There are probably people who spent longer waiting on line in City Hall to get married than the mayor spent working there.

Last May, he thought he would pull a fast one with a surprise event at Trump Tower announcing his version of the Green New Deal. I guess it never crossed his mind that there might be pro-Trump people in Trump Tower or that word of the event might leak out beforehand. By the time his pop-up presser was ready to go, we had the sound system cranked playing Tony Bennett's "Stranger in Paradise" and Frank Sinatra's "I've Got You Under My Skin." Meanwhile, dozens of protestors, including a pro-Trump lesbian group, rode up and down the escalators holding signs and chanting "Worst. Mayor. Ever!"

Now, if you're like me, you might be asking yourself why in the world de Blasio would think he could be president. Maybe it's because his head is so high in the atmosphere that he's not getting enough oxygen. Luckily, his odds aren't great. According to the polling analysis website FiveThirtyEight, the mayor has a negative favorability rating. That mean he has a less-than-zero chance to win the nomination.

Odds of being the nominee: less than zero.

———

Unless my publisher gets hacked by Russians, this book should be on the shelves of your favorite bookstore in early November 2019, eight months before the Democratic National Convention in Milwaukee. In that time, candidates will make countless references to racism, sexism, transphobia, Islamophobia, and whatever the new giveaway of the day is. All they'll do is prove that nothing has changed, that the Democrats are still obsessed with identity politics over real progress, proposing harebrained socialist plans instead of real solutions, and pandering to the fragile emotions of social justice warriors.

It's the same old story.

17.

—————

TRUMP 2020

IN CASE YOU HAVEN'T NOTICED, I'm not exactly a Hallmark card type of guy. I've never thought there was much value in sentimentality, in getting all misty about the past or whatever. *Bleh.*

But every once in a while, I do look back at what my father—and the rest of my family and friends—have managed to accomplish these past few years, and even I am taken slightly aback. Together, we took on the most corrupt political machine in the history of the United States and won. It was the greatest upset in the history of American politics, and I got to be the tip of the spear, or at least the tip of one of the spears. Then we weathered a political storm unlike anything this country has ever seen before, from the fake collusion allegations to biased reporters combing through every moment of our lives, to an investigation that seemed to go on longer than *Game of Thrones*, and we came out the other side leaner, meaner, and stronger than ever. Even for a not-so-sentimental guy like me, that's pretty impressive. It's definitely something I'll be telling the grandkids about (if they're not taken away from me by the gender-neutral AOC administration because I believe in binary genders).

Then again, my grandkids might find it all hard to believe. I know I do sometimes. For instance, if you had come and told me, say, during my gap year, when I was camping in the woods by day and pouring pints of Coors Light by night, that my father and I would someday become the target of our nation's top intelligence agencies, I would probably have told you to take it easy on the mushrooms.

But you're not tripping; it is all too real.

Even now, there are forces deep inside our government trying to bury evidence of wrongdoing against my father. They're sweeping the phony Steele dossier and the illegal FISA warrants under the rug and trying to pretend that none of it ever happened. If those people have a hand in writing the history of the Russia hoax—and believe me, they will try—they will say that the Mueller investigation was based on real evidence and that Donald Trump and his administration really did commit obstruction of justice. They'll forget names such as Christopher Steele, James Comey, Andrew McCabe, Peter Strzok, and Lisa Page—as Mr. Mueller of the eponymous report seems to have done during his very own congressional testimony—and they'll remember made-up Russian oligarchs and the people who supposedly turned us into spies.

If you don't think something like that could ever happen, consider this: it's happened before—to, of all people, Martin Luther King Jr.

J. Edgar Hoover and the FBI kept a file on Dr. King for years. They cooked up a story that he was—get this—an agent of Russia, sympathetic to Communists, and out to destroy the United States with his speeches and boycotts. (Go ahead and stop me if any of this sounds familiar.) They tapped his phones. They planted evidence in his hotel rooms. They made his life a living hell and then sent him letters saying the only way out of that living hell would be suicide. Then, in what is perhaps the worst part of it all, they covered the whole thing up. For fifty years, the records of the FBI's many operations against Martin Luther King Jr., were sealed by federal order, accessible only to people at the highest levels of the intel community. Whenever anyone tried to have them unsealed, the request was denied by whatever establishment politician was in charge. Only in 2007, when most of the documents were released—I say "most" because many of them are believed to have been destroyed—did we discover the extent to which our law enforcement institutions had targeted one of our greatest citizens. No one was punished. Many of those responsible are dead, never having been held accountable for the crimes they committed. After living through the past three years, can you honestly say that anything has really changed? Or is it just more of the same?

I don't know if the FBI has records of the secret operations it conducted against the Trump campaign and administration. But I wouldn't trust the top brass at the FBI to unseal them if they did. Remember, this is the organization that was led by James Comey, a man who elevated leaking and lying to an art form. As I write this, the DOJ's inspector general has just released a blistering report saying that Comey leaked to the press official documents describing interactions between the US president and the FBI director, a crime that, according to our friend Rudy Giuliani, a former federal prosecutor, should have landed Comey in jail. I have no doubt that if he were a Trump supporter, or at least not a member of the permanent political class, he would be in a jail cell right now. But just like Hillary Clinton, just like Peter Strzok and Lisa Page and Andrew McCabe, Comey is given every benefit of the doubt when it comes to whether or not he broke the law. He, like the others who orchestrated the attempted coup, won't ever be punished. Instead, he'll probably end up on CNN as a paid contributor! People like him are given hours and hours to prepare for interviews, and then, at the end of it all, when we're deciding how to punish (or not punish) them, we think about their families, their years of service, and how much it would hurt their feelings to be prosecuted. If you believe that any member of the Trump administration would ever get that kind of leniency, you haven't been paying attention.

Now, before someone at HuffPost starts typing up a "Don Jr. Hates the FBI" headline (which, no doubt, they're already doing), I want to make it clear that I'm not talking about the rank-and-file people who work at our intelligence organizations—people who handle the real work and make sure we're kept safe from domestic and international threats. They are decent, hardworking people, and I would trust most of them with my life. In fact, I do just that. I have no problem with the door kickers, the men and women of our law enforcement agencies whose boots are on the ground. Those amazing men and women do a great job, and many I've talked with are disgusted by the Clappers and Comeys of the world—people who would "tarnish their badge." In my experience, they are overwhelmingly MAGA. But I do have a huge problem with the lawyers and political hacks who make up agencies' top ranks. They're just career bureaucrats who've been given too much power by the system for too long. Their motives are self-serving. They care little about America and everything about their own interests.

In fact, if you're reading these words between the hours of about seven and ten in the evening, there's a pretty good chance you can turn on your television right now and see John Brennan, a former director of the CIA; James Clapper, a former director of national intelligence; or Andrew McCabe, James Comey's former deputy at the FBI, continuing to spew lies about my father, trying to bury the truth of their crimes in real time in front of a network news audience. Oh, and by the way, they've all written books. (Okay, I know what you're thinking: "Well, so did you, Don." Apples and oranges. They wrote books about the lies they told, and I wrote one because they told them about me.) Obviously, the fake-news media weren't content to sit back and cover the criminals who were trying to take down my father, so they gave them parking spaces, press passes, and book contracts instead. If you're on their side, you're not punished for wrongdoing. In fact, you're rewarded with lucrative commentator roles on CNN and MSNBC.

That's why I have absolutely no faith that the real story of what the FBI (in conjunction with the DNC and Hillary Clinton's campaign) did to my father will ever see the light of day. I've simply been through too much to believe it will. I mean, sure, there have been some good reporters and private citizens who've uncovered parts of it. We now know that the FISA warrants used to spy on our campaign in Trump Tower were not obtained legally and that several agents at the highest levels of the FBI breached protocol when going after targets in the Trump administration. We know that just about every one of Robert Mueller's Nineteen Angry Democrats was a Trump-hating hack looking for any reason they could find to nail him and me, and we also know that Mueller himself—a sorry old man well past his prime, who was used like a rented mule by Democrats in Congress—was the author of his report in name only. But is anything going to come of it? Are we ever going to get an apology or see any of the people who pushed the fake conspiracy theory for years punished for the fraud they perpetrated on the American people? Will *anyone* be held accountable? Ever?

I'm not holding my breath.

———

Today, as we gear up for the 2020 election, the fake-news media are bigger and more invasive, and their audiences more brainwashed, than ever. Have you ever seen a story—just *one* story—that broke in favor of Trump instead of the other way around? Of course not. Back when my father first announced he was running for president, the lies the media told about him usually pertained only to the small stuff: our family business, his financial history, his personal life. Few in the media accused him of being a Russian spy or colluding with foreign oligarchs. Today, those unsubstantiated rumors have become the gospel truth of the left and things are only getting worse. The media continue to lie despite definitive proof to the contrary, and they're not going to stop.

If you don't believe me, pick up a liberal newspaper or tune your television to one of those failing three-letter liberal news stations. CNN, NBC, ABC—doesn't matter, just as long as you rinse your eyes thoroughly with clean water after you're done. I'm sure you won't enjoy what you see, but it's good to get a sense of the nonsense the other side continues to push.

If you'd been watching NBC News, for example, on the evening of Tuesday, August 28, 2019, you would have seen Lawrence O'Donnell, a man who's been telling blatant lies about my father since long before he announced he was running for president, talking in a split screen with Rachel Maddow. With obvious glee, O'Donnell told Maddow and all her ultrawoke viewers about documents that had been reviewed by "a single source close to Deutsche Bank" that would prove once and for all that yes, it was true, all of it—Donald Trump really had colluded with Russia! "This single source close to Deutsche Bank," O'Donnell said, "has told me that Donald Trump's loan documents there show he has cosigners. That's how he was able to obtain those loans and that the cosigners are Russian oligarchs."

Please. If you believe that, I have "a single source" close to

Lawrence O'Donnell who tells me that he likes to dress up in women's clothes and sing karaoke on weekends. See how easy it is to make this crap up? I could do it all day. (And they do!) Even Rachel Maddow, the liberal queen of the conspiracy theories, seemed a little hesitant to believe him. Take it from me: if you make an accusation against my father and *Rachel Maddow* isn't buying it, whatever you've got is probably nonsense. It should have been a tip-off that O'Donnell's staff didn't even try to call Trump Org for comment or verify the story in any other way.

Sure enough, O'Donnell was on television the very next night, crying and telling the world that nothing he had said was even remotely true. For some people, that little half-assed nonapology was enough. But for me, it wasn't even close. When O'Donnell posted an initial tease of the story on Twitter, it was shared tens of thousands of times. When he later posted a tweet saying that the whole thing had been a lie and admitting that he hadn't even run it by the fact-checking team at NBC News—which, I would imagine, is probably three chimpanzees sitting around a table with an encyclopedia—that message was retweeted a mere eight thousand times. And O'Donnell is only a tiny cog in the left's propaganda machine.

Though the onslaught of lies continues, it will not slow DJT down. From the moment he stepped onto the stage in the atrium of Trump Tower to announce his run for president, my father had his mind set on one thing and one thing only: the American people. And if you think for a second that he didn't know when he descended the golden escalator exactly what lay ahead for him— the constant attacks by the left and right, the two-faced elites in the swamp who'd pretend to be his best friends—you don't know my father. From the moment he decided to run, he knew exactly the hell he was about put himself through, and he did it anyway. Because it was the right thing to do.

He'll continue doing the right thing in 2020 and beyond. That fight isn't over, and for the sake of the men and women who put my father into the White House in the first place, it has to continue.

I know it will for me.

———

When I hit the road with the Trump campaign in 2015, the first thing I noticed was that people were fed up with liberal censorship and political correctness. All over the country, folks were tired of being talked down to by the elite political class, told over and over again that their concerns didn't matter and their voices weren't going to be heard. I met proud factory workers who had watched as Democratic policies had torn their lives apart; I met conservative college kids who were terrified to identify themselves in class for fear that liberal professors would retaliate; I met women who were shunned by friends because of their political views. If this seems to you to be a theme that I've hit time and again in this book, you're right. Those stories are seared into my memory. They were living in a country that was ruled by what the left did or did not find offensive, and they were sick of it. So was I.

I don't know if I can point to an exact date when it happened, when I realized what was at stake and started to view politics on a personal level. I'm sure it happened the way most things do—bit by bit and then all at once, like a nonreinforced chair giving out under Michael Moore. Over time, I began to realize that the Bush and Obama administrations had done damage to the things I believe in. President Obama, especially, had attacked free markets and free speech in ways I couldn't stand for.

Then, when my father announced, I realized that some of my liberal friends—or people I had thought were friends—began to retreat to the echo chamber of the left. They read only the *New*

York Times and watched only MSNBC. They became like a cult. Suddenly, conservatives were their enemies. Compromise was impossible. The list of things they wouldn't talk to me about got longer and longer. The jokes they told were no longer funny but mean-spirited. Their outrage was ridiculous and hollow. I had never had a deep emotional attachment to Manhattan, but now I felt like a stranger in a strange land.

Out on the road, I had the opposite feeling. When my father's campaign went into a city or town, I saw the first glimmer of hope in eyes that had for too long been without it. In my dad, not only did they see someone who understood their problems, they saw someone who was willing to fight for them, someone who would never give up fighting for them. His voice was like the first roll of thunder you hear before a storm begins. By the time he was finished on stage, lightning had struck. Look, I'm aware that there's an unhealthy amount of division and divisiveness in this country right now, and I know many people blame my father for that. With so many media organizations trashing him day and night, I'm not surprised. But this kind of bitter division predates my father's announcement speech by a long, long time. People all over the country had been feeling it for years; all he did was bring the fight from the small towns and diners of America into the halls of Congress and the White House.

Of course, I didn't see my dad on the trail often, especially toward the end of the campaign. As you might have noticed, when DJT enters a room, his energy fills every square inch of it. I learned quickly that the best place for me to be during the final days of the 2016 campaign was wherever he wasn't. Luckily, I had friends who were willing to leave their jobs and families for days at a time to travel with me. And the work wasn't always glamorous. We took thousands of selfies a day, practically begged for money, and coordinated our own movements and the movements of thousands upon thousands of people who came to see us at campaign stops.

But guess what? We crushed it.

We pulled in over $100 million at a time when we didn't have the relationship with the RNC that we do today. We did that without its Rolodex, using just our own relationships. We slept in motels around the country; we met real Americans who were fed up with Washington elites; we went days without food at times. Not that we minded. We had our fair share of testosterone, adrenaline, and Red Bull to keep the momentum going. But more importantly,we had loyalty, friendship, and will.

Out on the campaign trail, I began to understand what politics really meant. At the very least, I saw why people who get a taste of the political life have a hard time giving it up. I watched it happen to many of my friends on the campaign trail—people who'd lived their entire adulthood in business and industry and then, once they got out on the road and started shaking hands with the voters of this country, found it impossible to go back and sit in their offices. It happened to Tommy Hicks, who's now a cochair of the Republican National Committee. It happened to others, too, including myself. I knew that there would be a time to make money, but as a patriotic American, there was no way I could squander the opportunity to help push the MAGA movement forward.

In a mostly false article by *The Atlantic* that focused on fictitious infighting between myself and Ivanka, various Republicans weighed in on my ability to connect with the base:

> "By November 2018, Don had appeared at more than 70 campaign events across 17 states—and powerful Republicans were abuzz. "I could very easily see him entering politics," Senator Kevin Cramer told me. "I think

his future is bright," said House Minority Leader Kevin McCarthy. Newsmax's CEO, Chris Ruddy, told me he'd personally encouraged Don to run for office; Sean Hannity called him "a born natural leader." Senator Rand Paul went so far as to say that Don was one of the best Republican campaigners in the country. "If you can't get the president," Paul told me, "he's a close second."

Even if you leave aside all the good my father has done for the country in terms of policies since he's been in the White House—and there is plenty, from the economy, to tax cuts, to our standing in the world, to appointing two great justices to the Supreme Court and countless lower court appointees, just to name just a few—there is one more lasting impression he's left on our political system: he's made people see that their principles are worth fighting for, that we don't have to roll over and die anymore just because the left says so. Somehow, he understood intuitively that politics is a game but what's at stake is anything but. For those of us on his campaign, and for the millions of people who followed him, he showed us by example that what we believe in matters. It might mean rough going, but if it's right, you do it anyway. Prison reform? Not exactly a conservative thing. Opportunity zones? Not something that directly benefits his base. There is no base for him in inner cities. (Although based on the results he's getting on the economy, there should be, and he's working hard to change that.) He did those things not because it was the right thing to do politically. That's the difference between this presidency and so many others. Donald Trump doesn't sit there and make a decision based on polling numbers. He listens to the people. He didn't run a campaign based on polling groups. He did it based on his gut, on decades of experience, and on the applause and cheers of the forgotten men and women of this country who were being heard for the first time in decades. When he talks of job growth, he does so with more experience than perhaps any other president. He has been signing the front of checks for forty years. What the hell would Hillary Clinton know about job growth? She hasn't created a job in her life. Maybe a pollster job. Maybe a position for someone who bleaches her servers for her or hammers her iPhones to bits. But a real job? Not a chance. Neither has Joe Biden, Elizabeth Warren, Bernie Sanders, Kamala Harris, Chuck Schumer, Nancy Pelosi, or any other Democrat in Washington.

Still, the campaign we face in 2020 is going to be an even greater test of both DJT's will and ours. Back in 2016, it was pretty much just Bernie shouting socialist nonsense. Today, there are card-carrying socialists leading a revolt in the Democratic Party. In 2016, there was only one corrupt Democrat, at least only one we had to worry about—admittedly, Hillary was the kind who can escape prosecution at the highest levels of the government despite clear evidence of crimes, the kind whose enemies always seem to "commit suicide" under mysterious circumstances—but still, she was only one person. And as the conservative comedians jokingly say, "she can't suicide us all." Today, there are twenty Democratic candidates in the race, each one representing a different horrible path for our country. Back in 2016, my father had the element of surprise on his side. Few on the left even took his campaign seriously, let alone noticed the movement he was creating. Today, the left, the liberal media, and the administrative state have their eyes wide open. They're like a trapped animal. They will do anything to regain power. Anything.

I also know that if they're spoiling for a fight, they came to the right place. Of all the lessons my father has taught me—and there have been plenty—the greatest one is this: There comes a time when you have to put up or shut up, to be a man, (or a woman; I don't want to be charged by the PC police) whether or not it's politically correct to do so, or walk away. To fight or be a coward. So the left can take whatever shots it wants at us. We'll do what we always do: hit back twice as hard. Fight or flight is a basic component of human evolution. What can I say? I guess in the Trump family, the flight instinct never really developed.

———

I began this book telling you I wasn't mad. I'm still not. After all, there's a lot to feel good about.

I hear from people all the time how much better their lives are. Last Valentine's Day, for instance, I took Kimberly to a nice restaurant on the upper East Side of New York City. Not exactly a bastion of conservatism. As the evening progressed, I could sense that all eyes were on us, and perhaps a scene would soon unfold. As we paid our tab, and made our way for the exit, a woman got up, pointed at me, and yelled, you! I thought, here we go, here comes a fight with grandma on Valentine's Day. And then it happened, she said to us and the entire restaurant, "You have the biggest balls in the world and you don't take crap from anyone. Keep it up!" She broke the ice, as the entire place erupted in applause. In a room that I thought, would be hostile and nasty, we found friendly supporters. It goes to show you, you never know where you might find a friendly voice. It took one person, with courage and conviction to break the ice and the rest followed.

My dad has accomplished an incredible amount in the less than three years he's been in office. Despite what you hear from the liberal media, those achievements have helped all Americans. As I write this, the job market is the best it's ever been. For the first time, there are more jobs available than we need. It used to be people went out and looked for a job; now jobs are looking for people. It's also the greatest time ever to get a better job than the one that you have. And the best time ever to start a career. Right now we have the lowest unemployment rate for both men and women in fifty years. We have the lowest unemployment rate ever for blacks, Latinos, and Asians, ever: 3.7 percent. Lowest youth unemployment in half a century, and veteran's unemployment is the lowest in twenty years. Never before has there been a more pro–American worker president. His Pledge to America and its workers has resulted in employers committing to train more than 4 million Americans. DJT is committed to vocational education. Ninety-five percent of US manufacturers are optimistic about the future—the highest ever.

President Obama once famously said that you would need a magic wand to bring back the manufacturing jobs lost during his administration. Well, abracadabra, Mr. Former President. The Trump administration has added 1 million manufacturing, construction, and energy jobs.

In total, my father has added 6 million jobs to the market and, amazingly, 6.2 million people are off food stamps. What will the Democrats do if Americans start becoming self-sufficient? It certainly won't be good for their failed policies!.

Still, if you subscribe to the liberal press bullshit, those gains are about to go up in a puff of smoke. As positive as my dad is about our roaring economy, the media is that much negative and worse. More than once in the preceding pages, I've told you that the MSM hates my father more than they love America, and there is no better example of this than how they "cover" the impending doom they say is coming.

Look, I've been in the marketplace my entire adult life. I know how it ebbs and flows. For the sake of millions of Americans who will suffer, however, I pray that a recession doesn't happen. But if it does, you can lay the blame squarely on the propaganda machine of the left. Not only do they believe an economic downturn will help them win the White House, but it would also provide them with a depressed America, the perfect setting to implement their social-ist plans. Remember what Bernie said: "There's nothing wrong with breadlines."

The Democrats have also pledged to repeal my father's tax cuts, which have been a godsend to the American middle class by doubling the Child Tax Credit from $1,000 to $2,000, doubling the standard deduction, and putting more than $2,000 back in the family wallet.

And while Democrats are for open borders and health care for illegal immigrants, my father's has budged not one inch on his immigration stance or his fight to build the wall. When you boil all the talking points down, what's left are a few immutable facts. My dad wants to keep criminals and illegal drugs out of America. He wants to stop the unlawful immigrant drain on our social safety net. DJT's not against immigrants. He just wants those who, like my Ethiopian friend from the Denver coffee shop, love America, not the ones who hate us. I don't see how anyone can argue with that.

Nor do I think anyone can argue with his Eexecutive order to cut two regulations for every new one—the Trump administration is the first in decades to cut more regulations that it has added. By greenlighting the Keystone Pipeline and the Dakota Access pipeline and by lifting regulations on $50 trillion worth of energy reserves, my father has blown the doors off of energy production.

After decades of inaction, my father has also taken the first steps toward a lasting peace in the Korean peninsula. Not that anyone will give him credit for it. One morning sitting with my two-year-old, Chloe and having breakfast, we saw on television an "expert" on North Korea who was ridiculing and criticizing

President Trump for his willingness to meet with the leader of North Korea. At that moment it dawned on me: my infant daughter has about the same level of success in achieving peace with North Korea as this expert on television.

He took us out of the costly and ineffective Paris climate agreement. He's gotten us out of lousy Obama and Clinton-era trade deals including the Trans-Pacific Partnership (TPP) and NAFTA. He took us out of John Kerry's horrendous Iran deal. He's restored America's respect on the world stage, and leaders around the globe know that the days of taking advantage of America are over.

Let me make it easy on you; here are some more of his accomplishments:

- The Trump administration is providing more affordable health care options for Americans through association health plans and short-term plans.
- The FDA approved more affordable generic drugs than ever before in history. And thanks to our efforts, many drug companies are freezing or reversing planned price increases.
- The administration has reformed the Medicare program to stop hospitals from overcharging low-income seniors on their drugs—saving seniors hundreds of millions of dollars this year alone.
- My father signed Right to Try legislation, greenlighting experimental drugs for terminally ill people.
- He's secured $6 billion in new funding to fight the opioid epidemic.
- He has reduced high-dose opioid prescriptions by 16 percent during his first year in office.
- He signed VA Choice Act and VA Accountability Act, and he has expanded VA telehealth services, walk-in clinics,

and same-day urgent primary and mental health care.

- He has done what no other president before him could: moved the United States embassy in Israel to Jerusalem.
- No American president has ever appointed two conservative justices to the Supreme Court who are better than Neil Gorsuch and Brett Kavanaugh.

I could go on, but I think you get the point. Look, I get it. I know there are plenty of people out there who don't like me and don't like my father. But just because you don't like the messengers doesn't mean you have to hate the message. That message is making the lives of millions and millions of American safer, richer, and more hopeful, and it has accomplished that feat in three short years. Imagine what my father can do with another four.

I got into politics by happenstance. Then I found that I liked the fight in it. But I've come to realize that it's not just a fight for the sake of a fight. It's even more than the daily battle with those who want to take my father and me down. It's a fight for the happiness and well-being of my children and yours.

That is what's at stake in 2020. In one very big way, the next presidential election is more important than the last. When my dad campaigned in inner cities in 2016 he'd remind minority audiences how past administrations, including Obama's, had failed them. He would then ask them to vote for him using this simple but brilliant logic: "What do you have to lose?"

Their answer, if they were truthful about it, was nothing.

Well, that's not the case anymore. It's not the case in inner cities, where the unemployment rate is at historic lows; it's not the case in the suburbs, where tax cuts increased wages and retirement accounts have doubled in some cases; and, despite what you may read in the *New York Times*, it's not the case in the Rust Belt and

West Virginia, where he's increased coal exports by 60 percent, or on America's great expanse of farmland, where renegotiated trade deals have provided a friendly future.

In this next election we have a lot to lose. From sea to shining sea, Americans across this great country of ours have a better life and more hope with Donald J. Trump in the White House.

I'd thought about ending this book with something sarcastic; I've been told that I can be that way sometimes. But beneath this snarky and handsome (hey, I'm a Trump; What did you expect?) exterior there lies one enduring truth: and that's my love of the United States of America.

Let's keep it great.

ACKNOWLEDGMENTS

TO MY FATHER, President Donald J. Trump: I am so proud of you. You were always there for us, and now you are there for our nation. Just like your amazing parents, you always took care of our family. When you decided to run for office, you stepped up to the challenge, and your grandchildren and millions of other kids will be better off because of it. You are one of the most incredible people I have ever known. Our country is blessed to have you as president with an incredible first lady by your side. Melania continues to bring poise and elegance to everything she does. Our nation is lucky to have her! Dad, I'd say keep fighting, but who are we kidding? You know no other way! Love you.

To my mother, grandmother, and late grandfather: Writing this book brought back many memories of summers spent in Czechoslovakia. I wouldn't be the man I am today if it weren't for those adventures and incredible memories. Thank you.

To my spectacular kids, Kai, Donnie, Tristan, Spencer, and Chloe: I love you more than anything. You were born into a unique family. We work hard and we achieve a lot, and there is little doubt in my mind that you will all do the same. Aim for success in all you do. I will be there for you every step of the way, always. To

Vanessa, thank you for our amazing children and the wonderful job you do with them.

To my siblings, Eric, Ivanka, Tiffany, and Barron: Only you can understand the craziness we have experienced in the last three years. We learned who our true friends are, and we learned the viciousness of fake news. Nothing could have prepared us for the lies. We are Trumps, we don't play the victim card, and we will succeed here as well. We are in this together.

To Kimberly: You always bring out the best in me and everyone else around you. You are such a special person. We have the best time together. Always know that I am thankful for you. Love you.

To Jared and Lara: You married into our family, but little did you know the roller coaster we would all embark on. I admire your dedication, work ethic, and desire to succeed, just like ours. We couldn't do this without you at our sides.

To my informal political team, who sometimes get me into more trouble than I can manage to get into myself, Sergio, Arthur, Andy, and Charlie: Being in politics with you makes it fun. Here's to many more adventures and memories over the coming years.

To my friends Tommy, Gentry, and Oz: When Dad decided to run, he told me on the elevator ride down to the announcement in Trump Tower that we would soon find out who our true friends are. I couldn't ask for a better group of friends to go into battle with, true friends!

To all my hunting, fishing, and shooting buddies, Jason, Rob, Rich, Trig, Don, Keith, Chuck, Gary, Jay, Dave, and the rest of the boys: I thrive in business, I choose to fight and win in politics, but I truly unwind when I am outdoors in the wilderness of our nation and our world. You keep me grounded at least a little—or till it becomes a competition. Thank you!

To Team Hachette, especially Rolf, Kate, Patsy, Brian, Sean, and Tom: Thank you for taking a chance on me! An extremely hard-working team who worked night and day to meet deadlines, make me shine, and make this book possible.

To my legal team, especially Alan Garten: Thanks for all you do in keeping me out of trouble despite bipartisan efforts to do the opposite.

To all those who work for the various Trump companies: You're the core of what we do. Real estate and hospitality don't necessarily mesh well with politics, yet you're part of this historic journey, too. I thank each and every one of you for all that you have done for my family and me over the years.

To every man, woman, and child who wakes up in this great nation and doesn't want to be a victim but wants to live the American dream, wants to win, succeed, produce, create, thrive, give back, and Make America Great Again!

ENDNOTES

CHAPTER 1: TRIGGER WARNING

Page 7: Megan Henney. "Mueller investigation by the numbers: 675 days, 500 witnesses," Fox Business, April 17, 2019. https://www.foxbusiness.com/politics/mueller-investigation-numbers-days-witnesses

CHAPTER 2: COUNTERPUNCH

Page 11: Adam Entous, Devlin Barrett, and Rosalind S. Helderman. "Clinton campaign, DNC paid for research that led to Russia dossier," *The Washington Post*, October 24, 2017. https://www.washingtonpost.com/world/national-security/clinton-campaign-dnc-paid-for-research-that-led-to-russia-dossier/2017/10/24/226fabf0-b8e4-11e7-a908-a3470754bbb9_story.html

11: Glenn Kessler. "Flashback: Obama's debate zinger on Romney's '1980s' foreign policy (video)," *The Washington Post*, March 20, 2014.

12: Karoun Demirjian. "'Undoubtedly there is collusion': Trump antagonist Adam Schiff doubles down after Mueller finds no conspiracy," *The Washington Post*, March 26, 2019. https://www.washingtonpost.com/powerpost/undoubtedly-there-is-collusion-trump-antagonist-adam-schiff-doubles-down-after-mueller-finds-no-conspiracy/2019/03/26/e972d9e8-4fdd-11e9-a3f7-78b7525a8d5f_story.html

13: Adam Entous, Devlin Barrett, and Rosalind S. Helderman. "Clinton campaign, DNC paid for research that led to Russia dossier," *The Washington Post*, October 24, 2017. https://www.washingtonpost.com/world/national-security/clinton-campaign-dnc-paid-for-research-that-led-to-russia-dossier/2017/10/24/226fabf0-b8e4-11e7-a908-a3470754bbb9_story.html

13: Nigel Chiwaya and Jiachuan Wu. "Mueller deflected questions 198 times. We tracked when he did it," *NBC News*, July 24, 2019. https://www.nbcnews.com/politics/politics-news/robert-mueller-house-testimony-tracker-july-2019-n1033166

14: Paul Krugman. "The Economic Fallout," *The New York Times*, November 9, 2016. https://www.nytimes.com/interactive/projects/cp/opinion/election-night-2016/paul-krugman-the-economic-fallout

14: Paula Firozi. "CNN president: Airing so many full Trump rallies was a 'mistake'," *The Hill*, October 14, 2016. https://thehill.com/blogs/ballot-box/presidential-races/301147-cnn-president-airing-so-many-full-trump-rallies-was-a

15: Ashley Parker and Nick Corasaniti. "Some Donald Trump Voters Warn of Revolution if Hillary Clinton Wins," *The New York Times*, October 27, 2016.

15: Christopher Mele and Annie Correal. "'Not Our President: Protests Spread After Donald Trump's Election," *The New York Times*, November 9, 2019. https://www.nytimes.com/2016/11/10/us/trump-election-protests.html

16: Michael E. Miller. "Antifa: Guardians against fascism or lawless thrill-seekers?", *The Washington Post*, September 14, 2017. https://www.washingtonpost.com/local/antifa-guardians-against-fascism-or-lawless-thrill-seekers/2017/09/14/38db474c-93fe-11e7-89fa-bb822a46da5b_story.html

17: John Bacon. "Suspect Killed After Steve Scalise, 4 Others Shot at Congressional Baseball Game," *USA Today*, June 14, 2017. https://www.usatoday.com/story/news/nation/2017/06/14/reports-congressman-others-shot-baseball-practice/102838314/

17: Julia Jacobs. "Rand Paul's Neighbor Is Sentenced to 30 Day sin Prison After Attack," *The New York Times*, June 15, 2018. https://www.nytimes.com/2018/06/15/us/politics/rand-paul-attack.html

18: Katherine Rosenberg-Douglas and Lisa Donovan. "Eric trump not pressing charges against waitress who spit on him at Chicago's Aviary, Trump Organization says," *Chicago Tribune*, June 26, 2019.

18: Jessica Chasmar. "Red Hen restaurant owner who kicked out Sarah Sanders says 'new rules apply' for Trump officials," *The Washington Times*, July 1, 2019. https://www.washingtontimes.com/news/2019/jul/1/red-hen-restaurant-owner-who-kicked-out-sarah-sand/

18: Joseph A. Wulfsohn. "Protestors gather outside McConnell's Kentucky home, one calls for his stabbing 'in the heart'," *Fox News*, August 6, 2019. https://www.foxnews.com/media/protestors-gather-outside-mcconnells-ky-home-one-calls-for-his-stabbing-in-the-heart

18: Christopher Mele and Patrick Healy. "'Hamilton' Had Some Unscripted Lines for Pence. Trump Wasn't Happy," *The New York Times*, November 19, 2016. https://www.nytimes.com/2016/11/19/us/mike-pence-hamilton.html

20: Ashe Schow. "Berkley Once Again Dissolves Into Chaos Over Free Speech," *The Observer*, April 17, 2017. https://observer.com/2017/04/berkeley-free-speech-patriots-day-turns-violent/

21: Christina Morales. "Conservative Writer Andy Ngo Details Attack at Portland Protest," Oregonlive.com, July 2, 2019.

22: Christopher Mele and Annie Correal. "'Not Our President: Protests Spread After Donald Trump's Election," *The New York Times*, November 9, 2019. https://www.nytimes.com/2016/11/10/us/trump-election-protests.html

CHAPTER 3: CRACKS IN THE FOUNDATION

Page 23: Melia Robinson. "A 58-story skyscraper in San Francisco is tilting and sinking—and residents say their multimillion dollar condos are nearly worthless," *Business Insider*, July 24, 2018. https://www.businessinsider.com/is-millennium-tower-safe-still-leaning-sinking-2017-9

26: https://www.britannica.com/topic/New-Left

26: https://www.fbi.gov/history/famous-cases/weather-underground-bombings

26: Bryan Burrough. "The Untold Story Behind New York's Most Brutal Cop Killings," *Politico Magazine*, April 21, 2015. https://www.politico.com/magazine/story/2015/04/the-untold-story-behind-new-yorks-most-brutal-cop-killing-117207

28: Wilson Andrews, Kitty Bennett, and Alicia Parlapiano. "2016 Delegate Count and Primary Results," *The New York Times*, July 5, 2016.

28–29: Michael Kranish. "Inside Bernie Sanders's 1988 10-day 'honeymoon' in the Soviet Union," *The Washington Post*, May 3, 2019. https://www.washingtonpost.com/politics/inside-bernie-sanderss-1988-10-day-honeymoon-in-the-soviet-union/2019/05/02/db543e18-6a9c-11e9-a66d-a82d3f3d96d5_story.html

35: Jamie Ballard. "Socialism is becoming more popular with Baby Boomers," YouGov, August 7, 2018. https://today.yougov.com/topics/politics/articles-reports/2018/08/07/socialism-capitalism-popular-baby-boomers

36: Myra Adams. "Unfunded Govt. Liabilities—Our Ticking Time Bomb," RealClearPolitics, January 10, 2019. https://www.realclearpolitics.com/articles/2019/01/10/unfunded_govt_liabilities_--_our_ticking_time_bomb.html

36–38: Day One Staff. "Update on plans for New York City headquarters," The Amazon Blog, February 14, 2019. https://blog.aboutamazon.com/company-news/update-on-plans-for-new-york-city-headquarters

38–39: Emily Witt. "The Optimistic Activists for a Green New Deal," *The New Yorker*, December 23, 2019. *https*://www.newyorker.com/news/news-desk/the-optimistic-activists-for-a-green-new-deal-inside-the-youth-led-singing-sunrise-movement

39: Matt Patterson. "Study Saul Alinsky to Understand Barack Obama," *The Washington Times*, February 6, 2012. https://www.washingtonexaminer.com/study-saul-alinsky-to-understand-barack-obama

39: Kevin Dayaratna and Nicolas Loris. "A Glimpse of What the Green New Deal Would Cost Taxpayers," *The Heritage Foundation,* March 25, 2019. https://www.heritage.org/environment/commentary/glimpse-what-the-green-new-deal-would-cost-taxpayers

33: Naomi Klein. "The Game-Changing Promise of a Green New Deal," *The Intercept,* November 27, 2018. https://theintercept.com/2018/11/27/green-new-deal-congress-climate-change/

41: Isabel Vincent and Melissa Klein. "Gas-guzzling car rides expose AOC's hypocrisy amid Green New Deal pledge," *New York Post,* March 2, 2019. https://nypost.com/2019/03/02/gas-guzzling-car-rides-expose-aocs-hypocrisy-amid-green-new-deal-pledge/

42: "Student Loan Question," CSPAN. https://www.c-span.org/video/?c4792658/student-loan-question

43: Cody Nelson. "Minnesota Congresswoman Ignites Debate On Israel And Anti-Semitism," *NPR,* March 7, 2019. https://www.npr.org/2019/03/07/700901834/minnesota-congresswoman-ignites-debate-on-israel-and-anti-semitism

43: Ian Schwartz. "Rep. Ayanna Pressley: 'We Don't Need Any More Brown Faces That Don't Want To Be A Brown Voice," *RealClear Politics,* July 14, 2019. https://www.realclearpolitics.com/video/2019/07/14/rep_ayanna_pressley_we_dont_need_any_more_brown_faces_that_dont_want_to_be_a_brown_voice.html

44: Hannah Hartig. "Stark partisan divisions in Americans' views of 'socialism,' 'capitalism'," *Pew Research Center,* June 25, 2019. https://www.foxnews.com/media/rudy-giuliani-ilhan-omar-september-11-comments

CHAPTER 4: CLASS WARFARE

Page 54–55: Michael Luongo. "The Ironic History of Mar a Lago," *Smithsonian Magazine,* November 2017. https://www.smithsonianmag.com/history/history-mar-a-lago-180965214/

64: "How Nafta Changed U.S. Trade With Canada and Mexico," *The New York Times,* August 15, 2017. https://www.nytimes.com/interactive/2017/business/nafta-canada-mexico.html

CHAPTER 5: GAP YEAR

Page 75–76: Jerry Dunleavy. "Top Democrat calling for full Mueller report had different view when Bill Clinton was investigated," *The Washington Examiner,* April 1, 2019. https://www.washingtonexaminer.com/news/top-democrat-calling-for-full-mueller-report-had-different-view-when-bill-clinton-was-investigated

79: "A Letter from GOP National Security Officials Opposing Trump," *New York Times,* August 8, 2016.

85: Nick Gass and Ben Schreckinger. "Donald Trump Jr. breaks out on national stage," *Politico,* July 20, 2016.

CHAPTER 6: NOT EXACTLY THE STATUE OF LIBERTY

Page 95–96: CIS, "The Legacy of the 1965 Immigration Act," Center for Immigration Studies, September 1, 1995.

96: Matt O'Brien and Spencer Raley. "The Fiscal Burden of Illegal Immigration on United States Taxpayers," *Fairus.com,* September 27, 2017. https://www.fairus.org/issue/publications-resources/fiscal-burden-illegal-immigration-united-states-taxpayers

96–97: Steven A. Camorota and Karen Zeigler. "Better Educated, but Not Better Off," Center for Immigration Studies, April 17, 2018. https://cis.org/Report/Better-Educated-Not-Better

97: Joel Gehrke. "State Department: At least 90 percent of heroin destined for the U.S. comes from Mexico," *The Washington Examiner,* March 2, 2017. https://www.washingtonexaminer.com/state-department-at-least-90-percent-of-heroin-destined-for-the-us-comes-from-mexico

97: Agencies in Mexico City. "Drug violence blamed for Mexico's record 29,168 murders in 2017," *The Guardian*, January 21, 2018. https://www.theguardian.com/world/2018/jan/21/drug-violence-blamed-mexico-record-murders-2017

98: Caitlin Dickerson. "Border at 'Breaking Point' as More Than 76,000 Unauthorized Migrants Cross in a Month," *The New York Times*, March 5, 2019. https://www.nytimes.com/2019/03/05/us/border-crossing-increase.html

99: Nicole Fuller. "MS-13 murders down on LI, but gang is trying to rebuild," Long Island *Newsday*, May 12, 2019. https://www.google.com/search?q=newsday+five+hundred+MS-13+2018&oq=newsday+five+hundred+MS-13+2018&aqs=chrome..69i57.11351j0j4&sourceid=chrome&ie=UTF-8

101: The White House. "Remarks by the President on Border Security and Immigration Reform," June 30, 2014. https://obamawhitehouse.archives.gov/the-press-office/2014/06/30/remarks-president-border-security-and-immigration-reform

102: Fareed Zakaria. "Democrats May Be Walking into an Immigration Trap," *The Washington Post*, June 22, 2018. https://beta.washingtonpost.com/

102: "Q: Do you support building a wall on the border with Mexico?," *The Washignton Post*, February 8, 2019. https://www.washingtonpost.com/politics/polling/mexico-building-support-oppose/2019/02/08/4d2ac40c-20cf-11e9-a759-2b8541bbbe20_page.html

106: Charles Fain Lehman. "More Than 700,000 Overstayed Visas in 2017," *Free Beacon*, August 20, 2018. https://freebeacon.com/issues/700000-overstayed-visas-2017/

CHAPTER 7: NOT YOUR GRANDFATHER'S DEMOCRAT PARTY

Page 114: Jillian Kay Melchior. "Philly Union Boss 'Johnny Doc' Has an Appointment With Justice," *Wall Street Journal*, February 8, 2019. https://www.wsj.com/articles/philly-union-boss-johnny-doc-has-an-appointment-with-justice-11549668706

114: Erin Shannon. "Report shows corruption continues to plague labor unions," Washington Policy Center, January 22, 2018. https://www.washingtonpolicy.org/publications/detail/report-shows-corruption-continues-to-plague-labor-unions

CHAPTER 8: BACK TO SCHOOL

Page 126: Lily Rogers. "Yale Needs to Stop Accepting Republican Students," *Yale Daily News*, April 13, 2018. https://yaledailynews.com/blog/2018/04/13/yale-needs-to-stop-accepting-republican-students/

127: Sudhin Thanawala. "Multiple Arrests at Ben Shapiro Berkeley Protests," *USA Today*, September 15, 2017. https://www.usatoday.com/story/news/nation/2017/09/15/ben-shapiro-berkeley-protest-arrests/669071001/

127: Madison Park and Kyung Lah. "Berkeley protests of Yiannopoulos caused $100,000 in damage," *CNN*, February 2, 2017. https://www.cnn.com/2017/02/01/us/milo-yiannopoulos-berkeley/index.html

129: Sudhin Thanawala. "Multiple Arrests at Ben Shapiro Berkeley Protests," *USA Today*, September 15, 2017. https://www.usatoday.com/story/news/nation/2017/09/15/ben-shapiro-berkeley-protest-arrests/669071001/

132–133: Jonathan Haidt and Greg Lukianoff. "The Coddling of the American Mind," *The Atlantic*, September 18, 2018. https://www.theatlantic.com/magazine/archive/2015/09/the-coddling-of-the-american-mind/399356/

134: Conor Friedersdorf. "The New intolerance of Student Activism," *The Atlantic*, November 9, 2015. https://www.theatlantic.com/politics/archive/2015/11/the-new-intolerance-of-student-activism-at-yale/414810/

135–136: Robby Soave. "Oberlin Students Want Below-Average Grades Abolished, Midterms Replaced with Conversations," *Reason*, May 24, 2016. https://reason.com/2016/05/24/oberlin-students-want-below-average-grad/

136: Robby Soave. "Survey: 58 percent of students want a campus where they are not exposed to intolerant or offensive ideas," *Reason,* October 11, 2017. https://reason.com/2017/10/11/survey-58-of-students-want-a-campus-wher/

136–137: David Frum. "Whose Interests Do College Diversity Officers Serve?," *The Atlantic,* September 8, 2016. https://www.theatlantic.com/education/archive/2016/09/americas-college-diversity-officers/499022/

CHAPTER 9: ELECTION NIGHT

Page 155: Adam Entous, Devlin Barrett, and Rosalind S. Helderman. "Clinton campaign, DNC paid for research that led to Russia dossier," *The Washington Post,* October 24, 2017. https://www.washingtonpost.com/world/national-security/clinton-campaign-dnc-paid-for-research-that-led-to-russia-dossier/2017/10/24/226fabf0-b8e4-11e7-a908-a3470754bbb9_story.html

CHAPTER 10: A DEADLY FORM OF HATE

Page 159–160: "Executive Order Protecting the Nation from Foreign Terrorist Entry into the United States," The White House.

160: "Christian Persecution," OpenDoorsUSA. https://www.opendoorsusa.org/christian-persecution/

161: Chris Mills Rodrigo. "Obama condemns attacks in Sri Lanka as 'an attack on humanity'," *The Hill,* April 21, 2019. https://thehill.com/blogs/blog-briefing-room/news/439904-obama-condemns-attacks-in-sri-lanka-as-an-attack-on-humanity

164: Samantha Schmidt. "Muslim activist Linda Sarsour's reference to 'jihad' draws conservative wrath," *The Washington Post,* July 7, 2017. https://www.washingtonpost.com/news/morning-mix/wp/2017/07/07/muslim-activist-linda-sarsours-reference-to-jihad-draws-conservative-wrath/

167–168: "Feinstein: 'The Dogma Lives Loudly Within You, and That's a Concern'," *The Washington Post,* September 7, 2017. https://www.washingtonpost.com/video/politics/feinstein-the-dogma-lives-loudly-within-you-and-thats-a-concern/2017/09/07/04303fda-93cb-11e7-8482-8dc9a7af29f9_video.html

168: John l. Jenkins. "Letter from Rev. John I. Jenkins, C.S.C. to U.S. Sen. Dianne Feinstein," *Notre Dame News,* September 9, 2017. https://news.nd.edu/news/letter-from-rev-john-i-jenkins-csc-to-us-sen-dianne-feinstein/

171: Olivia B. Waxman. "The 1995 Law Behind President Trump's Plan to Move the U.S. Embassy in Israel to Jerusalem," *Time* Magazine, December 5, 2017. https://time.com/5049019/jerusalem-embassy-history/

CHAPTER 11: MISS GENDERED

Page 174: Ed McConnell. "Mum arrested in front of her children for calling transgender woman a man," *Mirror.co.uk,* September 1, 2019. https://www.mirror.co.uk/news/uk-news/mum-arrested-front-children-calling-19120272

176–177: Victor Morton, "Transgender hurdler easily wins NCAA women's national championship," *The Washington Times,* June 3, 2019. https://www.washingtontimes.com/news/2019/jun/3/cece-telfer-franklin-pierce-transgender-hurdler-wi/

179: Dave Collins. "High school athletes file complaint over transgender policy," *AP News,* June 18, 2019. https://www.apnews.com/3966a7d34fc64dd886aa12116795c7b7

181: Alex Morris. "It's a Theyby! Is it possible to raise your child entirely without gender from birth? Some parents are trying," *The Cut,* April 2, 2018. https://www.thecut.com/2018/04/theybies-gender-creative-parenting.html

181–182: "Trans Student Resources," http://www.transstudent.org/definitions/

CHAPTER 12: THE ENEMY OF THE PEOPLE?

185: Joshua Bote. "Trump baby blimp rises again," *USA Today,* June 3, 2019.

185–186: Matthew Butcher. "Flying the Sadiq Khan balloon is not an exercise of free

speech—it is a party for bigots," *Metro.co.uk*, August 31, 2018. https://metro.
co.uk/2018/08/31/flying-the-sadiq-khan-balloon-is-not-an-exercise-of-free-speech-
it-is-a-party-for-bigots-7900396/

188: Laura Spadanuta. "Donald Trump Plays Hardball," *Penn Today,* December 2, 1999.
https://penntoday.upenn.edu/node/148712

190: Margaret Hartmann. "Trump Under Fire for Improper Fish-Feeding Technique," *New
York Magazine,* November 6, 2017. http://nymag.com/intelligencer/2017/11/trump-
under-fire-for-improper-fish-feeding-technique.html

191–192: Steve Cortes. "Trump didn't call neo-nazis 'fine people.' Here's proof," *RealClear
Politics,* March 21, 2019. https://www.realclearpolitics.com/articles/2019/03/21/trump_
didnt_call_neo-nazis_fine_people_heres_proof_139815.html

192: Drew Magary. "Donald Trump's Family Is Just as Bad as Donald Trump," *GQ,* July 19,
2016. https://www.gq.com/story/donald-trumps-family-as-bad-as-trump

193: Mckay Coppins. "The Heir," *The Atlantic,* October 2019. https://www.theatlantic.
com/magazine/archive/2019/10/trump-dynasty/596674/

196–199: Jim Sciutto, Carl Bernstein, and Marshall Cohen. "Cohen claims Trump
knew in advance of 2016 Trump Tower meeting," *CNN,* July 27, 2018. https://www.
cnn.com/2018/07/26/politics/michael-cohen-donald-trump-june-2016-meeting-
knowledge/index.html

204: Dave Goldiner. "Donald Jr. and Eric Trump pay bill after walking out on 'round's on
us' tab at Irish pub," *New York Daily News,* June 8, 2019. https://www.nydailynews.
com/news/politics/ny-donald-trump-jr-eric-irish-pub-bar-tab-20190608-
li7c3jk3pben5obgwyuwaawmrm-story.html

CHAPTER 13: SHADOW BANNED

Page 221: Benjamin Goggin. "YouTube's week from hell: How the debate over free speech
online exploded after a conservative star with millions of subscribers was accused of
homophobic harassment," *Business Insider,* June 9, 2019. https://www.businessinsider.
com/steven-crowder-youtube-speech-carlos-maza-explained-youtube-2019-6

222: Richard Hanania. "It Isn't Your Imagination. Twitter Treats Conservatives More
Harshly Than Liberals," *Quillette,* February 12, 2019. https://quillette.com/2019/02/12/
it-isnt-your-imagination-twitter-treats-conservatives-more-harshly-than-liberals/

224: "Jack Dorsey Says Twitter Unfairly Filtered 600,000 Accounts," *Bloomberg,* September
5, 2018. https://www.bloomberg.com/news/videos/2018-09-05/jack-dorsey-says-
twitter-unfairly-filtered-600-000-accounts-video

CHAPTER 14: THE LATE-NIGHT KING OF COMEDY

Page 225–226: "Jussie Smollett: Timeline of the actor's alleged attack and arrest," *BBC,*
June 25, 2019. https://www.bbc.com/news/newsbeat-47317701

229–230: *Ibid.*

235: "Ten Days After: Harassment and Intimidation in the Aftermath of the Election,"
Southern Poverty Law Center. https://www.splcenter.org/20161129/ten-days-after-
harassment-and-intimidation-aftermath-election

236–238: Andy Ngo. "Inside the Suspiscious Rise of Gay Hate Crimes in Portland," *New
York Post,* March 30, 2019. https://nypost.com/2019/03/30/inside-the-suspicious-rise-
of-gay-hate-crimes-in-portland/

238: "Hate Crime Statistics, 2017," FBI. https://www.fbi.gov/news/pressrel/press-releases/
fbi-releases-2017-hate-crime-statistics

238: Wilfréd Reilly. "Hate Crime Hoaxes Are More Common Than You Think," *Wall
Street Journal,* June 25, 2019. https://www.wsj.com/articles/hate-crime-hoaxes-are-
more-common-than-you-think-11561503352

240: Ian Schwartz. "Capeheart: Smollett Case 'Fit In With A Reality" Under Trump That
A Lot of People Wanted to Believe," *RealClear Politics,* February 18, 2019. https://

www.realclearpolitics.com/video/2019/02/18/capehart_jussie_smollett_case_fit_
in_with_a_reality_under_trump_that_a_lot_of_people_wanted_to_believe.html

CHAPTER 15: JOE CHINA

Page 246: Peter Schweizer. "The Troubling Reason Why Biden Is So Soft on China," *New York Post,* May 11, 2019. https://nypost.com/2019/05/11/the-troubling-reason-why-biden-is-so-soft-on-china/

248: Adam Edelman. "Biden's comments downplaying China threat to U.S. fire up pols on both sides," *NBC News,* May 2, 2019. https://www.nbcnews.com/politics/2020-election/biden-s-comments-downplaying-china-threat-u-s-fires-pols-n1001236

249: Peter Schweizer. *Secret Empires: How the American Political Class Hides Corruption and Enriches Family and Friends,* 2018.

251: Victor Davis Hansen. "What Drove the Mueller Investigation?," *National Review,* April 25, 2019. https://www.nationalreview.com/2019/04/mueller-investigation-pious-hypocrisy/

252: Peter Schweizer. "The Troubling Reason Why Biden Is So Soft on China," *New York Post,* May 11, 2019. https://nypost.com/2019/05/11/the-troubling-reason-why-biden-is-so-soft-on-china/

CHAPTER 16: THE OPPOSITION

Page 258: Jim Geraghty. "Bernie Sanders: China Has Done a Lot of Things for the People!," *National Review,* August 27, 2019. https://www.nationalreview.com/corner/bernie-sanders-china-has-done-a-lot-of-things-for-their-people/

261: Christopher Cadelago, *Kamala's attack on Biden was months in the making, Politico.* June 28, 2019. https://www.politico.com/story/2019/06/28/kamala-harris-joe-biden-debate-1390383

262: Liam Quinn. "Young Beto O'Rourke Wrote 'Murder Fantasy' About Running Over Children, Was Part of Famed Hacking Group: Report," Fox News, March 15, 2019. https://www.foxnews.com/politics/beto-orourke-wrote-murder-fantasy-children-was-part-of-famed-hacking-group-report

263: Eliana Johnson. "Cory Booker's Imaginary Friend," National Review, August 29, 2013. https://www.nationalreview.com/2013/08/cory-bookers-imaginary-friend-eliana-johnson/

264: Polly Mosendz. "Bill de Blasio Implicated in Tragic Groundhog Death," *The Atlantic,* September 24, 2014.

265: Erin Durkin. "Bill de Blasio details talk with biracial son about interacting with police: You 'train them to be careful when they have…an encounter with a police officer," *New York Daily News,* December 8, 2014. https://www.nydailynews.com/news/politics/de-blasio-details-talk-son-dealing-cops-article-1.2036870

265: Post Editorial Board. "Mayor Bill de Blasio's seven-hour work month," *New York Post,* September 3, 2019. https://nypost.com/2019/09/03/mayor-bill-de-blasios-seven-hour-work-month/

265: William Neuman. "A Mayor Walks into Trump Tower. A Circus Follows," *New York Times,* May 13, 2019. https://www.nytimes.com/2019/05/13/nyregion/de-blasio-trump-tower-protesters.html

CHAPTER 17: TRUMP2020

Page 269: "Federal Bureau of Investigation," The Martin Luther King, Jr. Research and Education Institute," March 19, 2019.

272: Brooke Singman. "Trump tears into Lawrence O'Donnell, media over 'totally false' Russia report: 'ALL APOLOGIZE!'," Fox News, August 29, 2019. https://www.foxnews.com/politics/trump-tears-into-lawrence-odonnell-media-over-totally-false-russia-report-all-apologize